COMMANDING

——— THE ———

PACIFIC

COMMANDING
THE
PACIFIC

MARINE CORPS GENERALS IN WORLD WAR II

STEPHEN R. TAAFFE

NAVAL INSTITUTE PRESS
ANNAPOLIS, MARYLAND

Naval Institute Press
291 Wood Road
Annapolis, MD 21402

Library of Congress Cataloging-in-Publication Data

Names: Taaffe, Stephen R., author.
Title: Commanding the Pacific : Marine Corps generals in World War II /
  Stephen R. Taaffe.
Other titles: Marine Corps generals in World War II
Description: Annapolis, Maryland : Naval Institute Press, 2021. | Includes
  bibliographical references and index.
Identifiers: LCCN 2021012742 (print) | LCCN 2021012743 (ebook) | ISBN
  9781682477083 (hardcover) | ISBN 9781682477090 (epub) | ISBN
  9781682477090 (pdf)
Subjects: LCSH: United States. Marine Corps—History—World War, 1939–1945.
  | Command of troops. | Generals—United States—Biography. | United
  States. Marine Corps—Officers—Biography. | Leadership.
Classification: LCC D769.369 .T33 2021 (print) | LCC D769.369 (ebook) |
  DDC 940.54/59730922—dc23
LC record available at https://lccn.loc.gov/2021012742
LC ebook record available at https://lccn.loc.gov/2021012743

♾ Print editions meet the requirements of ANSI/NISO z39.48-1992 (Permanence
of Paper).
Printed in the United States of America.

29 28 27 26 25 24 23 22 21   9 8 7 6 5 4 3 2 1
First printing

To Cynthia

Contents

Maps

Acknowledgments

Innumerable people assisted me during the four years it took to research and write this book. My department chair, Professor Troy Davis, secured funds for me to travel to Marine Corps University, in Quantico, Virginia, to examine Marine Corps records. The folks at the university's History Division, especially Fred Allison, Betty Mayfield, and Alisa Whitley, helped me locate important sources.

My good friend and colleague Professor Philip Catton read through the manuscript and offered his usual sage advice. Another colleague, Brookford Poston, kept me from working ceaselessly and obsessively on the manuscript by visiting my office most weekdays to discuss anything but the Marine Corps. Still another friend, Ken Arbogast-Wilson, drafted the maps for me. I am grateful that Susan Brook and the staff at the Naval Institute Press were willing to publish this manuscript.

Finally, I could not have written this book without the help of my wife, Cynthia. It recently occurred to me that she is the only person who has read all of my scholarly work over the past twenty years, which makes her the epitome of the long-suffering academic spouse.

INTRODUCTION

Perched on Iwo Jima's southwestern corner, Mount Suribachi looms ominously over the island's eight square miles of volcanic ash and barren ridges. By the time U.S. Marines landed there on 19 February 1945, Iwo Jima's 21,000 Japanese defenders had honeycombed Suribachi and the rest of the island with an intricate and interlocking network of pillboxes, gun emplacements, tunnels, and machine-gun nests. From these positions they rained fire on the Marines struggling to establish a beachhead and bring ashore the supplies, equipment, and reinforcements necessary to secure the island. The Marines in turn gave as good as they got, pounding Suribachi and the rest of Iwo Jima with artillery, naval gunfire, and airstrikes.

On 23 February, four days after the Marines first came ashore, Japanese resistance on Suribachi appeared to soften. On that cool and blustery morning, a small Marine patrol reached Suribachi's summit unopposed. Rather than test their luck, the leathernecks opted to withdraw. Even before that patrol had returned to U.S. lines, however, a larger, platoon-sized force started up the mountain. Riflemen pushed cautiously uphill while keeping a wary eye out for snipers, uncovered cave entrances, and landmines. Stretcher-bearers, Navy corpsmen, and a camera crew trailed behind. Like the Marines in the first patrol, they drew no fire as they reached Suribachi's peak and fanned out over the crest of the mountain. Someone scavenged a section of drainage pipe, attached a small American flag to it, and raised it into the stiff breeze.

Marines throughout the area saw the flag flying over Suribachi and cheered it as a sign that they were winning the battle. Sailors offshore spotted it as well, and soon vessels protecting and succoring the Marine foothold on the island blared their horns to acknowledge the good news. The information traveled along the beachhead and to the remainder of the fleet via radio and loudspeakers. On a Higgins boat headed to shore, Secretary of the Navy James Forrestal, who had crossed the Pacific for a firsthand view of the war, also noticed the flag. He lowered his binoculars, turned to his companion, Gen. Holland Smith, and said, "Holland, the raising of that flag on Suribachi means a Marine Corps for the next five hundred years."

As Forrestal finished talking, the Japanese troops still holed up inside Suribachi opened fire on the marines on the summit, forcing them to take cover. Renewed Japanese opposition could not, however, negate that the Marines held the mountaintop. Later that morning, another Marine patrol scaled Suribachi with a second, much larger, American flag. The press photographer Joe Rosenthal immortalized the otherwise routine raising of this flag in an iconic photo that won the Pulitzer Prize and became one of the most recognized representations of the conflict.

The raising of the American flags over Mount Suribachi is an oft-told story, part of Marine Corps lore. The Battle of Iwo Jima was, after all, not only the biggest Marine operation in World War Two, but it also encompassed everything the Marine Corps purported to represent: courage, sacrifice, honor, comradery, persistence, and discipline. Despite the engagement's renown, even World War II buffs remain unfamiliar with the Marine commander at Iwo Jima who fought and won the battle—Gen. Harry Schmidt, head of the V Amphibious Corps. Smith had led the Fleet Marine Force in the Pacific, but he exercised almost no direct authority over tactical operations on the island. Instead, it was Schmidt who bore the leadership burden on Iwo Jima, but he has received little acknowledgment for his role and actions even in detailed accounts of the operation.

The anonymity of Marine Corps World War II commanders is not limited to Schmidt on Iwo Jima. Although such Marine battles as Guadalcanal,

Tarawa, and Iwo Jima are well known, most military enthusiasts are unaware of the generals who led the leathernecks through these horrific engagements. This contrasts sharply with the experience of the Army and the Navy. Army generals George Marshall, Dwight Eisenhower, Douglas MacArthur, and George Patton are readily recognized among people with even a passing familiarity with World War II. Even the naval commanders Ernest King, Chester Nimitz, and William Halsey ring a bell with the historically literate. The names of Marine Corps generals such as Schmidt— men who led tens of thousands of leathernecks through some of the Pacific War's most important and difficult battles—have been all but forgotten.

There are various reasons for the anonymity of these Marine Corps combat commanders. One is size. During World War II, the Marine Corps was much smaller than the Army and the Navy. By the end of the conflict, the Army had nearly 8.3 million personnel and the Navy 3.3 million. Marine Corps strength, on the other hand, peaked at about 477,000. Whereas the Army sent overseas ninety 15,000-man divisions organized into twenty corps, the Marines' contribution consisted of only six divisions and two corps deployed to the Pacific. Thus it was primarily the Army that waged and won the war against Germany and Italy for the United States. Even in the Pacific, the Army deployed far more divisions, twenty-one, and conducted more amphibious assaults than the Marine Corps. This meant that the Marines engaged in fewer operations than the Army and Navy, giving Marine generals limited opportunities to distinguish themselves.

Moreover, Marine generals lacked a prominent voice in strategic planning for the Pacific War. The Marine Corps, as part of the Navy, was subject to that service's general authority and had no representation in the interservice Joint Chiefs of Staff, which determined grand strategy for U.S. forces. Marine generals did not command any of the geographic theaters of war. In short, Army and Navy officers determined strategic objectives and expected their Marine counterparts to carry out their decisions. As a result, Marine generals had little opportunity to dazzle contemporaries and historians with the strategic acumen that Army and Navy officers such as Nimitz, MacArthur, and Eisenhower displayed—or, as some critics argued, failed to demonstrate.

The Marine Corps' emphasis on amphibious warfare also hindered its combat generals from achieving renown. Marine amphibious assaults against

Pacific islands were relatively simple in conception and required little tactical finesse to conduct. In other words, the geography and terrain the Marines confronted usually called for direct assaults that provided Marine generals with few opportunities to display the kind of brilliant tactics that won Patton and other army generals fame. To be sure, these amphibious operations were extraordinarily difficult to organize, but the logistical, training, and planning skills that Marine officers needed to make them successful were not sufficiently glamorous to attract kudos from those interested in tactics and strategy.

In some respects, Marine generals were simply "victims" of American success. As the conflict progressed, the United States' overwhelming materiel and numerical superiority over targeted Japanese island garrisons virtually guaranteed Marine victory before the first leathernecks hit the beach. The outcome was rarely in doubt. It was instead just a question of casualties and time—how many marines would die and how long it would take. There was little of the drama that characterized the desperate struggles Army generals faced at the Battle of the Bulge or that admirals confronted at Midway and Leyte Gulf. Marine doctrine and the circumstances of World War II may have offered the average leatherneck and the Corps as a whole plenty of chances for glory, but not so much for the Marine generals who, in the broader scheme of things, merely reaped the harvest planted by their Navy colleagues.

Despite being fated to historical obscurity, the men who led the Marine Corps' largest units played a major role in defeating the Japanese. Although some portray large organizations like the Marine Corps as impersonal entities over which even powerful individuals exert little influence, this is usually not the case. People can impact an organization's culture and effectiveness and many do. Indeed, an organization is no better than its leaders, and superior resources and technology rarely compensate for poor leadership. This was certainly true of high-level Marine Corps combat commanders in the Pacific War. Their control over the institutional machinery of the Corps consisted of implementing decisions made by others. The Joint Chiefs of Staff and theater commanders may have decided which Japanese-held islands to target, but the Marine combat generals determined the proper tactics, weaponry, planning, organization, timetable, and training for the ground portion of the operation. They also selected staff officers and subordinates to assist them. They were therefore directly responsible for the success or failure of their missions. Through this, they left their marks on their units and, through them, the war. Comments by Eisenhower on the relationship between high-ranking Army commanders and their outfits apply just as well to the Marine Corps:

> I have developed almost an obsession as to the certainty with which you can judge a division, or any other large unit, merely by knowing its commander intimately. Of course, we have had pounded into us all throughout school courses that the exact level of a commander's personality and ability is always reflected in his unit—I did not realize, until opportunity came for comparisons on a rather large scale, how infallibly the commander and unit are almost one and the same thing.[1]

The upshot is that the Marine Corps could not have won its war against the Japanese without the particular leaders in charge of its divisions and corps during the conflict.

Although the Marine Corps played an important part in defeating Japan in the Pacific War, one can still question the selection and performances of its high-ranking combat commanders. The Marines Corps suffered heavy casualties in many of its operations. Around 3,200 leathernecks fell in four days of fighting for the tiny island of Tarawa, 14,500 on Saipan, 6,300 on Peleliu, and 26,000 on Iwo Jima. In some engagements, Marine losses were so high that officers scoured rear areas for personnel to throw into the fight as run-of-the-mill riflemen. In fact, Marine casualties at Iwo Jima and Okinawa so crippled the Corps that it would have had to cannibalize some of its units to bring those remaining up to strength for the climactic assault on the Japanese Home Islands. On the other hand, the Army's losses in its campaigns against Japan were often lighter than those sustained by the Marines. For example, only 11,300 soldiers fell in MacArthur's dash across New Guinea's north coast from February to September 1944, less than the almost 20,000 the Marines sustained in concurrent operations in the Mariana Islands. Moreover, although the Marines wrapped up some operations in short order, others lasted longer than necessary because of Marine generals' reluctance to ask the Army for help or to commit sufficient reinforcements. Securing Saipan, Guam, Peleliu, and Iwo Jima took weeks, not days, leaving one to wonder whether different commanders might have overcome the geographic and strategic limitations placed on the Marine Corps and achieved their objectives with fewer casualties and in less time.

The Army and Navy arguably misused the Marine Corps during the conflict. Some of the Corps' most difficult assignments were not only prohibitively costly, but also, in hindsight, of questionable strategic value. The Marine generals' willingness to take on almost any assignment therefore sometimes came at a stiff price. They acquiesced in part because they had little say in Pacific War strategy, but also because they were eager to demonstrate their value to the military establishment. If the Marines had balked at some of their missions, it might have shaken the Navy's confidence in the Corps and allowed the Army a greater role in the war.

Despite these criticisms, the Marine Corps' high-level combat commanders on the whole performed well during the Pacific War. Although they drew some of the conflict's most arduous and complex assignments, they emerged victorious in all of their operations during the U.S. counteroffensive across the Pacific. Marine generals certainly made mistakes, but none serious enough to affect the ultimate outcome of their battles. Those few who failed usually did so not on the battlefield, but in the equally difficult job of preparing for incredibly complicated amphibious assaults. Their success is a credit not only to Marine Corps doctrine and culture, but also to the service's commandants, who relied on their firsthand knowledge of the officer corps to appoint the right people to the right posts. These generals deserve more attention from historians than they have been given for their roles in victory over Japan.

SEMPER FI

An Anomalous Organization in Search of a Mission

The Marine Corps represents an anomaly in U.S. military history. It is an army more or less subject to a navy's authority that has throughout its history sought a mission to justify its existence and to differentiate itself from the rest of the armed forces. Although Congress authorized the establishment of a continental marine force during the Revolutionary War, it disbanded the outfit at the end of the conflict. In 1798, however, Congress reconstituted it for the Quasi-War with France, put it under the command of a commandant, and eventually made it part of the Navy. It became, in effect, the Navy's bodyguard. The new Marine Corps' duties included protecting Navy yards, serving as shipboard police, manning masts as sharpshooters during battle, and providing personnel for gun crews and landing parties. Marine detachments also fought alongside Army units from the War of 1812 to the Civil War. During this time, its strength gradually increased from several hundred to almost two thousand men. Its record, while solid, was hardly stellar, and it was anything but an elite force. Indeed, its biggest accomplishment was carving out an autonomous role for itself separate from the Navy while remaining a part of it. The early Marine

Corps suffered from an uneducated and bickering officer corps, substandard enlisted personnel (even by nineteenth-century standards), inferior and secondhand equipment, and a byzantine bureaucracy.

To make matters worse, advancing naval technology and societal reforms in the mid-1800s rendered the Marine Corps increasingly obsolete. Steam-powered warships with fewer and more powerful cannons eliminated the need for Marine sharpshooters and gun crews. Moreover, many ship captains concluded that they could control their men through force of personality and common adherence to duty, not through an intimidating Marine detachment maintaining order. Because of these developments, the Marine Corps played an insignificant role in the Civil War. It produced no notable officers, won no major battles, and contributed little to Union victory. Its officers squandered opportunities to carve out new missions, such as spearheading the Navy's amphibious assaults on Confederate coastal positions. By the end of the conflict, the Marine Corps was a quaint and antiquated force of questionable value.

Fortunately for the Corps, its situation improved at the end of the century under the leadership of Commandant Charles Heywood. In addition to creating the School of Application to train officers, Heywood upgraded the equipment and living conditions for enlisted men. At the beginning of the Spanish-American War in 1898, a Marine detachment seized Guantanamo Bay, Cuba, and then repelled a Spanish attack. Although a minor engagement, the skirmish received a disproportionate amount of coverage from a news-hungry press and helped the Marines build a reputation as an elite force. In this case, the image created the reality. The quality and quantity of recruits increased, so that by 1917 the Corps consisted of almost 13,000 men. During World War I, Marines fought valiantly as infantrymen in France, most notably at the Battle of Belleau Wood in June 1918. At the end of the conflict, though, the Marine Corps confronted a mission problem. Because Marine and Army troops essentially performed the same tasks on the Western Front, to many the Corps seemed to be an expensive and unnecessary redundancy in the frugal postwar era.

The Marines reacted to charges of being superfluous by reinventing themselves. Before World War I, the Navy had pressured the Corps to focus on securing and defending overseas bases that the Navy wanted to use for projecting power around the world. In response, the Marines created the Advanced Base Force in 1913. After the conflict, some Marine officers, among them Maj. Earl Ellis, zeroed in on Japan as the most likely future adversary of the United States. War Plan Orange, the Navy's contingency plan for fighting Japan, called for the U.S. fleet to steam across the Pacific to rescue the American-held Philippines and defeat its Japanese counterpart in a climactic naval battle. Ellis recognized that doing so would require someone to seize and hold island bases in the Central Pacific to succor the Navy's offensive. In the 1921 report "Advanced Base Force Operations in Micronesia," Ellis advocated that the Marine Corps fill this difficult role. As he convolutedly put it, "To effect a landing under the sea and shore conditions obtaining and in the face of enemy resistance requires careful training and preparation, to say the least, and this along Marine Corps lines. It is not enough that the troops be skilled infantry men or artillery men of high morale: they must be skilled water men and jungle men who know it can be done—Marines with Marine training."[1] The Marine commandant, Gen. John Lejeune, endorsed Ellis' report, thus giving the Marine Corps a new mission: amphibious operations.

In embracing amphibious operations, the Marines committed themselves to waging a most difficult and intricate form of warfare. Storming a hostile beach from vessels offshore was (and is) not for the faint of heart. Organizing such an assault would require Marine generals, working with their staff officers, to gather and disseminate intelligence, determine training regimens, coordinate with Navy counterparts, assign objectives, delineate unit boundaries, allot resources, and combat-load transports and cargo vessels. Simply selecting the proper beach to attack necessitated an understanding of enemy defenses, offshore reefs and other underwater obstacles, tides, gradients, and sand composition. The Navy was responsible for escorting and protecting the invasion fleet, securing the seas around and skies above the target, and delivering a preliminary bombardment. At that point, Marines boarded specialized landing craft designed to deliver troops and supplies onto the beach. Herding the landing craft to their lines of departure in roiling seas and keeping them in place until they received orders to head for the coast was no easy task. Once ashore, Marines would find the beach loud, confusing, and littered with landmines, the dead and wounded, damaged and destroyed equipment, and detritus of every kind. Amid this, the leathernecks had to find their officers, collect their equipment, and push inland, often under enemy fire so intense that it was all but impossible to communicate, gather bearings, and deduce the tactical situation. While the infantry headed inland, beachmasters, shore parties, and others struggled to bring order to chaos by directing reinforcements, establishing communication centers and command posts, emplacing artillery, distributing ammunition and supplies, and tending to the wounded. Once the battle lines shifted away from the beach, operations became more conventional, but that did not make them any easier or less deadly.

The Marines soon learned that accepting their new amphibious mission and preparing for it were two different things. Small interwar budgets prevented them from developing and purchasing the specialized equipment amphibious warfare required. In addition, the Corps was stretched thin providing ship detachments, garrisoning China and the Philippines, and pacifying Haiti, the Dominican Republic, and especially Nicaragua. Many questioned whether amphibious operations were even feasible. The failed British campaign against the Ottoman Empire at Gallipoli during World War I convinced many military thinkers that modern technology had rendered successful amphibious assaults impossible because the defenders could so quickly summon reinforcements to the threatened beach via railroads. The Marines, though, did what they could with the limited means at hand, even if much of it was theoretical.

In 1934, Marine and Navy planners produced the *Tentative Manual for Landing Operations*, explaining in detail how to conduct effective amphibious assaults. It became the amphibious warfare bible not only for the Marine Corps, but for the Army as well. As such, its importance can scarcely be underestimated. As Archibald Vandegrift, a future commandant, put it in the aftermath of World War II, "Despite its outstanding record as a combat force in the past war, the Marine Corps' far greater contribution to victory was doctrinal: that is, the fact that the basic amphibious doctrines which carried Allied troops over every beachhead in World War Two had been largely shaped by the US Marines."[2]

Changes in U.S. foreign policy in the 1930s and early 1940s permitted the Marines to invest more time and resources in their new amphibious mission. The withdrawal of Marines from Haiti and Nicaragua freed up personnel to participate in annual exercises to test amphibious techniques. The outbreak of World War II in September 1939, however, would prove to be even more important to the Marine Corps. Although President Franklin Roosevelt declared the United States neutral, he also initiated a military buildup in case the situation changed. Bigger budgets enabled the Marine Corps to increase its strength from 19,400 men in 1939 to 65,000 men by November 1941 and to start purchasing the specialized landing craft necessary to transport troops and cargo from ship to shore in amphibious operations. To accommodate the growth in personnel, Headquarters Marine Corps (HQMC) organized the service's brigades into two 15,000-man divisions. There was nothing easy about this process. Officers faced equipment shortages, conflicts with their naval counterparts over the division of responsibilities, and an inability to grasp the enormous adjustments waging modern war would require. On top of all this, the Roosevelt administration sometimes interfered with the Corps' efforts to focus on amphibious warfare, by, for example, dispatching Marines to occupy Iceland in July 1941. By the time the Japanese attacked Pearl Harbor on 7 December 1941, the Marine Corps' progress had been impressive, but the outfit was still a long way from being prepared for war.

THE OFFICER CORPS

Despite the Marine Corps' substantial growth from 1939 to 1941, its top-level officer corps remained a small and insular group. In July 1941 the Corps had five major generals, nine brigadier generals, and seventy colonels. The service's fortunes in World War II depended as much on the abilities of these men as on anything else. They constituted the only source for the Corps' division and corps commanders, department chiefs, senior staff officers in the field and at HQMC, liaison officers with the Army and Navy, and high-ranking logistical personnel. As it turned out, there were never enough of them to go around because no one else could do these important jobs. The men came from a variety of geographic and socioeconomic backgrounds, but the institutionalized racism and sexism of the Corps limited them to white males. The Marine Corps may have instilled in them the same sense of duty, a ferocious commitment to their branch, loyalty, and self-reliance, but their personalities were hardly uniform. Vandegrift observed, "Senior officers do not conform to a standard mold, as some people like to think. Certainly in the prewar Marine Corps almost the reverse held true."[3] Indeed, the Marine Corps did not so much change personalities as it accentuated them, in the process producing a large number of colorful characters.[4]

The small number of high-ranking officers affected the Marine Corps' institutional culture and its performance in World War II in various ways. Of particular note, these men all knew each other personally or by reputation. Most of them had worked and socialized together for years, sometimes decades, and were therefore thoroughly cognizant of each other's backstories, strengths, weaknesses, habits, foibles, and eccentricities. Thus they had no need to closely read personnel files in evaluating senior officers. This familiarity enabled them to better assign people to jobs that best suited their talents, be it combat command, staff, logistics, and so on. These tight relationships also spawned back channels that allowed officers to speak frankly to and about each other without putting opinions on the record. On the other hand, these longstanding bonds sometimes interfered with the honest and rigorous evaluation of abilities. Officers sometimes hesitated to criticize or remove underperforming subordinates from their posts for fear of jeopardizing friendships and reputations. The Corps' insularity also generated numerous overlapping cliques and factions that bickered over and competed for the limited available resources. One officer later referred to the prewar officer corps as "clannish as hell."[5] On the whole, though, most officers believed that this familiarity benefited the Marine Corps in World War II. Vandegrift for one concluded that it made managing personnel easier: "[I] not only knew every officer in the Marine Corps but knew a great deal about them. From time to time we erred in their placement; generally, I feel we did not."[6]

Some of the cliques among high-ranking officers revolved around shared experiences while fulfilling prewar missions. Most of the officers had spent time on board warships commanding Marine detachments. These experiences introduced them to the Navy's way of doing things as well as to the naval officers with whom they would later work. Other officers had participated in pacification operations in Haiti, the Dominican Republic, and Nicaragua. There they learned about civil-military relations, logistics, small unit actions, and self-reliance. Still others served as so-called China Marines garrisoning Peking and Shanghai, where they gained exposure to officers from other countries and to complicated international situations. Some Marine officers bonded over their time together in Army and Navy schools or at HQMC. Most of these men appreciated their immersion in high-level military thinking and developed a jaded view of the Marine Corps' more rudimentary educational system. Their educational stints separated them from some of their more action-oriented colleagues and others less intellectually inclined. A common commitment to air power or artillery connected some officers. In addition, fighting in World War I united a cadre of Marine officers who gained considerable prestige in the Corps from surviving the worst of early twentieth-century combat.[7]

Regardless of clique, most officers embraced the Marines Corps' commitment to amphibious warfare. To them, it was a unique and challenging mission to master what no one else dared attempt. One officer remembered, "I think that period in the Marine Corps was the greatest thing that ever happened to it. . . . We were caught up in a tremendous enterprise of leading the way into something, pioneering, doing something that people said couldn't be done, and if there was anything that could shake an outfit out of its rut or out of intellectual sloth it was doing that sort of thing, going out into new frontiers."[8] Two events in the 1930s drove these efforts. First, a 1934 law replaced promotion by seniority with promotion by merit. Senior officers passed over by selection boards were forced into retirement after thirty-five years of service, leaving behind the most physically and mentally capable to ascend to the top of the Marine Corps hierarchy. This cleared away a lot of the deadwood in the officer corps. Second, gathering war clouds in the second half of the decade provided a sense of urgency for what appeared to be an increasingly likely and hazardous eventuality. This perceived danger focused institutional and personal attention like nothing else.[9]

The Marine Corps would pay a price for its small size, action-oriented attitude, and emphasis on amphibious warfare. Its rudimentary educational system, which one officer later described as "Mickey Mouse," failed to prepare officers for the large-scale operations they would encounter in the

Pacific. Unless they secured tours of duty at the more advanced and sophisticated Army and Navy schools, Marine officers often learned little about international affairs, commanding large units, staff work, logistics, and strategy. Such deficiencies were not serious when the Corps rarely fielded anything bigger than a battalion, but during the Pacific War, Marine generals found themselves running brigades, divisions, and even corps, all of which, to function smoothly, required specialized skills that few Marines initially possessed. In addition, the Corps neglected to instill in many of its officers a level of professionalism that promoted independent and unconventional thinking, self-awareness, and an ability to assess the viewpoints of others. As one World War II Marine division commander remembered, "The Marine Corps wanted to be small, it wanted to be good, but I must say that I didn't feel even then as a young officer that they were looking to the future in the proper way of being prepared and thinking about these things before we got into a situation and have so few people with any background that could understand the magnitude of the operation."[10] Some officers managed to overcome these deficits and performed admirably, but others did not.[11]

COMMANDANT THOMAS HOLCOMB AND HQMC

Maj. Gen. Thomas Holcomb held the post of Marine Corps commandant when the United States entered World War II in December 1941. Born in Delaware in 1879 but raised in Washington, D.C., Holcomb accepted a Marine Corps commission in 1900 after two unfulfilling years in the business world. He participated in Panama's American-manufactured war for independence against Colombia, gained Corps-wide fame for his role in Marine marksmanship programs, served the first of several tours of duty in China, and worked as an aide to commandant Gen. George Barnett. He saw considerable action in World War I at Belleau Wood, Chateau Thierry, St. Mihiel, and the Argonne as a battalion commander and then brigade executive officer. After the conflict, he rectified his lack of formal military education by attending the Army's Command and General Staff College. He also spent two years leading the Marine legation detachment in Peking and eventually ran Marine Corps Schools. Between these assignments, he supplemented his military education with stints at the Naval War College and Army War College. In 1936 President Roosevelt surprised everyone by selecting the relatively junior Holcomb as the seventeenth commandant of the Marine Corps. Holcomb likely owed the appointment to his commitment to amphibious doctrine as well as his longstanding acquaintance with Roosevelt.

Holcomb, a stocky man of medium height with graying hair and piercing eyes, owned four pipes that he constantly smoked, one after another, in rotation. With steel-rimmed glasses and a gentlemanly, formal, and reserved personality, he rarely raised his voice or addressed men by their first names. His good judgment, plain-spokenness, and common sense inspired confidence, but he possessed no charisma. In fact, although Holcomb sometimes demonstrated a quiet sense of humor, a cold-blooded, dour, and self-interested aspect to him prompted one officer to note that he lacked the milk of human kindness. For example, Holcomb was once angered to learn that an officer's transfer to China had been delayed so that he could tend to his cancer-stricken wife. A colleague noted that Holcomb's actions usually benefited his career as much as they did the Marine Corps. He was a good administrator who could see things through to completion, believed in the value of education, and emphasized that officers and enlisted men stay in their lanes. When one young officer tried to impress Holcomb by shoveling a snowy street, Holcomb remarked, "Let me tell you something, young man. You are a commissioned officer; you get paid to use your brain and not your hands. Now put that shovel away and get an orderly to do it."[12] Holcomb was in most respects a classic early twentieth-century Marine officer—dedicated, self-disciplined, and self-reliant. There may not have been anything brilliant about him, but he was the right man at the right time. One Marine general recalled after the war, "He was one of the finest commandants the Marine Corps has ever had, and it was through his intelligent and energetic guidance that the Corps was able to prepare for and make the contribution that it did make in the prosecution of the war."[13]

As commandant, Holcomb faced some obstacles and challenges foreign to his higher-ranking Army and Navy counterparts. Because the Marine Corps was organizationally part of the Navy and subject to its authority, Holcomb had to consult with and in many instances to secure approval from the Navy before making important decisions, including personnel changes. Holcomb and Adm. Ernest King, the Navy's hard-nosed and fero-cious Chief of Naval Operations, unfortunately hated one another. Hol-comb privately referred to King as "that son-of-a-bitch" and the "bastard." Even so, the two men developed a grudging respect for each other, but their mutual antipathy was not conducive to a cooperative and transparent rela-tionship between the Navy and HQMC. Indeed, the Navy short-circuited the Marine Corps out of the strategic decision-making process during the war. Naval officers expected Marines to keep their mouths shut and seize targets identified by naval planners and the Joint Chiefs of Staff. Without much input in determining strategy, Holcomb's role was limited mostly to administration rather than command. Because Army officers believed that every leatherneck was one less man eligible for their service branch, Holcomb had to fight the Army tooth and nail for every augmentation of Marine Corps strength. At the same time, Holcomb had to accommodate pressure from Roosevelt's administration to organize specialized units of paratroopers, raiders, and others. Holcomb opposed such outfits because they undermined morale among those not selected to serve in them and diverted strength from the regular units that did most of the fighting. Even so, he acquiesced at the war's start and authorized their development.[14]

The scope and scale of World War II put immense pressure on the Marine Corps and its commandant. To prevent being overwhelmed with the work-load generated by the conflict, Holcomb kept regular hours, walked for exercise, got to bed reasonably early, and made time for relaxation. There was, however, nothing easy about it. Although Holcomb's responsibili-ties were primarily administrative, the bureaucratic infighting that swirled around Washington in general and the Navy Department in particular was nonetheless stressful. Indeed, Holcomb referred to Washington as a "snake pit" of intrigue. Fortunately for Holcomb, he had the support of HQMC to help him deal with problems.

In peacetime, a triumvirate of commandant, adjutant and inspector, and quartermaster dominated HQMC. During the war, however, the Plans and Policies Division assumed a powerful role. Dubbed "Pots and Pans" by Marine wags, the division, established in 1918, gradually developed into a general staff that served as the Corps' institutional brain. It did so because it seemed more efficient and effective than other parts of HQMC.

Its sections—engineering, artillery, communications, and so on—evolved into little empires whose tentacles reached into the field and sometimes interfered with the prerogatives of local commanders. Holcomb disliked the rigmarole all this bureaucratic growth generated and responded by decentralizing as much authority as possible. When a problem arose, he usually assigned it to the section of HQMC most affected by it to let staff there develop a solution, and then he backed its efforts at implementation. However, identifying a solution acceptable to everyone sometimes created considerable paperwork. Holcomb efforts to square this circle remained a work in progress when he left office at the end of 1943.[15]

Assigning personnel to high-level posts was among Holcomb's most significant responsibilities. World War II spawned innumerable new and important positions for Holcomb to fill, including command of the six divisions and two corps that the Marines deployed during the conflict. On the one hand, the pool of talent from which he could draw was limited to around a dozen generals and seventy colonels. On the other hand, the small number of available officers meant that Holcomb could closely track them, assigning them to the tasks that he felt best suited their abilities. He knew almost all of them personally and relied on this knowledge more than on their personnel records to make his decisions.

Holcomb adopted certain criteria for appointing combat commanders. For one thing, he believed that the relevant tasks required young and healthy officers. Holcomb recognized the tremendous physical and mental strain of command—insight gained from his World War I experience—so he paid close attention to senior officers' medical reports and passed over most of those who came up short in that regard. He also wanted combat commanders who could cooperate with others, especially naval officers, and stay in their bureaucratic lanes. He looked for men who had experience both with troops and at HQMC and who had succeeded in their previous missions. Most of all, he sought officers who could take the initiative and get things done.

Once the officers appointed to combat commands went overseas to assume their duties, it became more difficult for Holcomb to evaluate their effectiveness. To keep tabs on them, he encouraged them to write to him informally about their concerns, including issues related to personnel. As he explained to one general, "I hope you will continue to find opportunities to write me frequently. Don't mind pouring out your troubles. I have my own, but I have been and always will be sympathetic with yours."[16] This approach enabled officers to speak freely about each other to Holcomb without placing anything in the official records. Holcomb could then take action against substandard officers and reward outstanding ones. One problem, however, was that some officers occasionally gave their subordinates glowing evaluations in official reports, but then damned their performances in informal correspondence with Holcomb. They did so to avoid jeopardizing longstanding friendships and careers. Holcomb disliked and complained about this subterfuge, but his efforts to stamp it out failed. As it stood, Holcomb rarely openly removed officers from their posts for cause. His policy was to rotate home those officers who had been overseas for a year or more so they could teach others, recuperate from their travails, and open up slots for their stateside counterparts eager to advance their careers through combat experience. Because rotations were so commonplace, Holcomb could bring officers back to the States without disgracing them or generating controversy if he felt that they had failed to measure up.

CONCLUSIONS

By the time the Japanese attacked Pearl Harbor, the Marine Corps had positioned itself to play an important role in any conflict with a naval dimension. It had laid the doctrinal groundwork and had begun acquiring the equipment necessary to conduct amphibious operations. Its officers were united in their commitment to its mission. It also had a commandant who understood the Corps and recognized the importance of appointing capable personnel to lead large combat units. These developments helped overcome deficiencies from having a small number of high-ranking officers, shortages in manpower and materiel, and widespread ignorance about the demands of global war. Although the Corps was unprepared at the start of the war to assail Japanese-held islands, it was developing the necessary resources and guidelines to do so.

WAGING WAR IN THE MOST REMOTE PLACE ON EARTH

The Pacific Theater

I n terms of geographic scale and terrain, the environment in which the Pacific War against Japan was waged proved to be unlike anything the U.S. military had ever encountered. The Pacific Ocean covers 62.5 million square miles, or one-third of Earth's surface. By comparison, the continental United States is a mere 3.12 million square miles. In short, the distances involved were staggering. Only 3,450 miles separates New York City and London, but there are 3,600 miles between San Francisco and Pearl Harbor, and from there, an additional 3,850 miles to Tokyo, 5,300 miles to Manila, and 5,500 miles to Melbourne. During the Pacific War, it took weeks for vessels to make the long, lonely trek across the Pacific. Even air travel sometimes required days of tedious hopping from one rudimentary airfield to another. For the millions of troops deployed in the Pacific theater, service was a long voyage that often terminated in brutal combat in remote and hellish landscapes at the far reaches of the planet. Even with technology shrinking the Earth, there was still a ways to go to make the Pacific seem anything other than enormous and intimidating.

There are thousands of Pacific islands of various sizes and terrains over which the Japanese and the Allies had the potential to fight. Some were steamy, fetid, jungle-covered masses with thin soil, jagged mountains, exotic animals, and deadly diseases. Others formed tiny, barren, windswept, and coral-crusted atolls surrounded by treacherous reefs. Still others had significant populations, towns and cities, temperate climes, hills and valleys, and well-cultivated fields. The dimensions varied. For example, New Guinea is considerably larger than Texas, while Betio is a mere 380 acres. Although the thirty-nine atolls comprising the Marshall Islands total less than seventy square miles of land, they extend across 3 million square miles of ocean. Indeed, if superimposed over the continental United States, they would stretch from Washington, D.C., to Ohio. To further complicate matters, much of the Pacific Ocean theater lacked adequate infrastructure—that is, railroads, airfields, port facilities, power plants, warehouses, and so forth. This made waging war a logistical nightmare for all involved because they had to bring with them, by boat, almost everything they needed to fight the enemy and sustain themselves.

Geography would obviously play an important role in planning the war against Japan in the Pacific, but national and bureaucratic imperatives emerged as factors as well. To wage the conflict, the Anglo-American Combined Chiefs of Staff, composed of the U.S. Joint Chiefs of Staff and its British counterpart, divided the world into military theaters and gave overall command of each theater to whichever nation invested the most resources. Thus, the United States came to dominate the Pacific theater, but the process was not so simple. Both the Army and Navy wanted to run the Pacific War, and neither was willing to take a backseat to the other. Being coequal components of the U.S. military establishment, neither could order the other around. Only the president, designated commander in chief by the Constitution, held authority over both branches. In March 1942 the Combined Chiefs of Staff resolved the issue by splitting the Pacific into two theaters, one controlled by the Army and the other by the Navy. The Army-led Southwest Pacific Area, under the control of Gen. Douglas MacArthur, included Australia, New Guinea, much of the Dutch East Indies, and the

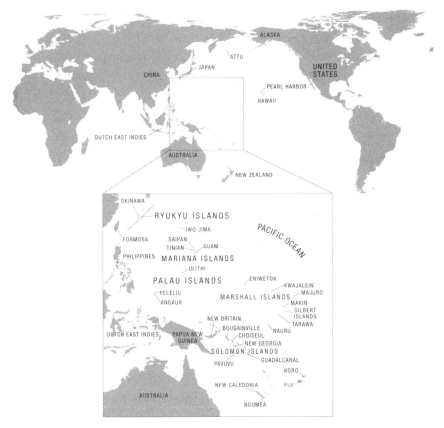

Map 1. *Pacific Ocean Area in World War II*

Philippines. The Navy-centric Pacific Ocean Area, encompassing most of
the rest of the Pacific and under Adm. Chester Nimitz's authority, was sub-
divided into three subordinate commands: the North Pacific Area, Central
Pacific Area, and South Pacific Area. Both theaters contained significant
Army and Navy resources that the Combined Chiefs of Staff placed under
the general authority of the theater commanders. Although this compromise arrangement complicated everything from logistics to strategic planning, it maintained interservice harmony and allowed the Army and Navy
to focus on defeating Japan. For a number of reasons during World War II,
the Marine Corps concentrated almost exclusively on the Japanese. The
Marines had anticipated and trained for years for a conflict in the Pacific
against Japan, and their emphasis on amphibious warfare was well suited

for operations in the island-rich Pacific Ocean. In addition, the Navy had a proprietary interest in the Pacific War, and the Marine Corps was part of the Navy. Despite all this, nothing was inevitable about the decision to focus on the Japanese.

Before the United States entered World War II in December 1941, the Marine Corps centered much of its institutional attention on Germany. In July 1941 President Franklin Roosevelt's administration had sent the Marines to occupy Iceland to keep it out of German hands and had later that year floated proposals to use leathernecks to seize various Atlantic and Caribbean islands. Even after the Japanese attacked Pearl Harbor, U.S. grand strategy continued to call for deploying resources against Germany while remaining on the defensive in the Pacific against Japan. Because of the Marine Corps' amphibious expertise, it could have spearheaded Allied efforts to invade German-occupied Europe, and once ashore, the Army and Marines could have worked together on the continent as they had during World War I. After the United States declared war on Japan and Germany, Navy Department officials contemplated dispatching the Marines to North Africa to fight the Germans there, but Marine officers at HQMC convinced Commandant Thomas Holcomb that any leathernecks sent to North Africa or Europe would lose their identity and specialized skills in a sea of Army soldiers. On the other hand, in the Pacific the Marines could continue to ply their trade and maintain their autonomy under the Navy's familiar authority. From this perspective, deploying the Marines in the Pacific became an easy recommendation for Holcomb to make to the Navy.[1]

Japan's surprise attack on Allied possessions in the Pacific and East Asia disrupted U.S. war plans. By crippling the American fleet at Pearl Harbor, Japan made it impossible for the Navy to immediately steam across the Pacific to rescue the Philippines and defeat its Japanese counterpart in the decisive battle envisioned by War Plan Orange. In addition, the Japanese offensive stunned everyone with its ferocity and scope. Instead of assailing a small number of targets, the Japanese simultaneously struck innumerable Allied positions throughout the region. By the end of May 1942, the Japanese had overrun the Philippines, Guam, Wake, Malaysia and Singapore, Hong Kong, Burma, and the Dutch East Indies. They captured around 85,000 British troops at Singapore alone, and another 76,000 Americans and Filipinos at Bataan, in the Philippines. The Japanese fleet spread across the Pacific and into the Indian Ocean, sinking dozens of Allied warships. On 23 January 1942, Japanese troops seized Rabaul, in New Britain, before pushing into Papua New Guinea and on to the Solomon Islands. In doing so, they expanded the theater of war far beyond anything U.S. military planners had anticipated when they created and periodically updated War Plan Orange.

GUADALCANAL

Japan's crushing naval defeat at the Battle of Midway in June 1942 did not immediately shift the Pacific War's momentum toward the United States. Despite this setback, the Japanese continued their efforts to round out and consolidate their newly won empire. On 6 July, Japan landed troops on Guadalcanal, in the southern Solomon Islands, and began constructing an airfield near Lunga Point. This news greatly alarmed Adm. Ernest King, the Navy's hard-nosed Chief of Naval Operations. King feared that after the airfield's completion, Japanese aircraft flying from it could threaten supply and communication lines between the United States and Australia. He therefore wanted to launch an offensive as soon as possible to retake the island and nip the problem in the bud. Unfortunately for King, Anglo-American grand strategy called for concentrating the bulk of Allied strength on the European War against Germany. Indeed, the Combined Chiefs of Staff was already formulating plans for an invasion of Vichy French North Africa that would consume a good chunk of available U.S. military resources. Even so, King hoped to take advantage of the opportunities created by the victory at the Battle of Midway and go on the offensive. In pursuit of this objective, he persuaded Gen. George Marshall, the Army's redoubtable chief of staff, not only to go along with his plan, but also to adjust administrative boundaries to put Guadalcanal in Nimitz's Navy-dominated Pacific Ocean Area. On 10 July, Nimitz issued orders for Operation Watchtower, a Navy-run operation to storm both Guadalcanal and the Japanese naval base on the small nearby island of Tulagi.

Guadalcanal had not figured in either Japanese or American prewar planning. Tucked away in the southern Solomon Islands, about 3,500 miles from

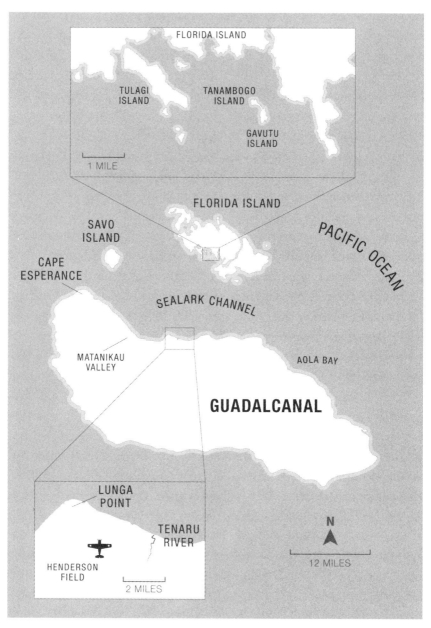

FLORIDA ISLAND

TULAGI
ISLAND

TANAMBOGO
ISLAND

GAVUTU
ISLAND

1 MILE

FLORIDA ISLAND

SAVO
ISLAND

PACIFIC OCEAN

CAPE
ESPERANCE

SEALARK CHANNEL

MATANIKAU
VALLEY

AOLA BAY

GUADALCANAL

LUNGA
POINT

TENARU
RIVER

HENDERSON
FIELD

2 MILES

N

12 MILES

Map 2. *Guadalcanal*

Tokyo and Honolulu, it was one of the most remote places on Earth. It contained two thousand square miles of dense jungle, mountains, swift streams, and occasional clearings. Its lush green foliage and surrounding clear blue seas gave the impression of an idyllic tropical paradise, but Japanese and American troops soon learned that Guadalcanal, like other South Pacific island battlefields, harbored nightmarish dangers for them. The trackless, smothering jungle was psychologically isolating and forbidding, inhabited by giant spiders, centipedes, snakes, rats, and crocodiles. Constant rains and the resulting steamy heat accelerated both growth and decay and gave the air a heavy, oppressive feel. Mud was everywhere and got into everything. Jungle rot turned scratches into infections that often produced oozing sores that never seemed to heal. The petri-dish environment spawned dengue fever, scrub typhus (carried by rodent mites), and other terrible diseases. Mosquito-borne malaria, which eventually afflicted almost everyone, sent thousands of feverish and shivering men to hospitals or graves. Guadalcanal was not, in short, the optimal place to wage a war.

Because Operation Watchtower was Admiral King's baby, the Navy was responsible for supplying the forces for its implementation. Fortunately for King, Gen. Archibald Vandegrift's 1st Marine Division was already deploying to the South Pacific. Born in Charlottesville, Virginia, in 1887, Vandegrift was raised around and inspired by Civil War veterans who filled his head with wartime adventures. He got an appointment to West Point but failed the physical, so his mother persuaded him to attend the University of Virginia while looking for another way into the Army. After graduating in 1901 Vandegrift secured a Marine Corps commission. He had not known about the organization until a senator mentioned it to him, but it seemed like the best way to satisfy his martial aspirations. While attending the School of Application, he was court martialed and convicted for returning late from liberty. As punishment he lost some seniority and received an unsatisfactory fitness report.

Vandegrift's early career progressed as any young Marine officer might expect in that era. He was stationed in the Panama Canal Zone, helped maintain law and order in Nicaragua, participated in the storming of Veracruz, and fought Cacos bandits in Haiti. On the other hand, he spent World War I in Haiti, rather than the trenches of France, so he did not become part of that clique of Marine officers who saw action on the Western Front. After returning to the States in 1923, he took the field officers' course at Quantico, Virginia, did a tour of duty in China, worked in HQMC's budget office, and served as a staffer in the Fleet Marine Force. In 1935 he returned to China for two years, during which he rose to lead the Marine detachment in Peking. Holcomb brought Vandegrift home in 1937 to become his military secretary and then assistant commandant. In November 1941 Holcomb rewarded Vandegrift for his good work by sending him to the 1st Marine Division as assistant commander. A few months later, Vandegrift became the division's commander.

A classic southern gentleman, Vandegrift was courteous, kind, graceful, and reserved. Although optimistic and superficially friendly, he kept a distance from most people. He never raised his voice and addressed almost everyone by their surnames. During the war, he refrained from denigrating the Japanese, but no one doubted his moral courage, determination, or his commitment to his country and the Marine Corps. Later as commandant, he personally signed all the condolence letters to the families of Marines killed in action. When his secretary suggested forging Vandegrift's signature for him, Vandegrift replied that if Marines could die overseas for their country, then he could stay up a few extra hours each night to affix his signature to a document expressing the Corps' sympathy.

Gifted with a sharp mind, Vandegrift was comfortable with responsibility. On the other hand, he was so hard of hearing and poor of sight that he sometimes did not understand everything said at meetings. His slow speech and deliberateness hampered his ability to readily articulate his views and therefore persuade listeners. He was sometimes so indulgent toward old comrades that he tolerated their inefficiency longer than he should have. Once Vandegrift made up his mind, though, he moved decisively to implement his decisions. He knew the Marine Corps, its doctrine, its personnel, and its limitations inside and out.[2]

Vandegrift owed his rise through the uppermost levels of the Marine Corps as much to his relationship with Holcomb as to his personal capabilities. Holcomb had kept close tabs on Vandegrift's career throughout the late 1930s and early 1940s. He selected Vandegrift to be his military secretary and then assistant commandant to groom him for the commandant's post.

Indeed, the two men were personally close. Holcomb admired Vandegrift's dedication and talent and used him as his sounding board. Vandegrift for his part liked and respected Holcomb. He was smart enough to recognize Holcomb's impact on his career, and his southern gentility enabled him to ingratiate himself and become a confidant without appearing cloying or sycophantic.

Holcomb had appointed Vandegrift head of the 1st Marine Division because its previous commander, Gen. Philip Torrey, proved unable to mold his subordinates into an effective team. It was a plumb assignment that further demonstrated to Marine Corps insiders Holcomb's partiality toward Vandegrift and one that thoroughly surprised the self-effacing Vandegrift. Holcomb regretted losing Vandegrift's services at HQMC, but figured it made military sense to send his most trusted lieutenant to the Corps' most important combat post.[3]

The Marines were by no means ready to implement Operation Watchtower. Although Marine units were en route to the South Pacific at the time, the Navy had deployed them to blunt an attack, not to launch one. Vandegrift reached Wellington, New Zealand, on 14 June. Less than two weeks later, the South Pacific Area commander, Adm. Robert Ghormley, summoned Vandegrift and his staff to Auckland, New Zealand, for a meeting. After Vandegrift took a seat in Ghormley's office, Ghormley handed him the dispatch authorizing Watchtower and said, "I have some disconcerting news." Vandegrift had not expected to take his division into action until the following year, so he was stunned to learn that the Navy wanted him to assail Guadalcanal in little more than a month. He did not even know the island's location. What Vandegrift did, however, know was that Watchtower would be an enormously risky and difficult undertaking for all sorts of reasons.

One big problem involved logistics. Vandegrift had to locate and load sufficient supplies, equipment, weapons, and ammunition for a slapdash mission of uncertain duration. Although the New Zealand government was accommodating, the Wellington longshoremen, unaware of Watchtower's nature and urgency, moved so lethargically that Marines took over many of their jobs. Because of the need to get under way, the Marines loaded their vessels without much rhyme or reason, often in cold drizzling rain. More than one leatherneck later recalled boxes of soggy cornflakes disintegrating on the docks.

To make matters worse, the 1st Marine Division was not concentrated. Although its 5th Marine Regiment was with Vandegrift in Wellington, the 7th Marine Regiment was on garrison duty in Samoa, and the 1st Marine Regiment remained en route. To replace the 7th Marine Regiment, King authorized Vandegrift to substitute the 2nd Marine Division's 2nd Marine Regiment, but it was just embarking from San Diego. There were also serious questions about the quality of the leathernecks and their officers. The 5th Marine Regiment seemed solid enough, but the 1st Marine Regiment was brand new. Moreover, the Corps had skimmed off some of the division's best personnel for raider and paratrooper battalions. Most of the officers were untested. One staffer recalled that the chaotic and stressful loading process broke a few officers mentally. On top of these problems, Vandegrift had almost no intelligence on Guadalcanal or its Japanese defenders, so his staff had to make educated guesses about geography, topography, hydrography, and expected enemy opposition. The uncertainly was enough to unnerve the most stalwart commander. Vandegrift, though, projected a serene confidence as he went about untangling the innumerable and inevitable snafus that plagued the planning process.[4]

Vandegrift's problems did not end there. On 18 July, Adm. Richmond Kelly Turner arrived to command the amphibious force responsible for transporting and supplying the Marines destined for Guadalcanal. This made Turner Vandegrift's immediate superior. The dour, gaunt, and balding Turner was a controversial figure in the Navy even before he reached the South Pacific. Almost everyone acknowledged his genius, determination, and phenomenal grasp of detail. He drafted plans almost singlehandedly and understood every aspect of them down to the smallest detail. Incapable of delegating, he drove himself to exhaustion and drink. Worse yet, he was loud, overbearing, opinionated, arrogant, and always certain that he knew better than everyone else. While often right, this was not the case with amphibious warfare. Once the first troops left their transports for shore, Turner was out of his element, but initially failed to recognize it. As Vandegrift later put it, "I knew from previous experience that Turner held certain strategic and tactical ideas which so long as they pertained to naval operations were valid enough. When he got into the work of the generals, however, he should have saved his time."[5]

Fortunately for the Americans, Turner demonstrated an ability to learn from his mistakes, but he committed many of those military sins from which he later learned during the Guadalcanal campaign. For example, he failed to understand that he and Vandegrift could not share control of most of the 2nd Marine Regiment as their reserve. Vandegrift and his staff were shocked to discover that Turner planned to establish his headquarters on Guadalcanal and, it seemed, direct the Marines in ground operations. Turner's ignorant self-assurance put Vandegrift in a difficult spot. After all, Turner was his boss and needed to be obeyed as such, but Vandegrift knew better than anyone that many of Turner's amphibious ideas for Watchtower were unrealistic and even dangerous. Had Vandegrift stood up and yelled, Turner might have backed down, but Vandegrift had neither the personality nor authority to behave in such a way toward a superior.[6]

Vandegrift and Turner were united in their commitment to Watchtower's success despite their differences, but they could not say the same of Turner's immediate boss, Adm. Frank Jack Fletcher, the overall commander of the expedition. On 26 July, Vandegrift and Turner met with Fletcher in the wardroom of Fletcher's flagship, the aircraft carrier USS *Saratoga*, near Koro Island, about a hundred miles south of Fiji. To Vandegrift, Fletcher appeared nervous and tired. He seemed to know little and care less about the operation. Fletcher, however, was sufficiently informed to complain that Watchtower had been hastily conceived, poorly planned, and undermanned. To make matters worse, Fletcher insisted that his carriers would remain in the vicinity of Guadalcanal for two days after the landing to provide air cover, not the five days Turner had slated for unloading the Marines and their materiel onto the island. Fletcher worried not only about Japanese air and submarine attacks, but also about fuel supplies. Retiring as always, and in more than a little pain because he had bruised his leg boarding *Saratoga*, Vandegrift explained his reservations dispassionately. Turner, on the other hand, made his unhappiness known loud and clear, to the point that the conference degenerated into a shouting match. Turner insisted that whatever Watchtower's shortcomings, the decision to undertake it had already been made, so it was their job to figure out how to implement it successfully. Fletcher found Turner's demands unrealistic and accused him of using the operation to further his career. Small wonder that one observer later noted that the meeting was more about fighting Watchtower's problems than solving them.[7]

Despite innumerable logistical, training, and command problems, the Marine task force gradually assembled off Koro Island. On 31 July, the expedition weighed anchor and steamed northwestward toward the Solomon Islands, camouflaged by low clouds and frequent rain squalls. There were approximately 19,000 Marines on board the twenty-three transport vessels escorted by Turner's warships. On the transport USS *McCawley*, Vandegrift hobbled about on his injured leg to inspect and encourage his men. He had been honest with his officers about the operation's difficulties but took comfort in the businesslike manner in which the leathernecks went about their preassault tasks. He wryly remembered that a few short weeks before he had never even heard of the island that had since consumed his thoughts and time. When he returned to his small, hot cabin on the evening before the invasion, he wrote to his wife, "Whatever happens you'll know that I did my best. Let us hope that best will be good enough."[8]

On the morning of 7 August the Marines landed on Guadalcanal and Tulagi after a cursory preliminary bombardment by Turner's warships. The landings went relatively well considering the Marines' inexperience with amphibious operations. The one thousand Japanese defenders on Tulagi and the nearby islet of Gavutu-Tanambogo resisted fiercely. It took the leathernecks, largely raiders and paratroopers, three days and 320 casualties to pry the Japanese from their caves. It was a shocking introduction to the skill and determination that Japanese soldiers would habitually display in subsequent engagements. Indeed, opposition was so strong that the Marine commander, assistant division chief Gen. William Rupertus, persuaded Vandegrift and Turner to commit their reserves from the 2nd Marine Regiment to finish the job.

Meanwhile, Col. LeRoy Hunt's 5th Marine Regiment and Col. Clifton Cates' 1st Marine Regiment faced almost no opposition when they splashed ashore on Guadalcanal. They met only a few hundred defenders, mostly Korean construction workers, who were disinclined to fight very hard. Even so, the leathernecks advanced inland sluggishly, failing to coordinate well or patrol effectively. Fire discipline was so poor that some of the Marines amused themselves by shooting coconuts out of trees. Such problems, hardly unusual for rookie troops, did not matter much in the end. The next day the Marines seized the unfinished airfield and captured considerable quantities of Japanese supplies and equipment in the process.[9]

Vandegrift remained onboard *McCawley* for most of 7 August so he could more easily keep track of events on both Guadalcanal and Tulagi. When he came ashore on Guadalcanal after his troops secured the beaches, he was not completely satisfied with what he found. Cates, for example, did not know the whereabouts of all of his units. Reserved as always, Vandegrift quietly emphasized the importance of occupying the airfield as soon as possible. Even so, both he and Turner were astonished by the ease with which the leathernecks had landed, considering their inexperience and lack of intelligence. The next day, when he visited Rupertus on the converted hospital vessel USS *Neville*, the sight of so many wounded Marines saddened Vandegrift, but their performance under fire also filled him with pride. Their condition reminded him of the awesome responsibility of his command.[10]

As it was, there were plenty of other occurrences to remind Vandegrift of his responsibilities. The day after the Marine landings, Fletcher decided to withdraw his carrier force from the area because he was concerned about fuel shortages and the heavy losses his aircrews had sustained from Japanese air attacks while defending the beachhead. Without air cover, the transports supplying the Marines were vulnerable, so Turner announced that he had to pull out as well. The Marines, however, had not yet finished unloading the transports. Although Turner assured Vandegrift that he would return as soon as possible, the fact remained that the Navy was for now abandoning the Marines. The news upset Vandegrift, but he concluded that he had enough supplies, troops, and weapons on hand to hold out for the time being.

That very night, however, the Americans learned how precarious their situation was. A Japanese naval force from New Britain and New Ireland slipped down the Solomons and inflicted a severe defeat on the Allies at the Battle of Savo Island. The Japanese sank one Australian and three American cruisers in a one-sided affair in which more than a thousand Allied sailors died. Japanese losses, on the other hand, were negligible. It was a sobering demonstration of the Japanese navy's night-fighting prowess. Fortunately for the Marines, the Japanese warships did not take the opportunity to destroy the transports off of Guadalcanal hurriedly preparing to leave. When the partially loaded transports set off on the afternoon of 9 August, they left the Marines with only enough ammunition for four days of fighting and a thirty-seven-day supply of food.[11]

With the transports gone, Vandegrift decided against attempting to secure all of Guadalcanal with his limited forces. After all, he already held the island's most important piece of real estate: the airfield, soon completed and renamed Henderson after a Marine aviator killed at Midway. Dispersing his troops would simply make the airfield more vulnerable to a Japanese counterattack. On the other hand, concentrating his leathernecks in and around Henderson Field enabled the Japanese to rush reinforcements to the island and secure a foothold there without interference. Vandegrift was honest with his officers about the Navy leaving them in limbo, but he insisted that their experience would not be a repetition of events in Bataan, in the Philippines, a few months earlier, when thousands of Americans and Filipino soldiers surrendered. To sustain morale, Vandegrift limped the lines daily to let the leathernecks see him. Such efforts by Vandegrift and his officers had the desired effect. Despite heat and rain, malaria, and reduced rations, the Marines remained determined. A few weeks after the landing, Vandegrift joined a group of Marines bathing in the Tenaru River. As he enjoyed the water, his eyes fell on a young leatherneck casually and confidently guarding the swimming hole with a machine gun. Vandegrift concluded that with men like these, the Japanese could never defeat them.[12]

For all the faith that Vandegrift placed in his leathernecks, he knew that their fate rested as much on the Navy as on their courage and determination. Guadalcanal may not have figured in American and Japanese strategic planning before the conflict, but once the Marines landed there, it quickly became the vortex of the Pacific War, sucking in far more American and Japanese resources than anyone anticipated.

Despite the United States' recent victory at the Battle of Midway, the Japanese navy remained quantitatively and qualitatively superior to its U.S. counterpart, as evidenced by its lopsided triumph at Savo Bay. While the Marines dug in on Guadalcanal, the Japanese and U.S. navies struggled to resupply and reinforce their forces in and around the island and prevent their opponent from doing the same. This resulted in a series of confusing naval battles that included everything from aircraft carriers and battleships to destroyers and submarines. Among the most important were the Battle of the Eastern Solomons (24–25 August), the Battle of Cape Esperance (11–12 October), the Battle of the Santa Cruz Islands (25–27 October), the Naval Battle of Guadalcanal (13–15 November), and the Battle of Tassafaronga (30 November). Each side suffered heavy losses in these engagements, but the Americans' growing materiel superiority and combat prowess gradually wore down the Japanese and turned the tide of the campaign. There was nothing easy about it for the sailors involved or for the Marines on Guadalcanal, who were periodically subjected to Japanese airstrikes and naval bombardment by vessels as large as battleships.

Vandegrift conducted most of his business with the Navy through Turner. Despite a bout of malaria and a poor diet, Turner was good to his word and periodically slipped vessels to Guadalcanal with enough supplies to sustain the Marines. Vandegrift recognized Turner's undoubted courage and commitment, but had problems with him habitually overstepping boundaries and going off on strategic tangents. At one point, for instance, he ordered Vandegrift to provide five hundred Marines to unload his ships. He also pushed for an invasion of Ndeni Island, east of Guadalcanal, which Vandegrift saw as a needless dispersion of limited resources. When Ghormley quashed the idea, Turner advocated establishing another beachhead on Guadalcanal, at Aola Bay. Most damningly in Vandegrift's eyes, Turner turned the leatherneck combat units left behind in New Caledonia into a raider battalion without consulting any Marine generals. Turner's unwise strategic ideas prevented Col. Amor Sims' 7th Marine Regiment from reinforcing Guadalcanal from Samoa until 18 September.

Vandegrift, as Turner's subordinate, was unable to do much about Turner's activities until Nimitz flew into Guadalcanal on 30 September for an inspection. Nimitz's plane touched down at Henderson Field just before nightfall in a blinding storm. After a late dinner, Nimitz and Vandegrift huddled in Vandegrift's tent to discuss the situation. Turner's name came up of course, but Vandegrift hesitated to voice his grievances, in part because of his reserved personality but also out of respect for the chain of command.

Instead, he talked circumspectly, limiting his criticisms to Turner's most egregious actions. Vandegrift's taciturn manner, though, belied a shrewd bureaucratic operator. Although Vandegrift was cagey with Nimitz, his chief of staff, Col. Gerald Thomas, at Vandegrift's behest spoke freely and bluntly, about Turner with Nimitz's Marine staff officer, who in turn conveyed this information to Nimitz. Turner, said Thomas, was Vandegrift's "hair shirt." Thomas' entreaties had their intended impact. When Nimitz returned to Pearl Harbor, he limited Turner's power ashore and drove the point home by getting King to reprimand Turner for exceeding his authority.[13]

Naval power was merely one dimension of the Guadalcanal campaign. Air power was another. Vandegrift understood as well as anyone that Henderson Field gave Guadalcanal its value. In American hands, the airfield represented an unsinkable aircraft carrier that could give the Marines control of the skies around the island; the nearest Japanese airfields were hundreds of miles away, on Rabaul and Bougainville. Although the Marines completed Henderson on 18 August with the help of captured Japanese equipment, it did not lead to immediate air supremacy. Constant Japanese air attacks damaged the airfield, and inclement weather, communication problems, fueling and arming difficulties, and a perpetual shortage of planes and spare parts hindered Marine efforts to dominate the local airspace. Moreover, most Japanese pilots and planes were superior to their American counterparts.

On 3 September, Gen. Roy Geiger arrived on Guadalcanal to assume command of what became known as the Cactus Air Force, operating out of Henderson. As soon as Geiger landed, he dropped off his gear and headed to Vandegrift's command post. Geiger greeted his old friend warmly and announced that he had brought along a case of Johnny Walker Scotch Whiskey. When Geiger returned to his tent a short time later to retrieve the liquor, however, he was irked to discover that someone had already absconded with it.[14]

Roy Geiger was a Marine Corps anomaly. Born in Florida in 1885, he graduated from Florida State Normal and went on to earn a law degree from John B. Stetson University in 1907. Instead of pursing a legal career, Geiger decided in favor of the Marine Corps. He was one of only two high-ranking World War II Marine combat commanders who entered the Corps as an enlisted man. He secured a commission in 1909, served as a recruiter, and deployed to Nicaragua, Panama, the Philippines, and China. In 1911 he received an unfavorable fitness report in which he was cited for "impertinence and flippance [*sic*]" after getting drunk at a party on a British warship celebrating the coronation of King George V and swimming back to the battleship USS *Delaware*.[15] He learned to fly at Pensacola Naval Air Station in 1916, and during World War I participated in bombing missions against German positions in Belgium and Germany. He was also arrested, but never tried, for making disparaging remarks about his superior right after the Germans surrendered. Following the war, he did a tour of duty in Haiti, worked in the judge advocate general's office, and in 1931 became head of Marine Corps aviation. Along the way he attended the Command and General Staff College, the Army War College, and the Naval War College, making him the only Marine World War II division or corps commander to darken the door of all three of those prestigious institutions. As Geiger explained to someone, "There are two places to be if you want to succeed in the Marine Corps—in time of peace, go to school and prepare for war—in time of war, get to the front and apply what you have learned."[16] After World War II began in Europe, he traveled to the Mediterranean as a naval attaché to observe and report on British air operations there. American involvement in the conflict brought him home, and from there Holcomb sent him to Guadalcanal to lead the Cactus Air Force.

Geiger did not make a good first impression. A tight-lipped, square-jawed chain-smoker with a penchant for cigars, he tended to unnerve people with his cold stare. Phlegmatic and unemotional, he was devoid of charisma. When Geiger spoke, it was always matter-of-factly, to the point, and without an ounce of eloquence. He disliked small talk and beating around the bush, which made conversing with him a challenge many junior officers preferred to avoid. Although he could be impish around old friends like Vandegrift, most of his subordinates found him intimidating, moody, and distant. Beneath the surface, however, Geiger had a first-rate intellect that enabled him to quickly grasp complex issues and see the flaws in any argument. While planning for the invasion of Guam, for example, he asked an officer for all the pertinent texts and tables on support artillery. The officer brought Geiger twenty pounds of instruction manuals and put them in a pile on the floor of Geiger's Quonset hut. Shortly thereafter at a

meeting on the subject, Geiger demonstrated that he had read and understood all the material. Geiger not only possessed a law degree and years
of aviation expertise, but he also attended the Army and the Navy's most
prestigious schools. In addition, he was hard-driving, aggressive, confident
and evinced no lack of physical courage. He frequently toured battlefields
right up to the front and even accompanied underwater demolition teams
in their boats on pre-landing missions to identify and clear beach obstacles.
It was small wonder that his fellow officers so respected him—except for
Turner, who questioned his intelligence—and joked that he was weaned
on aviation fuel.[17]

Given Geiger's distant demeanor, working for him was not always easy.
Though generally fair, he demanded a lot from his staff officers and could
be unforgiving of their mistakes or failure to live up to his exacting standards. Despite Geiger's thickset, doughy appearance, he believed in and
practiced physical fitness, even ordering his staff to play volleyball with him
to stay in shape. More seriously, Geiger often made up his mind and acted
without consulting or informing his staffers, leading to confusion and delay.
The good news was that Geiger respected the autonomy of his subordinate
commanders and did not interfere unduly in their operations. Whatever
his foibles, most agreed that Geiger was a fine combat leader. One officer
noted years later, "I was one of those who wondered why the Commandant would pick a man to lead a corps who had no experience as a ground
unit commander in his career. But, after serving under him in his four
campaigns, I was absolutely sure he could not have picked a better man. . . .
If you had a son or daughter going into battle, you would hope they had a
commander like Geiger."[18]

Because Geiger was an old and trusted friend, Vandegrift gave him carte
blanche over air operations from Henderson. Geiger worked tirelessly to
overcome the innumerable problems he came up against. He reduced the
vulnerability of his aircraft by tearing down structures near the airfield that
the Japanese had used for registering their artillery fire, deployed wrecked
planes as decoys, and constructed a secret airstrip to hide aircraft. He led
through personal example and force of personality. When a newly arrived
pilot insisted that Japanese naval guns had rendered Henderson Field inop-
erative, without a word Geiger walked down to the airstrip, commandeered

a dive bomber, took off (dodging shell holes), flew northward, bombed a Japanese antiaircraft battery, and returned safely.

There was nothing easy about Geiger's job. At one point in late October, for example, he had only thirty serviceable aircraft left. Conditions gradually improved though. Turner continued to bring in supplies, weapons, and equipment to replace materiel destroyed in combat and in accidents, and Navy aircrews arrived from carriers sunk or damaged in the battles around the island. The quality and quantity of planes and pilots got better. By early November, it was clear that the Americans were gaining the upper hand in the skies over Guadalcanal. At about that time and over Vandegrift's objections, Adm. Aubrey Fitch, air commander for the South Pacific Area, ordered an exhausted Geiger to Espiritu Santo for administrative duty. Six months later, Holcomb summoned Geiger to HQMC to direct Marine aviation. Although Geiger was on Guadalcanal for only two short months, his work there not only helped win the campaign, but also gained the respect of Holcomb, Vandegrift, and almost everyone else with whom he came into contact on the island.[19]

While Geiger struggled to secure the skies over Guadalcanal, Vandegrift focused on protecting Henderson Field from the Japanese army. To do so, he initially had three infantry regiments—the 1st, 2nd, and 5th—as well as the 11th Artillery Regiment to deploy on Tulagi and around Henderson. The Marines may have been intermittently cut off and isolated, but they were also dug in and increasingly prepared. Moreover, they benefited from a series of Japanese tactical blunders. After the Marine landings, the Japanese decided to counterattack as soon as possible to eliminate the Americans' foothold. The first Japanese troops came ashore at Taivu Point, east of the Marine perimeter, on 18 August. They mistakenly believed that there were only a couple of thousand Marines defending Henderson Field, when in actuality more than 11,000 were in the area. Thus, the 1st Marine Regiment easily repelled an assault on Henderson Field by fewer than a thousand Japanese soldiers at the Battle of Tenaru on the night of 20–21 August.

The Japanese, redoubling their efforts to bring in more troops to Guadalcanal, resorted to nighttime convoys that the Marines dubbed the Tokyo Express. Unfortunately for the Japanese, Vandegrift augmented his troops as well. He summoned his assistant division commander, Rupertus, and much of the Tulagi garrison to reinforce the defensive perimeter around Hender-son. On 12–14 September, approximately six thousand Japanese soldiers assailed the Marines at the Battle of Edson's Ridge. Col. Merritt Edson's battalion of raiders and paratroopers bore the brunt of the assault, and their superior firepower won the day. At the end of the engagement, several Japanese soldiers who had slipped through Marine lines charged Vandegrift as he stood in front of his command post reading messages, but nearby Marines killed them before they reached their target. The decimated remnants of the Japanese force retreated westward to the Matanikau Valley. Although Vandegrift had every reason to be proud of his leathernecks for their recent victories, they not only outnumbered and outgunned their opponents in both battles, but they also fought from prepared positions against an ill-equipped and tired enemy. Indeed, when the Marines undertook limited offensives into the Matanikau Valley in August and September, they failed to display much tactical prowess and achieved only limited success.

The fighting around Henderson Field gave Vandegrift the opportunity to evaluate his staff officers and subordinate commanders under combat conditions, and he was not completely happy with the results. He decided that his original chief of staff, Col. Capers James, was not measuring up. One officer remembered that James lacked the practical education necessary to keep a staff operating smoothly. In addition, Vandegrift felt that some of his battalion commanders were not sufficiently aggressive, and he was disappointed with the head of the 5th Marine Regiment, Col. LeRoy Hunt, a brave and bold officer with a fine World War I reputation. The Guadalcanal operation, though, revealed that Hunt could not control his battalions and was too easy on his men. During one of Turner's inspections, for example, Hunt demonstrated that he did not understand the tactical situation or his unit's deployments. As far as Vandegrift was concerned, he lacked the necessary hardness to lead men into battle and make tough decisions.[20]

Vandegrift was an indulgent man who disliked making difficult personnel decisions unless absolutely necessary. After the Battle of Edson's Ridge, though, he worried that Turner might relieve him from his command unless he got his divisional house in order. Still, Hunt in particular was an old and personal friend whose companionship Vandegrift valued. Mulling things over, Vandegrift resorted to the kind of bureaucratic subterfuge he had learned at HQMC. That autumn, HQMC had promoted a good many men to colonel to accommodate the Corps' expansion. In fact, the 1st Marine Division currently had a surplus of officers holding that rank. Holcomb wanted Vandegrift to send some of these men home to train and organize new units. There was no urgency to the order, but Vandegrift seized upon it to purge his divisional roster of underperforming high-level officers. Although he claimed that he was by and large returning colonels who had been with the division the longest, doing so also achieved his real goal of ridding the division of colonels such as Hunt, whose performances *NOT REALLY TRUE*   *UNUSUAL INTERPRETATION!* he had found wanting. Vandegrift's insistence that he had been motivated by fairness fooled no one. Hunt for one was upset by his removal as 5th Marine Regiment commander and never forgave Vandegrift for derailing his career.[21]

During the purge, Vandegrift also identified and rewarded several men who had proven themselves to his satisfaction. One was his operations officer, Col. Gerald Thomas, who took over as 1st Marine Division's chief of staff after James' departure. Vandegrift and Thomas were close. In fact, people described Thomas as Vandegrift's alter ego, confidant, and even as his brains. Their tight relationship aroused resentment and jealousy among some 1st Marine Division officers. Thomas' hard-driving and unforgiving personality did little to soothe bruised egos. Col. Pedro del Valle, the 11th Artillery Regiment commander, was another officer who earned Vandegrift's approval. Because he had been with the 1st Marine Division for such a long time, del Valle should have rotated stateside, but Vandegrift made an exception because he so respected his abilities. Vandegrift not only retained him on Guadalcanal, but also recommended his promotion to brigadier general. Despite the uncertain health of General Rupertus, the 1st Marine Division's assistant commander, Vandegrift continued to value him for having led the successful assault on Tulagi. Vandegrift likewise approved of his 1st Marine Regiment chief, Clifton Cates, whose outspoken commitment to defense-in-depth convinced Vandegrift to give his regiment the most vulnerable parts of the Marine perimeter to defend. In endorsing these and other officers in the Marines' first major World War II campaign, Vandegrift helped to create a "Guadalcanal clique" that dominated the Corps in the postwar years.[22]

[handwritten note at top:] ✗ RICHMOND TURNER WAS very intelligent but generally a "BIG" EGO AND MADE SOME CRITICAL MISTAKES AND ESCAPED CENSURE

On 21 October another important visitor arrived on Guadalcanal. Commandant Holcomb made the long flight across the Pacific to take a firsthand look at the Marines' war and to try to disentangle the complicated amphibious command relationship between the Marines and the Navy. Although Vandegrift worried about Holcomb's safety, he was happy *[handwritten:] WHAT THIS WWII → WAR?!]* to see his old friend and unburden himself to someone in a position to understand his problems and provide the necessary assistance. Holcomb complimented Vandegrift on his generalship and related the good news that Admiral King had promised to rein in Turner. They also discussed Nimitz's recent decision to replace the South Pacific Area commander, Ghormley, with the pugnacious Adm. William "Bull" Halsey. Holcomb planned to fly to Nouméa, New Caledonia, to confer with Halsey at his headquarters and insisted that Vandegrift accompany him to plead his case directly. Vandegrift resisted because intelligence indicated that the Japanese were preparing for another big assault on the Marine perimeter around Henderson, but Holcomb said that the fight could wait until Vandegrift returned. Besides, Rupertus could run things capably enough in his absence.

The next evening at Nouméa, Holcomb and Vandegrift met with Halsey, Turner, Army generals, and staffers. Vandegrift complained about *[handwritten:] ↓ SOB HE BLAMED EVERYBODY ELSE* the lack of logistical support, and Turner defended his efforts to keep the Marines supplied. After hearing everyone out, Halsey asked Vandegrift whether the Marines could stay on the island. Vandegrift responded that they could if the Navy provided more assistance. "All right," Halsey said. "Go on back. I'll promise you everything I've got."[23] With that, Halsey did what Ghormley had not: He committed the Navy wholeheartedly to victory on Guadalcanal.[24]

While Vandegrift and Holcomb conferred with Halsey, the largest and last Japanese assault on Henderson Field materialized. The Japanese had increased their troop strength to 20,000 on Guadalcanal but continued to seriously underestimate the number of Americans there. An Army regiment had just arrived on the island, giving Vandegrift approximately 23,000 soldiers and Marines, more than twice as many troops as the Japanese thought he possessed. The attack by less than six thousand *[handwritten:] HAD MORE* men was therefore doomed before it began. Vandegrift had delegated the job of repelling the anticipated offensive to Rupertus, but he had come down with dengue fever just before Vandegrift left. The disease so debilitated him that he could scarcely leave his bed for a week.

Geiger was senior to Rupertus, but as an airman, had not expected to take an active role in the ground battle. Rupertus' illness did not change Geiger's attitude. Geiger was so confident of the Marines and their defenses that he told Thomas, the 1st Marine Division's chief of staff, "Jerry, you know what you're supposed to do. You go ahead and do it. I'll be at the wing, and if you need me I'll come, but if you don't need me, I'll come to see you every morning at 8 o'clock."[25] The Japanese assailed the Marine perimeter on 23 October, but as before, their attacks broke down in the face of American firepower, numbers, and determination. More than 3,500 Japanese soldiers died in the three-day engagement as opposed to fewer than five hundred American casualties. By the time a chagrinned Vandegrift returned to Guadalcanal, most of the fighting was over, and the surviving Japanese were retreating.[26]

The failed Japanese assault marked a turning point in the Guadalcanal campaign. Growing U.S. naval and air power in the region made it increasingly difficult for the Japanese to supply and strengthen their forces on the island. Moreover, Halsey made good on his commitments. American reinforcements arrived, including the remainder of the 2nd Marine Division and the Army's Americal and 25th Divisions. By January 1943 there were some 50,000 American military personnel on Guadalcanal. The augmentation made it possible to finally relieve the 1st Marine Division. No one had envisioned the outfit staying on the island for such a long time, and Vandegrift had called for its relief in early September. King authorized its withdrawal in late November, and the following month the Navy evacuated its survivors to Melbourne to recuperate. Although the 2nd Marine Regiment had been on Guadalcanal since the invasion began, it stayed on because it was organizationally a part of the 2nd Marine Division.

By the time the 1st Marine Division reached Australia, it was in deplorable shape. The unit had suffered fewer than two thousand casualties during its sojourn on Guadalcanal, of whom 650 were fatalities. This was not a lot compared with subsequent Marine losses in the Pacific War, but another 8,550 1st Marine Division leathernecks had fallen ill to various diseases, especially malaria. Indeed, the maladies were so debilitating that some

_35 !_

wondered whether the unit would ever again be battleworthy. As it was, the
division had covered itself with glory in the campaign, so much so that its
officers put "Guadalcanal" on the divisional patch. One officer later asserted
that the 1st Marine Division did not accomplish as much as other Marine
divisions during the war, but it gained great esprit de corps by having the
right men in the right place at the right time.[27]

Vandegrift and his staff departed Guadalcanal for Nouméa on 16 December. He left on a somewhat unhappy note because the limited offensives he
undertook after the climactic Japanese attack had not been as successful as
he had hoped. The soldiers and Marines taking part were too inexperi-
enced or unaccustomed to fighting outside prepared positions to achieve
ABSOLUTE BS REVISIONISM AT IT'S WORST!
all their objectives. Despite Vandegrift's disappointment, the results had
no impact on his reputation. More than anyone else, he was the victor of
Guadalcanal. President Roosevelt was merely the most prominent of his
many boosters. Holcomb was of course another. Holcomb was so proud of
Vandegrift that he lobbied successfully to secure him the Medal of Honor
and promotion to lieutenant general. Neither Roosevelt nor Holcomb saw
any logic in sending Vandegrift to Australia to perform the routine work of
rehabilitating the 1st Marine Division for its next assignment. They instead
ordered him stateside to raise morale by giving speeches and making public appearances. He made an especially good impression testifying before
congressional committees. There was no doubt that Vandegrift was a man
going places, but only a select few realized how high he would climb.
When Holcomb had visited Guadalcanal in October 1942, he told Vandegrift that he planned to recommend him as his successor as commandant
when the time came.[28]

After Vandegrift's departure, the 2nd Marine Division replaced the 1st
Marine Division in what now became an Army-run operation conducted
by its XIV Corps to secure the island. The 2nd Marine Division commander, Gen. John Marston, had expected to take his unit into battle, but
he outranked Gen. Alexander Patch, the head of the XIV Corps. Even
after Marston offered to waive his seniority, Halsey refused to let Marston
accompany his division to Guadalcanal. Instead, Gen. Alphonse "Frenchy"
DeCarre, the 2nd Marine Division's assistant commander, traveled to the
island to lead the outfit.[29]

On 10 January 1943 Patch launched a final offensive to drive the Japanese off Guadalcanal for good. The Army bore the brunt of the fighting inland while the Marines advanced westward along the island's north coast. The Japanese had decided that the situation was hopeless even before the attack began and therefore withdrew their surviving troops under the cover of darkness. The last of their remaining 13,000 soldiers slipped away under the U.S. Navy's nose on the night of 7–8 February. Their successful evacuation put a somewhat downbeat coda on the operation for the Army and the Marines. Indeed, the 2nd Marine Division failed to shine in its first campaign for several reasons. For starters, the division's only experienced regiment, the 2nd, had been sent to Australia on 15 January, leaving behind green outfits whose officers unsurprisingly made plenty of rookie mistakes in coordinating and directing their men. Moreover, the division did not fight as an integrated force. Patch lumped part of it into a conglomeration dubbed the Composite Army–Navy Division, which could hardly be expected to operate smoothly. Finally, officers criticized DeCarre for his ineptitude in handling his division. He was not well respected to begin with—Holcomb, for example, regretted that Marston had asked for him as his assistant division commander—and he did not handle his leathernecks particularly well. One officer remembered that the 2nd Marine Division's performance on Guadalcanal "was a pretty sad show that the Marine Corps has nothing to be proud of."[30]

Whatever the attendant disappointments, the Guadalcanal campaign was nonetheless an important victory for the United States in general and for the Marine Corps in particular. It lasted six long months, during which each side sustained significant damage. Of the approximately 37,700 Japanese soldiers committed to the island, around 25,000 failed to return. The Japanese also lost twenty-four warships totaling 134,839 tons and well over six hundred aircraft in and around Guadalcanal. The Americans suffered 7,100 combat casualties, of whom four thousand were leathernecks. Allied naval and air losses were about the same as Japan's: twenty-four warships and around six hundred planes. The big difference was that the Americans could far more easily replace their men and materiel than the Japanese could. By inadvertently provoking the Japanese into a brutal war of attrition, the United States compelled Japan to fight a war it could not afford.

The campaign's other details were equally grim for Japan. Victory at Guadalcanal secured the communication and supply lines between the United States and Australia and provided the Americans with a new base from which to launch further offensives in the Solomon Islands. It also put the Japanese on the defensive once and for all. Having lost the initiative, and increasingly outnumbered and outgunned, Japan could do little more than wait for the next American blow to fall. Although the Japanese inflicted significant losses on the Americans, the survivors learned many valuable lessons that they applied in future operations.

For the Marine Corps, the Guadalcanal campaign held great relevance and not only in terms of the Pacific War. It put the Marines in the public eye and snagged them plenty of good press. It was, after all, the Marine Corps, not the Army, that undertook the first American counteroffensive against Japan and the Corps that garnered most of the credit for winning it. That meant something to an organization trying to justify its existence and value. Although the operation took far longer than the Marines expected, it also taught them a good deal about logistics, interservice coordination, and jungle fighting. It forged the 1st Marine Division into a veteran outfit and schooled a cadre of high-ranking officers such as Vandegrift, Rupertus, del Valle, and Cates who went on to play significant roles in the conflict. Indeed, Vandegrift emerged from Guadalcanal not only as a decorated hero, but also in a position to ascend to the top of the Marine Corps' hierarchy. In the bigger picture, the campaign provided the Marine Corps with the opportunity to dominate amphibious operations in the Pacific War, an opportunity that it almost squandered in 1943.

AN INSTITUTIONAL CRISIS

Allied military fortunes had improved significantly by early 1943. In February, more than 90,000 German soldiers surrendered to the Soviets at Stalingrad. Their captivity marked the end of a disastrous campaign for the German army that cost it enormous casualties and demonstrated the Red Army's growing proficiency. Three months later, in May, some 230,000 German and Italian troops laid down their arms in Tunisia to American, British, and Free French forces. This victory not only secured North Africa for the Allies, but also exposed Axis positions in the Mediterranean to further Anglo-American attacks. Despite these successes, the Allies still had a long way to go toward winning the European War. The Germans and Italians retained control of most of Western Europe, the Balkans, Norway, Denmark, the Baltic states, and the western Soviet Union. Finland, Hungary, Romania, and Bulgaria remained loyal German satellites. Although the United States was beginning to flex its economic power, the Anglo-American strategic bombing campaign over Western Europe had barely started, and German U-boats continued to threaten Allied transatlantic supply lines. Germany had undoubtedly suffered serious setbacks, but its defeat was by no means a foregone conclusion.

A similar situation prevailed in the Pacific War. In addition to seizing Guadalcanal, American and Australian forces had stormed and taken Buna-Gona, in northeastern New Guinea, in January 1943. These victories gave the Allies footholds in the Solomons and on New Guinea's northern coast that they could use for future operations. Moreover, the Japanese had suffered heavy casualties in the air, at sea, and on the ground. In geographic terms, however, these successes were relatively minor. The Japanese still controlled Manchuria, eastern China, Burma, Indochina, Malaysia and Singapore, Formosa, the Philippines, the Dutch East Indies, most of Micronesia, New Britain, half of New Guinea, and the northern and central Solomons. The U.S. Navy had hardly begun its submarine war against Japanese merchant shipping, and the Army Air Forces had yet to find air bases from which to conduct strategic bombing missions against the Japanese homeland. Moreover, the Allied decision to focus on defeating Germany hindered efforts to fight the Japanese. The Joint Chiefs of Staff did not, however, want to surrender the initiative that the Americans and Australians had so painfully wrested from Japan. With this in mind, on 28 March 1943 the Joint Chiefs authorized Operation Cartwheel against the big Japanese base at Rabaul, on New Britain. As South Pacific Area commander, Halsey's part of the plan was to ascend the Solomon Islands ladder, the next rung of which after Guadalcanal was New Georgia Island.

To implement his part of Cartwheel, Halsey had at his disposal an increasing number of Army, Army Air Forces, Navy, and Marine units. Marine combat strength was somewhat deceptive. Both the 1st and 2nd

Marine Divisions, recuperating from their ordeals on Guadalcanal, were in no shape to fight anytime soon. Moreover, the Joint Chiefs eventually assigned the 1st Marine Division to General MacArthur's Southwest Pacific Area. On the other hand, the new 3rd Marine Division began deploying to the area. It had been activated in September 1942 at Camp Elliott in California and was sent first to New Zealand and then to Guadalcanal.

Gen. Charles Barrett led the 3rd Marine Division. The Kentucky-born Barrett labored on a railroad until he gained a Marine Corps commission in 1909. During shipboard duty, he participated in the 1914 Veracruz occupation. He fought in France in World War I, but not with the Marines. Rather, he led a battalion in the all-black 92nd Division in the Argonne. After the conflict, he chased bandits in the Dominican Republic and attended the École de Guerre in Paris. From 1929 to 1933 he taught at the Marine Corps Schools and cowrote *Tentative Manual for Landing Operations* (1934), both of which marked him as a pioneer in amphibious operations. One Marine later stated, "In my opinion, Barrett was one of the most imaginative and ingenious officers in the Marine Corps and his forward thinking was responsible for many of the concepts of amphibious warfare. Frankly, I don't believe General Barrett has ever been given full credit for many of his ideas subsequently incorporated into our amphibious doctrine."[31] Barrett then worked in the War Plans Section of the Office of the Chief of Naval Operations, commanded a Marine battalion, and in 1940 became director of the Plans and Policies Division at HQMC. Holcomb appointed Barrett assistant commandant just before the United States entered World War II.

Barrett was one of the most admired and respected officers in the prewar Marine Corps. His amphibious warfare expertise accounted for much of this acclaim, but there was more to it than that. People such as Holcomb lauded Barrett's brilliance, sincerity, attentiveness, friendliness, work ethic, and tact. He was also a fine instructor who did much to spread the amphibious warfare gospel throughout the Corps. He once explained to a class that landing on a hostile beach was easy; the hard part was staying there. Barrett should have made a wonderful combat general, but he had a weakness that ultimately undermined his effectiveness. For all his talents, Barrett lacked a hardness of character, that ability to do whatever it took to win, regardless of the sufferings of his troops. He was simply too soft-hearted to lead men into battle. Years later one Marine officer summed up Barrett's shortcomings: "He was a man who just didn't have any iron in his soul whatsoever."[32]

These weaknesses were not yet apparent when Holcomb selected Barrett to command the 3rd Marine Division. Holcomb had been a Barrett supporter for years. Barrett was, after all, an innovator in amphibious warfare and well respected throughout the Corps. Moreover, Holcomb had received numerous positive testimonies about Barrett's efficiency. In August 1939, for instance, Adm. Harold Stark wrote Holcomb, "I have had contact two or three times with Colonel Charles Barrett. The first time he impressed me as rather exceptional, the second time more so, yesterday outstandingly so, and I just sat back and let my chest expand in pride of the Navy's presentation and knowledge of subjects under discussion at which he had it all over everybody else. He was clear, definite, and I know everybody there must have been impressed with him."[33]

In fact, in 1940 Holcomb considered recommending Barrett as his possible successor as commandant if Roosevelt sought to replace him. Holcomb's commitment to Barrett remained firm even after Barrett suffered a collapsed lung in early 1942. When Marine units deployed to the South Pacific, Holcomb gave Barrett a brigade to garrison Samoa. Barrett kept his leathernecks free of malaria and other tropical diseases by protecting them from mosquitoes and segregating them from the local population. To Holcomb, Barrett's personality and record made him the best candidate to run the 3rd Marine Division.[34]

Neither Barrett nor Vandegrift was the top Marine combat commander in the South Pacific in early 1943. Holcomb gave that job to Gen. Clayton Barney Vogel. Born in Philadelphia in 1882, Vogel procured a Marine Corps commission several months after he graduated from Rutgers in 1904. Before World War I, he served in China, at the School of Application, as an adjunct, in Panama, shipboard, and in the White House as an aide. He spent World War I occupying and pacifying Haiti. Afterward he took the Field Officers' course, worked in the judge advocate general's office, and was stationed in Nicaragua. He also participated in national rifle matches and studied law at Georgetown University. The 1930s found Vogel back in Nicaragua and then at HQMC. In 1937 Holcomb appointed Vogel Marine Corps adjutant and inspector general. He was running a brigade when World War II began in Europe. In February 1941 Holcomb elevated him to lead the 2nd Marine Division. After the United States entered the war, Vogel became commander of the Pacific Amphibious Force, after which in October 1942 he traveled to New Caledonia at the head of the new I Amphibious Corps.

Vogel was a solid, heavy-set man who enjoyed horseback riding and partying. Although some considered him capable and nice enough, others were less complimentary. One officer later called him a "drunken lecher" more interested in alcohol and womanizing than in doing his job. Another opined that the overall high quality of the Corps hid Vogel's shortcomings for much of his career. Whatever his failings, Holcomb either overlooked or was unaware of them when he assigned Vogel to lead the I Amphibious Corps. He had heard good things about Vogel after the United States entered the war and later pushed for Vogel's promotions to first major general and then lieutenant general. Holcomb continued to back Vogel for overseas duty even after Vogel broke his leg in the spring of 1942. Holcomb's support seems to have been due primarily to his respect for seniority, of which Vogel had plenty. Holcomb never exhibited toward Vogel the kind of affection he had for Barrett and especially Vandegrift. It took him time to realize that Vogel, while a perfectly acceptable general in peacetime, lacked the required level of ruthless efficiency, total commitment, organizational ability, and decisiveness to command large numbers of men in wartime.[35]

Some of Vogel's less admirable traits surfaced in October 1942 when he set up headquarters for the I Amphibious Corps in Nouméa. He seemed more interested in having a good time than in running his outfit and prioritized his own comfort. Some felt that his personal staff enabled his more selfish behaviors. There was nothing inherently wrong with enjoying life's finer things, but Vogel also demonstrated an unhelpful stubbornness and indecisiveness. His lack of initiative infected his staff officers, who bickered with each other and became increasingly apprehensive about their roles and prospects. Worst of all, Vogel was sometimes hard to find. He hated flying and traveled by boat whenever possible, a completely impractical practice in the far-flung South Pacific. At one point he found himself stranded in New Zealand, unable to procure a ship to take him back to New Caledonia, after weeks spent inspecting Marine units. Small wonder that the I Amphibious Corps struck many observers as thoroughly dysfunctional.[36]

Halsey was among those with increasing doubts about Vogel. The I Amphibious Corps was the logical outfit to conduct the invasion of New Georgia, but Halsey disapproved of Vogel's plans for the operation. Vogel, anticipating significant Japanese opposition, had demanded resources for the assault that were simply not available in the South Pacific. On the other hand, Gen. Millard Harmon, Army commander for the South Pacific Area, said that the XIV Corps could seize New Georgia with fewer troops and more flexible tactics than those proposed by Vogel. To Halsey, Harmon and the Army possessed the can-do attitude that assailing New Georgia required, so he gave the job to them. In doing so, Halsey froze the Marine Corps out of its defining specialty. As far as Halsey was concerned, the problem was that Vogel was too stubborn, uncooperative, and antiquated to wage war in the South Pacific. Although subsequent events proved Vogel to be correct—the New Georgia campaign lasted longer and necessitated greater resources than Halsey and the Army anticipated—vindication came too late to salvage his career.[37]

Halsey believed that short-circuiting the I Amphibious Corps out of the New Georgia invasion was a short-term solution because he still envisioned using Marine units in future operations. He felt that the resolution to the problem was to secure a new commander for the outfit. Although Halsey had the authority to request Vogel's removal, he hesitated to interfere in Marine Corps business. He instead opted to nudge Holcomb through innuendo and indirect persuasion to replace him. For example, he complained to Vandegrift about Vogel in a confidential conversation in the hope that Vandegrift would convey his unhappiness to Holcomb. In late April, Halsey colluded with one of his Marine staffers, Gen. DeWitt Peck, to up the pressure by convincing Peck to send a letter to Holcomb expressing concerns about Vogel. Peck wrote, "The [I Amphibious] Corps command here has since its inception been characterized by an almost total lack of initiative and punch. It seems to lack that old spirit of 'up and at 'em.'" Speaking through Peck, Halsey recommended that Holcomb kick Vogel upstairs to some worthy stateside command as soon as possible, and make it appear that the orders originated at HQMC, not the South Pacific Area headquarters.[38]

News of Halsey's ongoing discontent with Vogel and the I Amphibious Corps greatly disturbed Holcomb. Holcomb most certainly did not want to see the Marines sidelined for Operation Cartwheel, but he was unsure how to proceed because Halsey had put him in a difficult position. The problem was that Halsey's fitness reports on Vogel had been glowing, so removing him without an official paper trail justifying the decision would appear to be arbitrary and unfair. Although Holcomb was willing to replace an underperforming officer, he wanted it done correctly and therefore resented Halsey's efforts to keep his hands clean.

In mid-March, Holcomb radioed Halsey to inform him that if he believed Vogel should be sent home, he needed to say so. To make Halsey's decision easier, Holcomb hinted that he would welcome such a request. "You are in a position to know," Holcomb wrote, "and it is perhaps unnecessary to say that I would expect to hear from you properly if Vogel, or any other Marine officer under your command, did not measure up. The radio is working!"[39] Nonetheless, Halsey hesitated to put his unhappiness with Vogel on the record and delayed in replying. Instead, Halsey complained about Vogel to Nimitz, who in turn communicated Halsey's grievance to Admiral King, who responded by ordering Nimitz to New Caledonia for a firsthand look at the situation.

Nimitz flew down to New Caledonia in June with Gen. Holland Smith, the top Marine officer in the Central Pacific Area, and carried with him a letter from Holcomb containing background information. Vogel was still stranded in New Zealand when Nimitz and Smith arrived, but they investigated anyway. Neither officer liked what he found, and both said as much to Holcomb. Nimitz and Smith lamented the lack of initiative at I Amphibious Corps headquarters and attributed it to Vogel's inadequate leadership. Nimitz admitted that Halsey should have asked for Vogel's relief and acknowledged the merit of Halsey's criticisms. Upon receiving a 29 June letter from Nimitz, Holcomb decided to act without waiting on Halsey. Three days later, after consulting King, Holcomb ordered Vogel to return to the States for reassignment.[40]

Vogel's tenure and removal as I Amphibious Corps commander had consequences. Most obviously, Vogel was deeply hurt by his relief. Halsey deflected Vogel's anger by claiming disingenuously that the decision to reassign him had originated in Washington among officials dissatisfied with the I Amphibious Corps' performance. Holcomb tried to soften the blow by putting Vogel in charge of the Fleet Marine Force in San Diego, but there was no disguising that Vogel's days as a combat leader were over. Vogel had never been popular among high-ranking Marine officers anyway, so his discomfiture generated little sympathy within the Corps. Of greater import, the imbroglio convinced King that there was no need for two corps in the South Pacific. Probably because the Army's XIV Corps seemed to have the situation well in hand, King wanted to disband the seemingly redundant I Amphibious Corps. Holcomb dissuaded King from such a drastic move, but the fact that Holcomb had to engage in such a bureaucratic battle demonstrated how far the Marines' fortunes had fallen since victory at Guadalcanal.[41]

It was clear to South Pacific Area insiders that whoever replaced Vogel as the I Amphibious Corps commander would have his work cut out for him. There was little debate about the right man for the job. Halsey had had Vandegrift in mind when he engineered Vogel's removal, and Holcomb was amenable to the idea. Vandegrift was not only the Marine Corps' most successful and prestigious combat general, but was back in the region with the 1st Marine Division after his stateside sojourn. Although Vandegrift claimed that his appointment to run the I Amphibious Corps surprised him, he had been well aware of, and even contributed to, the drama surrounding Vogel's relief. Vandegrift understood that unless he restored Halsey's faith in the I Amphibious Corps, the Army might dominate the campaign against Rabaul and render the Marines unnecessary. As Vandegrift wrote to Holcomb, "For reasons of which I know and some of which I do not know confidence has been completely lost and this has recently become an Army show."[42] Considering the stakes involved, Vandegrift felt that he had to be ruthless. He relieved underperforming officers down to the divisional level, tackled and cleared the backlog of paperwork Vogel left behind, established a new logistical network, and visited subordinate units. His late July promotion to lieutenant general additionally encouraged him in his work. By the time he was finished, he had resurrected the I Amphibious Corps.[43]

Vandegrift's tenure as I Amphibious Corps commander lasted two months. That summer Roosevelt tapped Vandegrift to succeed Holcomb as commandant and wanted him to tour Marine installations in the Pacific and stateside before assuming his new post. Fortunately, there was a consensus among Holcomb, Vandegrift, King, Nimitz, and Halsey on who should lead the I Amphibious Corps on a more permanent basis: Charlie Barrett, head of the 3rd Marine Division. Barrett had impressed everyone since the war's start. Gen. Charles Price, while the local garrison commander on Samoa, had rated Barrett as outstanding, writing "Of all the general officers in the Marine Corps, this officer is best suited for the highest command the Corps can afford and his early promotion thereto is recommended."[44] Vandegrift and Smith both lauded Barrett's handling of the 3rd Marine Division. Holcomb's only reservation was that Barrett had not had the opportunity to take his division into battle. Such combat experience, Holcomb believed, would make Barrett more effective at the corps level. The fact was, however, that Vandegrift was to date the only Marine general who had led a division in sustained action in the conflict, and he was slated for bigger responsibilities. That being the case, Holcomb felt comfortable with selecting Barrett, who assumed his new post with the I Amphibious Corps on 15 September.[45]

Barrett's elevation meant that the 3rd Marine Division needed a new leader. Finding one proved somewhat problematic. Vandegrift initially recommended Gen. Allen Turnage to Holcomb after he heard that Turnage was doing a good job as assistant commander of the division. Vandegrift did so reluctantly, however, because he worried that Turnage lacked the necessary initiative to run a division. Indeed, the more Vandegrift thought about it, the more convinced he became that Turnage was not the right fit. Shifting gears, he instead suggested that Holcomb detach Gen. Harry Schmidt, the assistant commandant, to the South Pacific to take over the division. Barrett had reservations about Turnage's decisiveness too, but he preferred him over Schmidt because he had worked with Turnage and barely knew Schmidt. He assured Vandegrift that Turnage would demonstrate more forcefulness at the top spot than in a subordinate role. Barrett said that if Vandegrift remained unconvinced about Turnage, he would support the current director of the Policies and Plans Division, Gen. Keller Rockey, as his replacement. As for Holcomb, he shared Vandegrift's doubts about Turnage, but he was unwilling or unable to provide someone more qualified. He had already slated Schmidt to lead the 4th Marine Division and had Rockey in mind as Schmidt's successor as assistant commandant. Holcomb therefore decided to give Turnage the 3rd Marine Division. Besides, Turnage was familiar with the outfit and had Vandegrift's and Barrett's admittedly reluctant endorsements. On 2 September, Holcomb issued orders for Turnage to assume command of the 3rd Marine Division.[46]

Born in North Carolina in 1891, Turnage attended a military academy while growing up. He left the University of North Carolina to accept a Marine Corps commission in 1913 and then fought Caco bandits in northern Haiti. He commanded a machine gun battalion in France during World War I, but the conflict ended before he saw combat. He returned to the United States to teach at Quantico before serving three years shipboard with the Pacific Fleet. In the mid-1930s he directed the Basic School in Philadelphia and then took over a battalion. In 1939 Holcomb put him in charge of the Marine contingent in northern China, a delicate mission that required navigating the complexities of the Sino-Japanese War. Holcomb brought Turnage home in the summer of 1941 to head up the Plans and Policies Division at HQMC. After the United States entered World War II, Holcomb sent him to run Camp Lejeune, newly established in North Carolina. He became Barrett's assistant division commander when HQMC activated the 3rd Marine Division and accompanied the outfit overseas to Guadalcanal.

Turnage was well liked by almost everyone in the Marine Corps. Young officers saw Turnage and his wife as parental figures. Vandegrift was a long-time friend. People lauded Turnage's calm, gentlemanly qualities and his innate friendliness. Before one operation, Turnage summoned all his officers to a small wardroom, shook hands with each one as he entered, and then gave a short speech emphasizing the need to occupy the high ground. His serene competence played no small part in his career success. On the other hand, as the debate over his appointment indicated, there were doubts about his dynamism, decisiveness, and aggressiveness.[47]

Vogel's inability to manage the I Amphibious Corps to Halsey's satisfaction cost the Corps much of the credibility and esteem it had earned with the Guadalcanal campaign. Fortunately for the Marines, Holcomb's willingness to remove Vogel and Vandegrift's ruthless reorganization of the unit helped get it back on track. By the time Vandegrift turned the I Amphibious Corps over to Barrett, the Marines were ready to resume an active role in the conflict.

BOUGAINVILLE

Halsey's next target in Operation Cartwheel was Bougainville Island, at the top of the Solomons' ladder, and at 3,600 square miles, the largest island in the chain. Although only thirty miles wide, it stretches 125 miles toward Rabaul on New Britain. Mountain ranges divide the island down its center. The flat plains on Bougainville's eastern side could accommodate airfields, but the western half contained swampy valleys carved out by streams that turned into silty marshes when they reached the ocean. Jungle and primeval forests covered most of the island. There were no roads and few tracks. After the Japanese arrived in March 1942, they concentrated their forces at Bougainville's two ends and constructed airfields there. Approximately 21,000 Japanese troops garrisoned Buin in the south and another 5,000 occupied the Buka-Bonis area in the north. Because of the presence of German Christian missionaries, Bougainville's 40,000 natives by and large sympathized with the Japanese. *SIMPLY A LIE / NOT TRUE NO NATIVE PEOPLES EVER SIDED WITH THE JAPS!*

Halsey assigned the Bougainville invasion, dubbed Operation Cherryblossom, to the I Amphibious Corps. He hoped that Vogel's removal, Vandegrift's reorganization, and Barrett's appointment had restored the Marines to their rightful place as the South Pacific Area's amphibious spearhead. The fact that the 3rd Marine Division was in splendid shape and that the amphibious force commander, Adm. Theodore Wilkinson, was far more cooperative than Turner had been increased optimism that the operation would prove successful.

Unfortunately, problems soon arose. Barrett had been intimately involved in the planning for Cherryblossom even before he took over the I Amphibious Corps in mid-September. Although he was now a corps commander, he and his chief of staff, Gen. Alfred Noble, continued to immerse themselves in the nitty-gritty details of Cherryblossom instead of leaving them to their staff. They used the staff officers only as sources of information. As a result, discussions between Barrett and his staff seemed to go nowhere and solve nothing. One officer recalled that Barrett and Noble worked themselves to exhaustion until the wee hours of the morning while the staff officers sat around drinking. Small wonder that Barrett became increasingly edgy and fatigued.[48]

GENERALS DO THINGS THEIR WAY! MOST PLAN IN DETAIL!

THIS AUTHOR HAS NO REAL KNOWLEDGE OF Fighting on these Islands - Topography - Climate AND soldiers THAT FOUGHT TO THE DEATH

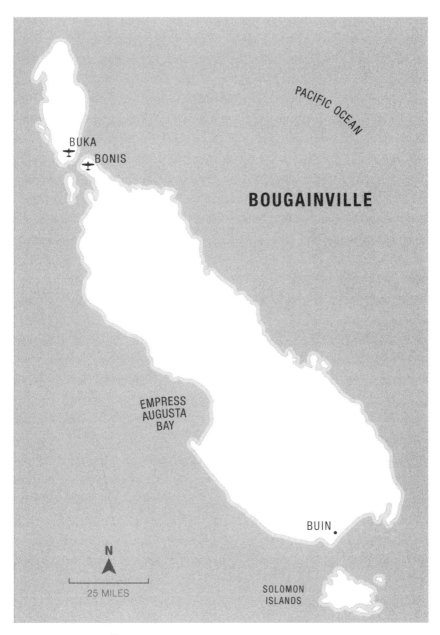

Map 3. *Bougainville*

THEY ALL DID ! DAH !!!

In addition, Barrett worried excessively about Marine casualties. To avoid and isolate large Japanese troops concentrations on either end of Bougainville, Barrett decided to land Marines at remote Empress Augusta Bay in the middle of the island's west coast. Once ashore, the Marines could establish a defensive perimeter behind which engineers could build the airfields necessary to gain air supremacy. If the Japanese wanted to destroy the airfields, they would have to march miles through trackless jungle, dragging their weapons and equipment with them, and assail well-defended Marine lines.

Like all plans, it was not risk free. The Marines would be dependent upon the Navy and its aircraft carriers to provide close air support until the airfields were up and running. Although Barrett designed the operation to keep American casualties low, he continued to fret about the dangers involved. He had a knack for spotting the flaws in any scheme, a trait that had served him well as a teacher, but one less useful as a combat *WRONG* general looking for the most cost-effective solution to a military problem. One officer remembered, "Despite all his brilliance, personality, and leadership, he increasingly allowed his humanitarian instincts to prevail over every dictate of a dire military necessity. In short, he had forgotten why he and his Marines were there."[49] When Gen. Millard Harmon, the Army commander in the South Pacific Area, suggested that the Marines focus on lightly defended Choiseul Island, southeast of Bougainville, Barrett ran with the opportunity to avoid a potential Japanese hornet's nest around Empress Augusta Bay.[50]

Barrett's prevaricating increasingly frustrated Halsey. Although he was not as bullheaded and impulsive as his reputation indicated, Halsey was still a man of action who believed in getting things done. He therefore had little patience for Barrett's concerns, but wanted instead to finish the Bougainville planning so he could get on with the war. To Halsey, Barrett seemed increasingly like an impediment to making progress in the South Pacific. Moreover, after his experience with Vogel, Halsey was less willing to tolerate inefficiency or timidity in his command. Halsey not only rejected Barrett's proposal to seize Choiseul Island, but also summoned Barrett to Nouméa from Guadalcanal for a heart-to-heart discussion. When Barrett arrived on 7 October, he went immediately to Halsey's headquarters. There Halsey informed him that he had decided to ask for his relief.[51]

The next morning Barrett appeared distracted and haggard as he went about the business of the day. He told no one about Halsey's decision but had a long conversation with Gen. David Brewster, a friend and I Amphibious Corps administrative deputy, that seemed to cheer him up. Indeed, Barrett asked Brewster to his quarters later for dinner and drinks. When Brewster arrived, Barrett was meeting with a couple of logistics officers. After dismissing them, Barrett greeted Brewster and several other officers whom he had invited over and told them to pour drinks while he went upstairs to wash up before they ate. A few minutes later, a Marine sentry burst into the house and yelled that Barrett had fallen from his second-story balcony. The officers rushed outside and found Barrett unconscious by the curb. Both a Navy doctor and an ambulance arrived within ten minutes to take Barrett to a hospital. Barrett never regained consciousness and was pronounced dead just before eight o'clock in the evening. The fall had fractured his skull, broken his neck, and caused a cerebral hemorrhage.[52]

High-ranking Marine officers grieved Barrett's passing. After all, Barrett had been well loved and well respected throughout the Corps. Holcomb wrote, "Barrett's death was the most severe blow the Marine Corps has had in my day."[53] There was considerable speculation about whether Barrett's fall was accidental or suicidal. Many of those who learned that Halsey had planned to ask for his relief concluded that Barrett had killed himself due to stress and humiliation. Because they did not want to upset Barrett's family or generate controversy, they opted to cover up what they thought was the truth. The court of inquiry that convened right after Barrett's death concluded that there had been no foul play, but it failed to interview Halsey, whose testimony would have provided a motive for suicide. Rumors nevertheless circulated that Barrett's death had been intentional, with people attributing it to everything from excessive drinking to overwork. In all likelihood, Barrett's death was probably a tragic mishap. If he had chosen to take his own life, there were more certain ways of doing so than leaping off a second-story balcony. Moreover, he left behind no note explaining himself. The most reasonable explanation is that an exhausted and overwrought Barrett fell to his death.[54]

Because Halsey had scheduled the Bougainville invasion for 1 November, the I Amphibious Corps needed a new commander as soon as possible after Barrett died. Halsey, having confronted this problem before, responded with a familiar solution: Vandegrift. He trusted Vandegrift, who had proven himself in winning at Guadalcanal and in cleaning up the mess Vogel had left. Although Halsey knew that Vandegrift would become commandant at the beginning of 1944, he radioed Nimitz and asked him to send Vandegrift back to the South Pacific to take over the I Amphibious Corps for now. Nimitz was amenable to the idea, as was Holcomb when he got the news.

Vandegrift had just reached Pearl Harbor after an inspection of Midway when Nimitz ordered him back to Nouméa. Vandegrift was saddened to learn of his old friend's death but jumped at the opportunity to participate in another operation. After attending Barrett's funeral and conferring with Halsey, Vandegrift flew to Guadalcanal to meet with the I Amphibious Corps staffers there. He found them in a state of shock about Barrett and had some difficulty getting them to focus on the immediate task. On the other hand, without Barrett's irresolution it was a relatively simple matter for the staff to put the finishing touches to the plan to land the 3rd Marine Division at Empress Augusta Bay. Vandegrift approved it with only one major change: The original proposal called for leaving one of the 3rd Marine Division's regiments behind at Guadalcanal for three weeks after the operation began, but Vandegrift persuaded Halsey to deploy it to Bougainville within three days after the remainder of the division came ashore.[55]

Since Vandegrift's tenure as I Amphibious Corps chief was a stopgap measure— Vandegrift had to return to the States by the end of the year to become Marine Corps commandant—Halsey needed someone to take over the corps on a more permanent basis after Cherryblossom began. One day Halsey and his war plans officer, the Marines' Gen. William Riley, discussed the matter and agreed that each would think about possible candidates before they conferred again. When they met in the hallway later, Riley said, "I have the very man!" Without batting an eye, Halsey responded, "You mean Roy Geiger, of course."

Geiger had impressed Halsey with his performance as head of the Cactus Air Force on Guadalcanal. He decided to ask for Geiger's appointment as Vandegrift's assistant corps commander, with the understanding that he would assume the top spot when Vandegrift departed for his new responsibilities in Washington. Halsey had no problem persuading Holcomb and

Vandegrift, who had in fact recommended Geiger for a corps to Holcomb the previous July. Holcomb had always been a Geiger booster and would write to a friend, "It gave me a great deal of pleasure to give the job to Geiger. I feel confident he can swing it."[56] Indeed, Geiger's selection met with universal approval among high-ranking Corps officers, and Geiger himself was happy to swap his job leading Marine Corps aviation in Washington for a more active combat post in the South Pacific.[57]

Despite the consensus within the Marine Corps that Geiger was the right man for the I Amphibious Corps, his selection was a Pacific War anomaly. Corps command was one of the most important and exclusive combat posts in the U.S. military. Its leaders were usually infantrymen or artillerymen who focused on tactics, not administration. Geiger, though, had spent most of his career as an airman. To be sure, he had participated in ground combat on Guadalcanal, but not as much as some believed. On the other hand, his experiences on Guadalcanal showed that he knew how to lead in combat. He also had had more than enough education for the job, having attended the Command and General Staff College, Army War College, and Naval War College. Ultimately, he was an intelligent man and a quick learner who impressed almost everyone with whom he came into contact. That Halsey, Holcomb, and Vandegrift had turned to Geiger also showed, however, that even after more than a year and a half of war, the Marine Corps still had only one officer—Vandegrift—who had proven himself capable of running a division, let alone a rarified outfit such as a corps. That being the case, Geiger's educational background, versatility, and reputation were enough to secure him the post.

On the afternoon of 31 October, Vandegrift assembled the 3rd Marine Division's officers for a short speech. He told them that the key to Cherryblossom's success was to know the mission, to be confident in the mission, and if not confident in the mission to keep that lack of confidence to themselves. The next morning, two of the division's regiments splashed ashore at Empress Augusta Bay on Bougainville's west coast. Col. Edward Craig's 9th Marine Regiment landed unopposed on the northern beaches, but Col. George McHenry's 3rd Marine Regiment encountered some resistance to the south. Differences aside, the Marine units quickly lost their integrity as soon as they entered the dense jungle. One leatherneck remembered,

"It was like running across thirty feet of the Sahara and suddenly dropping off into the Everglades."[58] Despite the natural and manmade obstacles, by the end of the day about 14,000 Marines were on the beachhead, among them Vandegrift, who was satisfied with what he saw. The Marines were advancing inland and a calm and serene Turnage seemed to have everything under as much control as a division commander could under the circumstances. Vandegrift was pleased with the progress the Marines had made in amphibious warfare in the fourteen months since Guadalcanal. That being the case, he opted to return to Guadalcanal that night and leave matters in Turnage's capable hands.[59]

The biggest military threats to the Marines on Bougainville came initially from the air and sea. Japanese air attacks interrupted unloading, but otherwise did little damage. The night after the landing, U.S. warships protecting the beachhead fought off a Japanese naval force from Rabaul. American land-based and carrier-based raids on Rabaul on 5 November further neutralized Japanese naval power in the region by damaging a half dozen Japanese cruisers there. While the Navy whittled down Japanese naval strength, the Marines on Bougainville brought in supplies and reinforcements, cleared the jungle, and expanded their perimeter. Doing so led to several engagements with Japanese troops in the area.

The major obstacles for the Marines were the jungle terrain and rainy climate. Even so, the first airfield was operational on 19 December, enabling land-based planes to dominate the skies over the island. By that time the Americal Division had arrived to augment the Marines, and Vandegrift had turned the I Amphibious Corps over to Geiger and headed back to the States. Geiger oversaw the transformation of the swampy Bougainville foothold into a well-defended bastion until the Army's Gen. Oscar Griswold arrived with his XIV Corps headquarters on 14 December to relieve the I Amphibious Corps. Geiger got along so well with Turnage that the two men sometimes discussed problems and decided on solutions in private meetings without informing their staffs. Soon afterward the 3rd Marine Division began its withdrawal from the island to make way for the Army's 37th Division; most of it was gone by 9 January 1944. As a result, the Marines were not on hand when the Japanese on the island launched their unsuccessful large-scale assault on the perimeter in March.[60]

The Bougainville operation completed the Allied climb up the Solomon Islands ladder and put them on Rabaul's doorstep. For the Marines, Bougainville showed how far they had come in the fourteen months since the jury-rigged Guadalcanal landing. Unlike Guadalcanal, on Bougainville the Marines worked well with the amphibious force commander, were sufficiently supplied and backed by a Navy capable of defending the beachhead, possessed enough air support to control the skies over the island, and were relieved early by soldiers who could better bear the burden of combat inland. Of course, some things remained the same. The Japanese fought doggedly as usual, and the fetid climate and jungle terrain made living conditions miserable. Fortunately, experience had taught the Marines to cope successfully with these challenges. The operation also blooded another Marine division, giving the Navy three combat-hardened divisions for future campaigns. Furthermore, it provided valuable experience for Geiger and Turnage. Geiger in particular impressed Vandegrift, who wrote to him in late January, "I want to congratulate you on the splendid work that you and your staff and the Corps did on Bougainville. . . . [T]hose of us who know the constant strain, danger, and hardship of continuous jungle warfare realize what was accomplished by your outfit during the two months you were there."[61]

CAPE GLOUCESTER

While Admiral Halsey's forces grappled with the Japanese in the Solomons, the 1st Marine Division was in Melbourne, recuperating from its Guadalcanal ordeal. It was not part of the I Amphibious Corps, and in fact, no longer belonged to Halsey's South Pacific Area. Because the division was one of the few units with amphibious experience, the Joint Chiefs had assigned it to MacArthur's Southwest Pacific Area for its operations against Rabaul.

The division was in deplorable condition when it arrived in Australia in January 1943. Around 7,500 of its leathernecks suffered from malaria, and almost all the others bore the physical or psychological scars of the Guadalcanal campaign. The good climate, local hospitality, and plentiful rations gradually restored the division. In March, the outfit started a retraining program to prepare for its next operation. The Marines received new M1 rifles and other equipment, engaged in small unit and amphibious drills, and absorbed replacements. By summer the division was in fine shape and ready for action. In late August, it moved in stages to New Guinea before embarking on its mission, an amphibious landing on New Britain Island.

After Vandegrift took over the I Amphibious Corps, General William Rupertus assumed command of the 1st Marine Division. Rupertus, born and raised in Washington, D.C., had served in the District of Columbia National Guard, graduated from the United States Revenue Cutter Service School (the future Coast Guard Academy), and in 1913 secured a Marine Corps commission. He passed World War I shipboard, but after the conflict ended he saw action against the Cacos bandits in Haiti as a company commander. He spent much of the 1920s either teaching or studying, the latter including a stint at the Army's Command and General Staff College. In 1929 he joined the Marine detachment in Peking, where his wife and two of his children died of scarlet fever. After working in the War Plans Section at HQMC, he returned to China—this time to Shanghai—when the Sino-Japanese War began. He was running the Marine barracks at Guantanamo Bay when his friend Vandegrift tapped him as assistant commander of the 1st Marine Division. In that role he led the Marine assault on Tulagi and the neighboring islets before enduring two bouts of dengue fever. Despite his impressive prewar record, perhaps his biggest claim to fame was writing the Marine Corps' famous Rifleman's Creed, which begins, "This is my rifle. There are many like it, but this one is mine."

Rupertus was perhaps the Marine Corps' most controversial World War II division commander. Rumor had it that his ultimate career goal was to become commandant. There was nothing unusual or wrong in aiming high, but Rupertus' pettiness, selfishness, and mercurial temperament made his ambition seem cloying and vindictive. His harsh opinions, tendency to play favorites, obvious moodiness, and ostentatious living while in the field also alienated many and generated little loyalty. Geiger eventually questioned Rupertus' basic competence. Some attributed Rupertus' off-putting personality to the loss of his wife and children while stationed in China. Whatever the reasons, he was not popular within the Corps. One officer remembered, "That guy was a loser. Christ, how the hell he got to be a division commander is astounding."[62] Fortunately for Rupertus, his

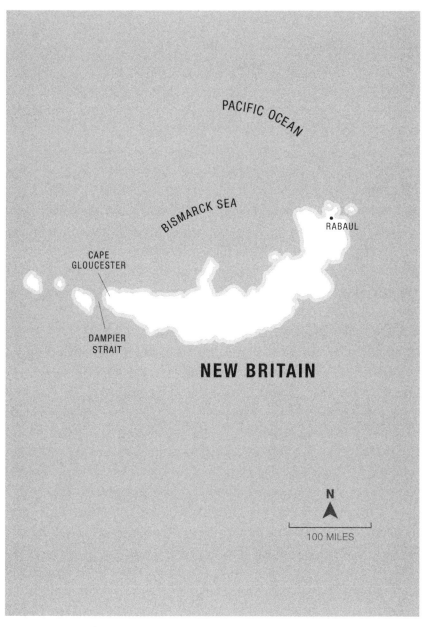

Map 4. Cape Gloucester

close friendship with Vandegrift—one officer later referred to it as Vande-grift's "blind spot"—provided him a degree of institutional protection and opportunity that helped explain his climb through the Corps' hierarchy after the Pacific War began.[63]

Holcomb's decision to appoint Rupertus to lead the 1st Marine Division made sense. Whatever Rupertus' shortcomings, he had done good work before the United States entered the war, earning praise from, among others, the exacting Gen. Holland Smith. Rupertus also gained credit for leading the assault on Tulagi. Besides, he was already the division's assistant commander and was therefore familiar with the outfit and its officers. Most influential of all, though, was Vandegrift's recommendation to Holcomb to select Rupertus as his successor. As it was, Holcomb needed little per-suading; he even opined to Vandegrift that Rupertus might someday make a good corps commander. Rupertus continued to impress after he took charge of the division. Vandegrift said that although he regretted leaving the division, he felt better knowing that it was in such capable hands. Army officers, including MacArthur, lauded the 1st Marine Division in general and Rupertus in particular.[64]

Rupertus' tenure at the head of the 1st Marine Division in 1943 was not trouble free. For starters, in August he came down with such a serious case of malaria that Holcomb contemplated ordering him home. Rupertus recovered, but that illness, combined with the bouts of dengue fever that had plagued him on Guadalcanal, meant that he was not in robust health. In addition, Rupertus clashed with Army officers. The 1st Marine Division was part of Gen. Walter Krueger's Sixth Army. Rupertus did not like the Army to begin with, and he disagreed with the initial plans for the invasion of New Britain. Sixth Army staffers wanted the 1st Marine Division to land on Cape Gloucester, on the island's western tip, and seize the two airfields in the area. Doing so would give the Allies control of the Vitiaz Strait between New Britain and New Guinea's Huon Peninsula and establish a foothold near Rabaul. MacArthur's headquarters sought to augment the operation with a simultaneous airdrop by a regiment of Army paratroop-ers, but Rupertus felt that this would clutter his logistics and disperse his resources. In the end, the Army canceled that part of the plan, but it did little to reassure Rupertus of the Army's competence.[65]

New Britain, a crescent-shaped island about 350 miles long, was covered in dense trackless jungle, had steep volcanic mountains, and was subject to intense humidity and considerable rainfall. Although the Japanese had more than 100,000 troops garrisoning their big base at Rabaul on New Britain's northeastern tip, the island's lack of roads meant that their 10,500 soldiers in the Cape Gloucester area were on their own. The Marines planned to assail both sides of the Cape Gloucester peninsula and then push on to the two local airfields that were the operation's chief objectives. On 26 December, elements of Col. William Whaling's 1st Marine Regiment landed on the eastern side of the peninsula while the remainder of his regiment and Col. Julian Frisbie's 7th Marine Regiment came ashore on the western side. Japanese opposition was sporadic. Three days later, Col. John Selden's 5th Marine Regiment arrived, pushed through the 7th Marine Regiment, and joined the 1st Marine Regiment in overrunning both airfields by the next day.

Rupertus, who had established his headquarters on terra firma several hours after the first Marines disembarked, was delighted to report on the last day of the year that the Marines had fulfilled their mission. The leathernecks spent the next few weeks establishing a perimeter around the airfields. Doing so required a series of sharp engagements with Japanese soldiers. Because of the stifling jungle, these engagements were even more isolating than those on Guadalcanal. One Marine remembered, "You'd step off from your line in the morning, take say ten paces, and turn around to guide your buddy. And—nobody there, Jap or Marine. Ah, I can tell you it was a very small war and a very lonely experience."[66]

The climate and terrain proved to be as much a challenge for the 1st Marine Division as the Japanese. The operation took place during the rainy season, so almost daily torrential downpours turned the ground into one big swamp. One Marine later said that it was like standing in a waterfall, adding, "As I was saying, water underfoot, water above, mud. Your clothes were dirty, there was no way really to take care of yourself, because of the elements."[67] Rotted trees, destabilized by the rain, fell and killed several leathernecks. By the time the division left the island in early May 1944, it had suffered almost 1,500 casualties.

Some questioned the operation's cost in time and casualties because the Southwest Pacific Area command opted not to develop the island logistically.

Even so, it was hard to quibble with the 1st Marine Division's performance. One Army observer noted, "The front line soldier was superb. These men were in splendid physical condition and spoiling for a fight. They were like hunters, boring in relentlessly and apparently without fear. I never heard a wounded Marine moan. The aid men, unarmed, were right up in the front lines getting the wounded. Fire discipline was excellent."[68]

As 1st Marine Division commander, Rupertus of course received much of the credit for seizing Cape Gloucester. Geiger praised the division, and by implication, Rupertus, for its good work. On the other hand, there were reasons to criticize Rupertus' performance, especially his handling of personnel. Rupertus was a mercurial man, alternately vindictive and gracious, and the stress of his responsibilities did little to alleviate this trait. He resented HQMC's habit of sending high-level officers to his division without consulting him and looked down on those who had not fought on Guadalcanal. For instance, halfway through the Cape Gloucester operation, HQMC dispatched the well-regarded Col. Oliver Smith to New Britain to serve as Rupertus' chief of staff. Rupertus had not asked for Smith, who had neither seen action nor gone through Guadalcanal. Instead, Rupertus intended to give the job to John Selden, head of the 5th Marine Regiment. Rupertus responded by transferring Smith to lead the 5th Marine Regiment and making Selden his chief of staff. After Smith gained some combat experience, Rupertus appointed him his assistant division commander, but froze him out of his inner circle, even suggesting that Smith set up a separate mess elsewhere. In some respects it was not personal; Rupertus had treated Smith's predecessor, Lemuel Shepherd, similarly, but it was hardly a good way to act toward subordinates upon whose fate an outfit depends. Small wonder one officer later recalled, "Gen[eral] Rupertus did several things like this which really made me think he was a small man."[69]

With two successful amphibious operations under its belt, the 1st Marine Division was a valuable Pacific War commodity. MacArthur certainly saw it that way. He hoped to keep the division in his theater for future campaigns, telling one Marine officer, "You will be my shock troops, my best division."[70] He also stated that he would give up the Marines only over his dead body. HQMC, on the other hand, viewed things differently. Marine officers believed that it was easier for the Corps to maintain control over its units in the Navy-dominated Pacific Ocean Area than anywhere else. After becoming commandant on 1 January 1944, Vandegrift worried that MacArthur would misuse and fritter away the 1st Marine Division on missions that did not involve amphibious assaults. MacArthur's insistence that the division remain on New Britain for mopping up duties seemed to confirm Vandegrift's concerns. Vandegrift appealed to King, who persuaded the Joint Chiefs to order the 1st Marine Division's return to the Pacific Ocean Area. When MacArthur dragged his feet, Nimitz pried it loose by assigning the outfit to invade the Palau Islands and telling MacArthur that his obstinacy was jeopardizing that undertaking.

The Marines eventually left New Britain for rehabilitation on the Russell Islands in early May 1944. Although its casualties had been relatively moderate, several months on the fetid island had seriously exhausted the division. One officer remembered, "The infantry was finally relieved. The guys were getting [into] the trucks to go up the other end of the island. They looked like death, they were pale, no life in them at all, shriveled up. You've never seen the likes of it—men looking like that. But they'd been in the jungle quite a long time."[71]

CONCLUSIONS

Although American military planners originally designed Operation Cartwheel to seize the big Japanese base at Rabaul, Allied successes in its implementation had so depleted Japanese air and naval assets in the region that in August 1943 the Joint Chiefs of Staff decided to instead neutralize and bypass the fortress and its 100,000 Japanese defenders. The Bougainville and Cape Gloucester operations were among the last pieces of the revamped Cartwheel puzzle to fall into place.

Cartwheel benefited the Marines in numerous ways. Most obviously, it served as a painful schooling in modern warfare. On Guadalcanal, Bougainville, and Cape Gloucester the Marines learned a great deal about tactics, training, logistics, interservice cooperation, and leadership. The campaign gave the Navy and Marine Corps three experienced divisions to use in future operations. These outfits saw enough action to get a taste of combat, but not so much as to render them ineffective.

In terms of high-level leaders, several were found wanting even before they took their divisions into battle. Holcomb relieved Vogel as I Amphibious Corps commander because he failed in planning. Barrett's inability to effectively plan doomed his career as well. Finally, DeCarre hardly shined at the head of elements of the 2nd Marine Division on Guadalcanal. On the other hand, Vandegrift emerged as the Marine Corps' star general for his performances on Guadalcanal and in twice reforming the I Amphibious Corps. Geiger earned kudos for his work with Marine aviation on Guadalcanal and for overseeing the I Amphibious Corps on Bougainville. Rupertus and Turnage turned in solid, if unspectacular, jobs as division commanders on Cape Gloucester and Bougainville. Even before Cartwheel ended, new Marine generals with new units were deploying in the Central Pacific for operations that would test the Marine Corps more severely than in the South Pacific.

═══ ★THREE★ ═══

CENTRAL PACIFIC OFFENSIVE

T he Navy never intended to wage war in the South Pacific. For naval officers, Operation Cartwheel against Rabaul was an expensive, if necessary, diversion of resources. Instead, the Navy had planned to fight the Japanese across the Central Pacific from their base in Hawaii. Doing so would provide plenty of room for the Navy to engage and hopefully defeat its Japanese counterpart in a climactic battle before going on to blockade Japan into submission. Such an offensive would also provide the Army Air Forces with airfields from which it could pulverize the Japanese homeland with its new B-29 Superfortress bombers. In the Central Pacific, the Marines could undertake the amphibious assaults against small islands for which they had long trained. Even before the Joint Chiefs of Staff decided to wrap up Operation Cartwheel and simply bypass Rabaul and its 100,000 Japanese defenders, the Navy had turned its sights back to the Central Pacific.

Unhappily for the Navy, Army officers, led by Gen. Douglas MacArthur, had their own plan for winning the conflict with Japan: advancing on Japan from Australia via New Guinea and the Philippines. This route would enable the U.S. military to use Australia as a base and cut Japan off from its Dutch East Indies oil fields. It would also permit MacArthur to redeem the pledge he had made in 1942 to liberate the Philippines. Both the Army and Navy's preferred strategies had merit, but the real issue was which service would lead in the Pacific War. Although the Joint Chiefs of Staff was inclined to endorse the Navy's approach and in fact gave it the initial go-ahead in 1943, MacArthur complained so doggedly and effectively that in March 1944 the Joint Chiefs agreed to revisit the matter. After a review, they opted to compromise with their Dual Drive Offensive. The Joint Chiefs authorized the Navy to undertake its thrust across the Central Pacific from Hawaii with the bulk of the available Pacific War resources, and permitted MacArthur to conduct his own campaign across New Guinea from Australia. The goal of the offensives was to reach the vaguely defined China-Formosa-Luzon area, at which time the Joint Chiefs would decide what to do next. The Dual Drive Offensive dispersed U.S. resources and doubled the number of Japanese objectives to take, but it also made it more difficult for the Japanese to predict and respond to attacks. Most important, it preserved interservice harmony by giving each branch its own offensive. For the Marines, this meant that they would continue operating under the Navy's familiar aegis.

The Navy and Marines began preparing for their offensive across the Central Pacific before Operation Cartwheel ended. Commandant Thomas Holcomb gave Gen. Holland Smith the job of leading the Marine contingent, which would eventually become the V Amphibious Corps. Sixty years old at the time, Smith would emerge as the Marine Corps' dominant personality in the Central Pacific offensive. Born in Alabama in 1882, Smith graduated from Alabama Polytechnic Institute nineteen years later, in 1901. His father wanted him to follow in his footsteps and become a lawyer, so Smith earned a law degree from the University of Alabama. A year in private practice convinced him, however, that he was not cut out for the legal profession. After Smith's efforts to secure an Army commission failed, someone suggested the Marine Corps as an alternative. Smith had never heard of the organization, but subsequent inquiries convinced him to seek a commission, which he obtained in 1905. Before World War I, he served in the Philippines, Panama, and the Dominican Republic. He fought in France in World War I, mostly as a staff officer, and remained busy throughout the 1920s, becoming a Naval War College graduate, Office of Naval Operations staffer, Joint Army-Navy Planning Board Committee member, Haiti pacifier, chief of staff for the 1st Marine Brigade at Quantico, instructor and student at the Marine Corps Schools, and quartermaster.

Smith embraced the Marines' post–World War I commitment to amphibious warfare and in the 1930s continued his ascension up the Marine Corps hierarchy. He spent time in the Pacific Fleet, directed HQMC's Operations and Planning Division, and served as assistant commandant. He was commander of the 1st Marine Brigade when World War II began in Europe, training the outfit in amphibious operations. Holcomb retained him at his post when the brigade evolved into the 1st Marine Division. In June 1941 Holcomb put him in charge of Marine amphibious forces in the Atlantic Ocean and in August 1942 assigned him to lead its Pacific Ocean counterpart.

Smith became the most prominent and divisive high-ranking Marine Corps combat general in World War II. The press dubbed him "Howlin' Mad," but his real nickname was "Hoke." With his steel-rimmed glasses and thinning hair, Smith reminded one person of a rural schoolmaster. On first acquaintance, he typically came across as crusty and hard-nosed. Blunt, opinionated, loud, and no nonsense, Smith dominated every conversation in which he participated. He certainly had the courage of his convictions, a trait that often generated as much anger as respect. His devotion to the Marine Corps and its amphibious mission was absolute. He sometimes suspected wrongly that others were out to denigrate both, and when this happened, he fought tooth and nail to protect the Corps' prerogatives, regardless of the consequences. His combativeness and impatience obscured a shrewdness, intellect, and decisiveness that made him a surprisingly good organizer and planner. There was nothing subtle about Smith's military philosophy. As he explained in his memoirs, "I have advocated aggressiveness in the field and constant offensive action. Hit quickly, hit hard and keep right on hitting. Give the enemy no rest, no opportunity to consolidate his forces and hit back at you. This is the shortest road to victory in the type of island war the Marines had to fight and is most economical of lives in the long run."[1]

Beneath Smith's rough exterior, he was actually a warm and compassionate man, full of kindness and sentimentality. He relaxed by hunting and playing cribbage and enjoyed animated and free-flowing conversation. As a devout Christian, he felt a moral obligation to all of humanity. During the Saipan operation in 1944, for example, he ordered an officer to feed and shelter a half dozen hungry and exposed Japanese prisoners he had come across, explaining, "We're supposed to be Christians. We have to act like Christians."[2] Smith claimed that controlled anger was a man's best weapon, but in his hands it was an imperfect armament that he frequently struggled to master. Despite his professionalism, his emotions often got the better of him, and he was prone to bouts of depression and self-pity. He tended to breathe heavily before losing his temper, giving plenty of warning to stand clear. He was no military genius, but his undisputed competence and administrative abilities made him an obvious selection for the complicated and intricate assignments he received during the war.[3]

Smith may have been an obvious choice for challenging amphibious tasks, but that did not make his appointment in 1943 as head of the V Amphibious Corps inevitable because he could be a difficult man to work with or for. That he was chosen stood as a testament to the respect that naval officers had for him. Smith's success in training Marines and soldiers in amphibious warfare had so impressed Adm. Chester Nimitz, head of the Pacific Ocean Area, that he took Smith with him on his June 1943 inspection trip to the South Pacific, during which he informed Smith that he planned to ask Holcomb for his services. When Adm. Richmond Kelly Turner passed through Pearl Harbor the following month, he suggested Smith to Nimitz as an amphibious corps commander. Turner later recalled, "I recommended Holland Smith for his job. He was the best man I knew for it. He was a marvelous offensively minded and capable fighting man. It was no mistake, and I would do it all over again."[4] Both the Secretary of the Navy, Frank Knox, and the Chief of Naval Operations, Adm. Ernest King, endorsed the idea. Smith had won King's respect a couple years earlier during fleet exercises in the Caribbean. He had so stridently resisted King's efforts to boss around Marines that King threatened to remove Smith from his post. Smith responded, "Relieved or not, as long as I am in command I am going to command."[5]

Holcomb and Smith, however, were not on very friendly terms. Indeed, in September 1942 Holcomb had complained to Vandegrift that Smith was becoming increasingly uncooperative. Like everyone else, though,

Holcomb valued Smith's abilities. He also approved of the job Smith had done preparing soldiers for the invasion of Attu, in the Aleutians, and knew that he had the support of the naval establishment. Holcomb had one last and overriding reason for authorizing Smith's new assignment. He explained to one Marine officer, "The reason I am appointing Smith is that there's going to be a lot of trouble with the Navy over rights and preroga-tives and such things and Holland is the one I know who can sit at the table and pound it harder than any naval officer."[6]

Smith's transfer to Hawaii and subsequent selection to command the V Amphibious Corps rescued him from more than a year of frustration. Although he had been busy training troops, what he really wanted was to lead them in battle. He had resented Vogel's appointment to run the I Amphibious Corps, attributing it to Holcomb's hostility. Moreover, an unfortunate mishap threatened to derail his career. On the night of 5–6 February 1943, he struck and injured an enlisted sailor with his car while driving in San Diego. He did not stop until a motorcycle cop pulled him over three miles down the road and arrested him for hit-and-run and drunk driving. The district attorney declined to press charges because the sailor had been jaywalking and there was no evidence that Smith was inebri-ated. Smith worried, however, that the incident would anger Holcomb and embarrass the Marine Corps. He worked hard to get into Holcomb's good graces by excelling in preparing soldiers and Marines for amphibious warfare. He accompanied the Army's 7th Division in its Aleutians cam-paign and derived great satisfaction in the accuracy of his unpopular and much-maligned prediction that the Japanese would evacuate Kiska Island rather than fight for it.

When Smith arrived at Pearl Harbor in 1943 to organize the V Amphib-ious Corps, he was dismayed by the Navy's dismissive attitude toward him and the Marine Corps. The Navy initially assigned him quarters in an area reserved for junior lieutenants until he complained. He was also displeased that no one seemed to take the war as seriously as he did. Despite such irri-tations, Smith was grateful to both God and Holcomb for the opportunity to ply his trade in its most direct manner. He wrote to Holcomb, "This job is growing in importance every day and increasing responsibilities are being placed on us. God being my helper, I will not let you or the Corps down.

. . . Some of these days I hope to adequately express my deep appreciation for all you have done for me."[7]

Holcomb's expectation that Smith would have to fight to protect Marine prerogatives proved accurate. The problem was not the genial Nimitz, with whom Smith had established a good rapport, but rather the amphibious force commander responsible for transporting the Marines to their objective: Turner. Although Turner had recommended Smith to lead the V Amphibious Corps, it did not mean they had the capacity to get along. In fact, many in the know expressed a morbid interest in the anticipated clash between the two officers, both of whom were ferociously loyal to their services, short-tempered, and convinced of the certitude of their ideas. King may have reined in Turner during the Guadalcanal campaign, but there were still plenty of things about which the Navy and Marines could disagree.

Smith had met Turner in Washington earlier in the war, and at first he compared Turner to an exacting schoolmaster. He soon learned, however, that Turner was aggressive, relentless, determined, and just plain ornery. The two men clashed from the start over a variety of issues, mostly related to the division of authority between the Navy and the Marines. Their meetings throughout the war often degenerated into shouting matches. On one occasion, an outraged Turner threw a six-inch-thick binder at Smith's chief of staff. On another, Smith yelled at Turner, "I don't try to run your ships and you'd better by a goddamn sight lay off of my troops."[8] Naval officers on friendly terms with both men became accustomed to one complaining about the other. There were, however, several good reasons why their relationship survived. For one, Smith and Turner genuinely respected one another and recognized each other's talents. Moreover, they both knew that if they failed to resolve their differences, they might lose their jobs. Their disputes remained professional, not personal. Indeed, they often socialized together, during which they appeared thick as thieves. The upshot was that no matter how much they yelled at each other, they compromised and got things done.[9]

Because the Marine Corps was organizationally part of the Navy, the disputes between Smith and Turner were, in institutional terms, domestic. Another powerful military entity in Hawaii, however, posed a threat to the

Marine Corps' amphibious mission. Although the Navy dominated the Pacific Ocean Area, it became clear early on that the Navy and Marines lacked the means to undertake an offensive across the Central Pacific without significant assistance from the Army. In fact, the Army invested considerable resources in the theater, including four combat divisions that would participate in every important operation of the campaign. To oversee the Army's interests, its chief of staff, Gen. George Marshall, dispatched Gen. Robert Richardson to Hawaii.

Nicknamed "Nellie" for his pompous and finicky manner, Richardson was the epitome of the frustrated staff officer. He had more rank than authority, but wanted not only to administer the soldiers in his jurisdiction, but also to lead them in battle. Unhappily for Richardson, Nimitz had already assigned Smith the job of overall command of ground troops in the Central Pacific offensive. Richardson was not convinced that this was a good idea. He suspected that Marine officers like Smith lacked the tactical, logistical, and administrative skills necessary to undertake the kind of large-scale operations called for by the Pacific War. He tried to get along with everyone, but his doubts about the Marines' basic institutional competence gradually hardened into a conviction that eventually helped poison Army-Marine relations in the Pacific Ocean Area.[10]

Smith leaned heavily on his chief of staff, Col. Graves "Robert" Erskine, in coping with the innumerable challenges he faced. They were close friends, and Smith considered Erskine a brilliant officer and valued his efficiency. Erskine appreciated Smith's independence, perceptiveness, and the burdens under which he labored. Erskine had little respect for the Marine Corps' educational system because he believed it did not do enough to prepare officers for staff work above the regimental level. He therefore worked hard to mold his staff into an effective team. For instance, he taught his staff officers that the best way to find out what was going on at the front was to go there themselves. If he was often overbearing and brusque, the positive results it obtained spoke for themselves. Erskine's role proved to be all the more important because Smith's responsibilities were so broad.

Although Erskine and Smith liked each other, the relationship was hardly trouble free. Erskine occasionally forgot to inform Smith about issues that Smith felt important. When Smith found out, he sometimes refused to speak to Erskine for days at a time. In fact, on two occasions Smith fired Erskine as his chief of staff, but when Erskine gathered his things and reported back to Smith for further orders, Smith responded, "Get back to work, goddamnit, you know I didn't mean that."[11]

TARAWA

The Joint Chiefs of Staff initiated the Central Pacific offensive on 20 July 1943 by authorizing Operation Galvanic, which called for simultaneous attacks on the islands of Tarawa and Nauru. Tarawa was one of the Gilberts, a chain of around sixteen islands running 420 miles north–south. Nauru was an isolated speck of land 450 miles southwest of Tarawa, just south of the equator. The Joint Chiefs wanted the two islands to serve as springboards for an offensive against the Marshall Islands, to the west. Smith had no problem with seizing Tarawa, but he did not think Nauru worth the effort. He believed that occupying Nauru would require more troops than those available, would be too far from Tarawa for the Navy to effectively support both invasions, and had beaches too poor for an amphibious landing. Turner and Adm. Raymond Spruance, the overall commander of the expedition, agreed. Putting their heads together, the three men recommended substituting another island in the Gilberts, Makin, for Nauru. Located 115 miles north of Tarawa, Makin was close enough for the Navy to support both assaults simultaneously. Moreover, it had a small Japanese garrison, was closer to the Marshalls than Nauru, and had flat terrain suitable for airfield construction. King and the Joint Chiefs agreed, and on 5 October Nimitz gave the reconfigured plan the go-ahead. The basic idea was for the Army to take Makin while the Marines stormed Tarawa.[12]

Chains of hundreds of atolls—islands of coral that enclose a lagoon—are a distinguishing geographic feature of the Central Pacific. Tarawa, a triangular-shaped atoll with a perimeter of forty-two miles, surrounds a two-hundred-square-mile lagoon. The Americans had no intention of seizing the entire atoll, but instead focused their attention on the southwestern-most island of Betio. Only three miles long and six hundred yards wide, Betio, like most atoll islands, lies just a few feet above sea level. At the time, its vegetation was limited to coconut trees and scrub brush. It derived its military importance

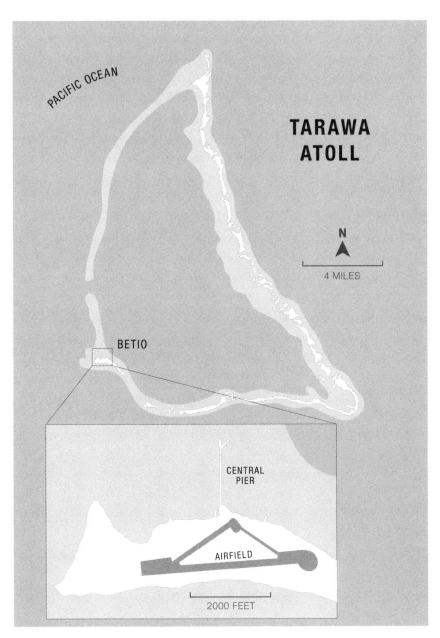

PACIFIC OCEAN

**TARAWA
ATOLL**

N

4 MILES

BETIO

CENTRAL
PIER

AIRFIELD

2000 FEET

Map 5. Tarawa

from an airfield guarded by more than four thousand Japanese troops and laborers who had been there since September 1942.

Nimitz needed the Army's help to implement Galvanic because there were not enough Marines in the Central Pacific for the job. The 1st Marine Division was busy preparing for the Cape Gloucester operation, and the 3rd Marine Division was similarly preoccupied getting ready to invade Bougainville. That left Gen. John Marston's 2nd Marine Division. It was an experienced outfit, having fought on Guadalcanal, but its performance had not impressed some Marine officers. Halsey had not allowed Marston to lead his troops to the island because he outranked the Army commander in charge there. By the time the division returned to New Zealand for rest and habilitation in March 1943, around 12,000 of its men had contracted malaria. Marston had been well respected in the prewar Corps as a nice, well-meaning, and kind-hearted officer. Holcomb appreciated the good job Marston did commanding the Marine contingent sent to occupy Iceland in the summer of 1941 and rewarded his efforts by assigning him the 2nd Marine Division. Once in the South Pacific, however, Marston lost control of his outfit. He spent too much time in his office immersed in trivial details instead of in the field inspecting his leathernecks. He also failed to ride herd over his officers. One Marine later said that division headquarters in Wellington had a brothel-like atmosphere, with women in various states of dress scurrying out every morning.[13]

In all likelihood, sickness explained at least some of Marston's inefficiency. Soon after the 2nd Marine Division returned to New Zealand, he came down with chills and fever. Although malaria was distressingly common in the mosquito-filled South Pacific, it took doctors several weeks to diagnose it in Marston. Proper treatment restored much of his health, but a medical board determined that he needed three more months of rest to completely recuperate. Marston felt that he was ready to resume his responsibilities, but also recognized that the 2nd Marine Division's well-being came first. As he put it in a 2 April 1943 letter to Vogel, "There is no need for me to express my regret about the entire affair, but you know well enough that if I am relieved, it will be one of the greatest disappointments of my life. However, I am still insistent that any action taken should give first consideration to the Second Marine Division and not to myself or any other person."[14] Holcomb agreed. He was not yet fully aware of the 2nd Marine Division's woes, but he had concluded that it would be "foolish" to keep Marston on as division commander when he might not be physically up to the job. That being the case, in early April he ordered Marston home. Holcomb tried to ease Marston's disappointment by assigning him head of the Department of the Pacific. It was a prestigious peacetime post, but as Marston recognized, a backwater during the war. Marston also resented what he saw as Holcomb's arbitrary treatment of his case. Nevertheless, he assumed his new position with as much grace as he could muster, while fully aware that he had missed the opportunity to play an important combat role in the conflict.[15]

Holcomb replaced Marston with another Smith—Julian. The Maryland-born Smith graduated from the University of Delaware in 1907 and secured a Marine Corps commission less than two years later. As a young officer he served in Veracruz, the Panama Canal Zone, Haiti, the Dominican Republic, and shipboard. He spent World War I stateside, training officers. A year after the conflict ended, he took a machine gun battalion to Cuba to help restore order there. In the 1920s Smith worked in the HQMC budget office and attended the Army's Command and General Staff College. The 1930s found him in Nicaragua, but he spent much of the decade back at HQMC in various capacities. After running a battalion, he traveled to London to observe World War II from that important vantage point. He became head of the Fleet Marine Force Training School in North Carolina after the Japanese attacked Pearl Harbor.

Julian Smith hardly fit the image of the stereotypical gung-ho Marine officer. Low key, courtly, and confident, he appeared older than his years. His serenity made him an excellent teacher. One officer recalled, "But he was a fine old gentleman, kindly person, not an inspiring leader in the sense of a 'Follow me, let's go' hard charger, but a fine leader nevertheless in that his moral fiber, so to speak, was such that you could just love him, and we did. You'd fight for him."[16] While commanding the Fleet Marine Training School at Camp Lejeune, North Carolina, Smith was awakened by an aide in the middle of the night to take a phone call from a Marine's father, who had insisted on talking to him immediately about his son. Smith could not provide the man with the information he wanted but promised to look into the matter the next morning. After Smith hung up, his wife complained about the father's impropriety. Smith responded, "There may be thousands of Marines on this post, don't you know, but to that mother and father in Washington there is only one, their son. No one knows in what condition their Marine might return, or if he will return at all."[17]

Smith's biggest career obstacle was his health, or, rather, perceptions of his health. While in Nicaragua Smith had contracted sprue, a rare and serious tropical malady that results in pernicious anemia, brought on by dietary deficiencies. The disease ruined his appetite, sucked the energy out of him, left him in constant pain, and landed him in the hospital for three months. He recovered with a strict diet, vitamins, and liver extract injections. Regardless, some officers wondered whether he was physically capable of performing combat duty overseas. Smith believed that concerns about his fitness delayed his promotion to general, and he remained convinced that rumors that he lacked stamina had limited his wartime opportunities.[18]

For Smith, the first seventeen months of the war was one disappointment after another. He wanted a combat command, but none was forthcoming. He had hoped that Holcomb would appoint him to lead the 1st or 2nd Marine Division and was dismayed when those jobs went to Vandegrift and Marston. He had asked Holcomb for the 3rd Marine Division, but Holcomb gave that one to Barrett. Smith was sure that his record justified at least a division and suspected quite accurately that doubts about his health explained Holcomb's unwillingness to send him overseas. In August 1942 he wrote, "I am afraid my standing with Headquarters is not any better than it used to be and I am not anticipating any attractive duty. However, as always, I shall do my best to render good service and continue taking it on the chin, if necessary."[19] To bolster his case, Smith got a special physical examination that gave him a clean bill of health. That, as well as the all-clear from two routine medical boards, finally persuaded Holcomb that Smith's constitution could withstand combat conditions.

Holcomb had planned to give Smith the new 4th Marine Division, but Marston's debilitation convinced him to instead dispatch Smith to New Zealand as Marston's successor. In May 1943 Holcomb summoned Smith from Camp Lejeune to Washington. When Smith entered Holcomb's office, Holcomb explained the situation and asked him how long it would take him to get to the South Pacific. Smith replied that he could leave immediately. Holcomb then expressed some last-minute reservations about Smith's sprue. Smith, with his goal in sight and not about to be deterred, reassured Holcomb that he was fit as a fiddle. Smith's upbeat response muted, but did not eliminate, Holcomb's residual reservations, so he gave him his blessing and issued the necessary orders.[20]

When Smith reached New Zealand, he was disappointed with the condition of the 2nd Marine Division in general and with the high-ranking officers in particular. As far as Smith could tell, these officers spent too much time living it up and not enough time training their men and tending to the division. Staff work was equally slipshod. The regiments were more accustomed to acting independently, as they often had on Guadalcanal, rather than working together as a team. Indeed, the division appeared organized from the bottom up, not the top down. Smith later noted, "There seemed to be no organization for me to grab hold of, you know. I was lacking an ADC [assistant division commander], chief of staff, and everything to turn things over to me."[21] Smith was especially concerned about the quality of the regimental commanders. The head of the 6th Marine Regiment, Col. Gilder Jackson, had left because of illness, but his bad attitude continued to infect the outfit. Malaria had also forced out another officer about whom many had doubts, assistant division commander Alfonse DeCarre. With Vandegrift's help, Smith brought in better officers. Merritt Edson became Smith's chief of staff, and Lt. Col. David Shoup emerged as Smith's mainstay as division operations officer. Smith initiated a retraining program that restored the division's morale, efficiency, and physical condition. By July he was optimistic that he had turned things around, and in September he pronounced the division ready to go. The only major outstanding personnel problem was illness. As late as September some 1,800 men remained on the sick list, including 856 with malaria.[22]

Galvanic was an intricate military undertaking, in part due to the abundance of resources now at Nimitz's disposal, but also because of complicated interservice relations. The Army, Navy, and Marine Corps all contributed forces to the operation, and although everyone pledged interservice cooperation, officers still jostled to protect their branch's prerogatives. This state of affairs interfered with clear and smooth lines of authority. Spruance was in overall command, with Turner, as head of the amphibious force, directly under him. From there things became convoluted. Holland Smith's V Amphibious Corps was equal to Turner's amphibious force in Galvanic planning, but Turner had priority in its execution. The Army did not want Smith giving orders to its 27th Division assailing Makin. Moreover, because Julian Smith would lead the 2nd Marine Division against Tarawa, Holland Smith and his V Amphibious Corps seemed like a superfluous link that would slow down the transmission of directives between Julian Smith and Turner. Nimitz's chief of staff, Adm. Charles McMorris, questioned whether Holland Smith should even accompany the invasion fleet and ordered him left behind at Pearl Harbor. An outraged Smith appealed to Spruance to intervene on his behalf. When things finally shook out, Nimitz permitted Holland Smith to go along, but he went with Turner on the battleship USS *Pennsylvania* to observe the Makin assault and had little direct authority over the actual fighting. Smith, unsurprisingly, found this enormously frustrating. One admiral remembered Smith saying, "All I want to do is to kill some Japs. Just give me a rifle. I don't want to be a commanding general. Just give me a rifle. I'll go out there and shoot some Japs. I want to fight the Japs."[23]

Other aspects of Galvanic were equally troubling. There were continuing questions about Tarawa's reefs, tides, and defenses, as well as debates and compromises over landing craft usage, preliminary bombardment particulars, and force allocations. The fact was that this was the first time the Navy and Marines were undertaking an amphibious assault in the teeth of enemy defenses. Although most officers expected overwhelming American materiel and numerical superiority to deliver victory, it was clear that translating doctrine from theory to reality was going to be messy and unpredictable. For the Marines, the stakes were particularly high. If the Tarawa assault failed, it could raise questions about the very need for the Corps. Small wonder that Holcomb for one believed that the Marine Corps' future was on the line.[24]

On 7 November, the transports carrying the 2nd Marine Division rendezvoused at Efate Island, in the New Hebrides, with the warships tasked with escorting them to Tarawa. They were part of Spruance's Fifth Fleet of around two hundred vessels, including thirteen battleships, eight heavy cruisers, four light cruisers, nine aircraft carriers, and seventy destroyers and escort destroyers. To maintain secrecy, intelligence officers had made arrangements and distributed invitations for a dance in Wellington dated for after the division was to return from what were supposed to be routine exercises at Hawkes Bay. One wag jokingly noted that the division left behind plenty of broken hearts and broken dates. After a week of last-minute rehearsals, the assembled fleet set sail for the Gilberts on 13 November.

Julian Smith had much to keep him occupied as he traveled on board the battleship USS *Maryland*. He knew that a direct attack on Betio in the thick of Japanese defenses was bound to be costly and was unhappy that Holland Smith had stripped him of his 6th Marine Regiment for use as the corps reserve. Moreover, two of his staff officers had warned him that the 2nd Marine Regiment commander, Col. William Marshall, was close to exhaustion. Smith invited Marshall to his stateroom for a chat. A relaxed Marshall arrived and told Smith an old Marine joke. Marshall laughed and laughed and then began crying uncontrollably. "General Smith," said Marshall, "I can't take them in." A saddened Smith responded, "You're not going to have to, Bill." Smith relieved Marshall and gave the regiment to Shoup as a reward for the good work he had done planning for the assault. Marshall's discomfiture was just another detail to occupy Smith's mind. Even so, he tried not to fret, writing to his wife the evening before the invasion, "It is now in the hands of Providence and the fighting hearts of the Marines; I have complete faith in both and am not worrying."[25]

The Marines assailed Betio on the morning of 20 November. Unfortunately, the preliminary naval bombardment and airstrikes inflicted little damage on Japanese troops manning machine gun nests, pillboxes, covered gun emplacements, and large concrete blockhouses reinforced by palm logs. After several delays, the first leathernecks hit the beach on Betio's northern side at around nine o'clock. Amtraks carried the first three waves over the coral reef directly ashore, and from there troops scrambled for cover behind log barricades near the waterline. Subsequent waves in trackless landing craft were unable to surmount the reef because, as some had feared, the incoming tide did not provide enough water. These leathernecks had to disembark and wade four to five hundred yards to the beach in water up to their waists and through a hail of Japanese bullets and shells that killed or wounded a good many of them. Once ashore the Marines could not locate their units or communicate with vessels offshore. With each passing hour fewer and fewer landing craft remained functioning due to enemy fire and mechanical breakdowns. At around noon Shoup arrived near a pier, established an impromptu and primitive command post, and took charge. Small numbers of tanks and artillery also came ashore. By nightfall the Marine beachhead was not a continuous line, but rather a series of shallow defensive perimeters held by small groups of tired men.

For Julian Smith, on board *Maryland*, 20 November was a frustrating day. Although he was the 2nd Marine Division's commander with the immediate responsibility for seizing Betio, bad communications made it difficult for him to understand the battle, let alone direct it. He issued orders that took hours to reach their recipients, if they did at all, and even longer for anyone to attempt to implement them. The one thing Smith knew for certain was that things were not going as planned. That being the case, he radioed Turner and Holland Smith to ask for permission to use the V Amphibious Corps' reserve, Col. Maurice Holmes' 6th Marine Regiment.

Holland Smith and Turner were one hundred miles away on board *Pennsylvania* observing the Army's assault on Makin. With the planning for Galvanic over, the two men were getting along famously. As far as Holland Smith was concerned, the Makin operation was just an insignificant skirmish taking the inept Army far longer than necessary to wrap up. On the other hand, he had worried about Betio from the start. Julian Smith's request for the 6th Marine Regiment confirmed his fears. He and Turner agreed to release the regiment because they had so much respect for Julian Smith. Even so, Holland Smith spent the night tossing and turning until he opened his Bible and read about Joshua and the children of Israel. He awoke the next morning feeling somewhat better but wishing that he were closer to the scene of the action.[26]

For all the Marines' woes, they were in better shape than Betio's Japanese defenders. U.S. naval gunfire had destroyed their communications and killed their commander, making it impossible for them to coordinate their actions. Japanese manpower and ammunition were finite and dwindling. On the morning after the Marine assault, 21 November, the incoming tide made it easier for the Marines to get their landing craft over the reef and directly to the beach with reinforcements and supplies. Throughout the day small Marine detachments used blocks of TNT and flamethrowers to destroy Japanese positions and slowly advance inland. They cleared enough ground for elements of the 6th Marine Regiment to land toward evening without excessive casualties. Edson also arrived to take general control of the battle and relieve an exhausted Shoup of some of his responsibilities. By nightfall it was clear that the Marines were winning. Even so, it took several more days to clean up remaining Japanese resistance, a process helped by an unsuccessful last-minute Japanese counterattack that wiped out most of the remaining garrison.

By the time the Marines secured Betio, the island was a shattered shell. Destroyed landing craft dotted the shoreline, discarded and demolished equipment littered the beach, and burned-out pillboxes and gun emplacements scarred the interior. When Holland Smith arrived for a firsthand look, he was shocked by the scene: "No words of mine can reproduce the picture I saw when the plane landed after circling that wrecked and battered island. The sight of our dead floating in the waters of the lagoon and lying along the blood-soaked beaches is one I will never forget. Over the pitted, blasted island hung a miasma of coral dust and death, nauseating and horrifying."[27] Smith found Julian Smith dirty and tired, but proud of his leathernecks. He too was distressed by the casualties. Indeed, more than one thousand Marines had died in the battle, and another two thousand were wounded. As for the Japanese, almost the entire garrison was killed. It was a stiff price to pay for a tiny island that almost no one had ever heard of.[28]

Indeed, many Americans were shocked to learn of the casualties the Marines sustained seizing such a small and obscure island. From their perspective, the operation seemed prohibitively expensive. By the time public criticism crescendoed, Vandegrift had replaced Holcomb as commandant and was as saddened as anyone else by the high human cost of storming Tarawa. He did not, however, try to downplay Marine losses or reassure concerned citizens that Tarawa was an anomaly unlikely to reoccur. As Vandegrift saw things, war required such sacrifices, and the public had to accept this harsh reality if it wanted to defeat Japan. He explained to one concerned senator, "A landing attack is recognized by all military experts as being the most difficult and costly of all forms of attack. Losses at Tarawa were heavy, and losses will be heavy in future attacks of this nature."[29]

Marine and naval officers who reviewed Galvanic after the capture of Tarawa did not question the need for amphibious assaults against strongly defended Japanese positions, but instead focused on conducting them better in the future. The consensus was that occupying Tarawa had been necessary to unlock the door to advancing farther westward. After the war, though, Holland Smith claimed that storming Tarawa had not been worth the high price. He called it a "terrible waste of life and effort."[30] He was not the only person who later argued that the Americans should have bypassed the Gilberts and directly attacked the Marshall Islands. That said, more thoughtful officers recognized that the Marines and Navy were bound to make serious mistakes the first time they assailed a well-fortified Japanese-held island, regardless of the location and time. After all, until Tarawa, Marine amphibious doctrine was mostly hypothetical because earlier Marine landings at Guadalcanal and Bougainville went largely unopposed. Tarawa served as an expensive classroom experiment that taught naval and Marine officers what amphibious practices did and did not work. One Marine officer noted that Tarawa "pointed out inevitable weaknesses in technique and paved the way for future successful operations." As far as he was concerned, "There had to be a Tarawa."[31] Tarawa therefore derived its value not so much from the strategic advantages its occupation provided, but from what the Marines learned from the errors they committed there.

Despite heavy Marine losses, neither Holland Smith nor Julian Smith suffered professionally from their roles in Operation Galvanic. Most high-ranking Marines refrained from criticizing their actions, and Holcomb congratulated each officer for jobs well done. On the other hand, both men definitely learned from the experience. Julian Smith was honest about the problems and mistakes, but also praised his leathernecks for overcoming them. The poor performances of two of his regimental commanders concerned him the most. As for Holland Smith, he used the battle to force changes in amphibious doctrine. To him, Tarawa proved the need for more of everything in subsequent amphibious assaults—more amtraks, longer and heavier and more accurate preliminary bombardments, and better communications and intelligence. He also recommended that as head of the V Amphibious Corps, he should actually lead the Marines into action, not serve as a trainer, planner, and observer. Happily, Turner endorsed almost all of his suggestions, though a cynical Vandegrift warned that Turner's sincerity might prove transitory.

Holland Smith condemned the Army for not securing Makin as quickly as he thought possible, even though the soldiers occupied the island in the allotted time. Smith's charges gained weight when a Japanese submarine sank the escort carrier USS *Liscome Bay* on 24 November, costing 640 sailors their lives. If the Army had wrapped up its conquest of Makin sooner, the *Liscome Bay* would not have been around when the Japanese submarine put in an appearance. Whatever the merit of Smith's accusations, they contributed to the already difficult relationship between Smith and the Army.[32]

A NEW COMMANDANT

President Roosevelt had selected Holcomb as commandant of the Marine Corps in 1936 and four years later reappointed him. By 1943 Holcomb had led the Marine Corps through the biggest expansion in its history, one that enabled it to play a prominent role in the Pacific War. Despite this accomplishment, Holcomb was unsure of his future role in the Corps. In August 1943 he would reach the Marine Corps' mandatory retirement age of sixty-four. Although Roosevelt could still keep him on as commandant because lieutenant generals were not subject to automatic retirement, there was no guarantee that he would. Holcomb wanted to continue at his post and see the conflict through to its victorious conclusion. He was not the only one who felt that way. For example, former commandant John Russell told Holcomb that the Corps needed his steady hand. There was, however, an important principle at stake that convinced Holcomb that he needed to step down, or at least offer to do so: He had not deployed retired Marine officers over sixty-four-years old to active duty because he believed younger men made the best wartime leaders. He worried that some might charge him with hypocrisy and self-aggrandizement if he remained on duty. For an honor-bound man like Holcomb, such things mattered. After his trip to the Pacific in summer 1942, he wrote to Secretary of the Navy Knox and informed him that he planned to apply for retirement on his next birthday and would bow out as commandant whenever Knox and Roosevelt thought best. The following June he elaborated to Undersecretary of the

Navy James Forrestal, "Reluctant as I am to drop the reins in the midst of a great war, should the President agree that a change is desirable, I am prepared to submit a request for voluntary retirement."[33]

Holcomb did not intend to just walk away from the Marine Corps; he wanted to leave it in good hands. To Holcomb, that meant doing what he could to ensure that Roosevelt selected Vandegrift as the next commandant. Indeed, Holcomb had been grooming Vandegrift for the job for years. In an undated personal memo, Holcomb wrote,

> One of my first official acts when I became Commandant of the Marine Corps on 1 December 1936 was to have orders issued directing the transfer of Colonel A. A. Vandegrift from the Embassy Guard, Peking, China, to Headquarters, for duty in one of the most important key positions at this Headquarters. On his promotion to Brigadier General three years later, I appointed General Vandegrift as Assistant to the Commandant. About that time I made up my mind that if I had the power to choose my successor, the choice would fall on General Vandegrift. I have never since wavered in that feeling.[34]

When Holcomb flew to Guadalcanal in October 1942, he talked privately with Vandegrift about the commandant's position. Holcomb told Vandegrift that although he hoped Roosevelt would reappoint him as commandant, he would recommend Vandegrift as his successor if the president preferred that he retire. Of course, there was no guarantee that Holcomb could persuade the unpredictable Roosevelt to see things his way, but he was reasonably confident that Vandegrift would get the job. Fortunately, Vandegrift's record made Holcomb's task easy. Vandegrift's victory at Guadalcanal had turned him into a Marine Corps hero and household name, and his subsequent actions as I Amphibious Corps commander had garnered him plenty of respect among naval officers. Holcomb invariably coupled his comments about retirement with assertions that this would open the way for a younger distinguished officer to take his place, criteria that only Vandegrift met. Holcomb was blunter when circumstances warranted. In December 1942 he told Knox straight out that Vandegrift was the man to replace him and was pleased that Knox seemed to agree. The final decision, though, remained the president's.[35]

On 9 July 1943, Holcomb attended a White House dinner honoring French Free leader Henri Giraud. After the meal the guests dispersed into three nearby rooms, with Roosevelt as usual sitting on a sofa in one of them. A short time later Adm. William Leahy, chairman of the Joint Chiefs of Staff, summoned Holcomb to see Roosevelt. Holcomb waited patiently until Roosevelt finished discussing business with several other people and turned his attention to him. Echoing Holcomb's statements on the issue, Roosevelt said that he would like to appoint Holcomb to another term as commandant but felt that it would be best to make way for younger men. That being the case, he had decided to acquiesce to Holcomb's request to step down and to submit Vandegrift's name to the Senate as his successor. Roosevelt wanted Vandegrift to bring himself up to speed before assuming his new post by touring Marine Corps operations in the Pacific. Holcomb and Roosevelt therefore agreed that 1 January 1944 would be the optimal date for the changeover. By way of compensation, Roosevelt also suggested that perhaps Holcomb could join the Joint Chiefs of Staff, but nothing came of the idea. Nearly five months later, on 1 December, Secretary of the Navy Knox formally and reluctantly accepted Holcomb's retirement application. Two weeks after that, the Senate confirmed Roosevelt's nomination of Vandegrift as the Marine Corps' eighteenth commandant.[36]

Vandegrift became commandant more than a year after Holcomb first mentioned that he might retire. During that time Vandegrift had kept busy visiting the States, touring the Pacific, and reorganizing and then leading the I Amphibious Corps. If he was impatient to ascend to the top spot, he did not show it. He was grateful for Holcomb's support, writing to him, "I only hope that should I succeed you that I will be able to take care of the Corps as well as you have done and with the same objective determination. It is useless for me to thank you for all that you have done for me, I only hope that my thoughts and feelings have been and I can assure you will continue to reflect my friendship and admiration."[37]

Vandegrift could also take comfort in the reaction to his appointment from high-ranking Marine officers. Ordinarily, Vandegrift's elevation would have generated charges of favoritism because he was junior to several capable generals, but his wartime record, which included the Medal of Honor, made it hard to question his selection. As one Marine later put it, "These [senior officers] just took it, because, remember, Vandegrift was the hero of Guadalcanal. You just couldn't get away from it."[38] Generals instead fell in line and adjusted themselves to the new order.[39]

On New Year's Day 1944, Holcomb, Vandegrift, and their families traveled to the Department of the Navy so Knox could read the orders officially authorizing Holcomb's retirement and Vandegrift's appointment as commandant. Holcomb and Vandegrift then hastened to the Commandant's House, where the Marine Corps Band performed what was traditionally a surprise serenade. When the band finished, Vandegrift thanked the members and invited them inside for hot rum and sandwiches. From there Holcomb and Vandegrift drove to HQMC. Holcomb gathered up his few remaining possessions and took his leave as commandant. At the door Holcomb placed his hand on Vandegrift's shoulder, smiled, and gave him some parting and somewhat contradictory advice: "Vandegrift, when I go out this door I am placing twenty years on your shoulders and taking them off mine. You won't realize it at first but you will finally learn what I mean. You have a good many friends in the Corps. I only hope that when you turn your job over to a successor you have the same number. The Commandant does not make many new friends if he does his job well."[40]

Having worked before the war as Holcomb's secretary and later as assistant commandant, Vandegrift was thoroughly familiar with HQMC. Moreover, he had spent December 1943 at Holcomb's elbow getting up to speed. Vandegrift was still startled by the sense of wartime urgency at HQMC. Before taking over as commandant, he had written to Geiger, "Things here are about as hectic as you told me I would find them; and many times I have longed, even in this brief space of time, for the peaceful calm of a bombing raid on Bougainville."[41] He tried to pace himself to avoid exhaustion. He usually got to work at eight o'clock in the morning to read dispatches and catch up on his correspondence. At nine o'clock he attended the Secretary of the Navy's conference and then the naval intelligence briefing on the latest military developments. After that he returned to his office and worked until lunch. He reserved his afternoons for dealing with subordinates and receiving visitors. He got home around six with a briefcase full of documents. He entertained often, figuring that it was easier to reason with admirals and legislators after a good meal in front of a drawing room fire than in his crowded and busy office.[42]

Vandegrift understood that the Marine Corps required an efficient headquarters staffed with quality personnel. He brought along his chief of staff, Gerald Thomas, to become director of the all-important Plans and Policies Division. He also secured Thomas' appointment to brigadier general even though he was a relatively junior colonel. Vandegrift figured that Thomas not only deserved the promotion, but also needed the heftier rank to get things done in his new job. As head of Plans and Policies, Thomas continued his role as Vandegrift's confidant, sounding board, spark plug, and hatchet man. Thomas's most important organizational reform was transforming Plans and Policies into a true staff organization. Doing so created some confusion and aroused resentment. In particular, the relationship between Thomas and the assistant commandant, Gen. DeWitt Peck, was not always clear. In the end, they divvied up HQMC between them, with Thomas running operations and Peck looking after administration.[43]

As commandant, Vandegrift worked hard to maintain good relations with those with power over the Marine Corps. Knox's increasingly poor health, though, forced him to turn over many of his responsibilities to Undersecretary of the Navy Forrestal. Fortunately, Vandegrift respected Forrestal as one of the most intelligent and honest men in the federal government. As for Congress, Vandegrift conferred periodically with Rep. Carl Vinson, chairman of the House Naval Affairs Committee, from Georgia, to discuss Marine Corps needs. A sympathetic Vinson almost always did what he could to help. Although Vandegrift had only a passing familiarity with the irascible Chief of Naval Operations, Adm. Ernest King, he knew enough of his abrasive reputation to tread carefully around him. At their first meeting, Vandegrift assured King that he would do his best to implement Navy directives, but he added that he would not pull any punches in defense of the Marine Corps or serve as King's rubber stamp. King glared at him for a moment before abruptly nodding his head. From that point on, Vandegrift usually avoided King and conferred instead with King's deputy, Adm. Charles Cooke Jr. When forced to deal with King, Vandegrift usually secured his cooperation by reminding him of everything the Marines had done for the Navy during the war. As Thomas recalled, "General Vande-grift's relations [with King] were pleasant, not familiar, but always on a really good sound basis, and never in my three and a half years with him there [HQMC] did I see him lose a battle. He won every one of them."[44]

Vandegrift was equally careful in his relationships with his high-ranking subordinates. Many of them had been his seniors before the war and his ascension to commandant. He knew them all, of course, and tried to be sensitive to their feelings. The biggest source of friction between them and Vandegrift was personnel. Even after the war began and the Corps swelled in size, its top level remained small and insular. Everyone knew everyone else. When officers failed in their duties on or off the battlefield, their commanders often wanted them transferred elsewhere without careers or feelings being hurt. To do so, they resorted to unofficial letters to HQMC and refrained from putting anything negative on the record. The problem was that this enabled men found wanting to continue to rise through the Corps' hierarchy to positions of increasing responsibility. Nimitz for one commented on the large number of underperforming Marine combat offi-cers who filled important Pearl Harbor billets. He warned that this practice, if continued, would ultimately hurt the Corps.[45]

Vandegrift was well aware of this practice and had in fact indulged in it himself. Holcomb had disliked and tried to combat it, but with limited success. When Vandegrift became commandant, he decided to stamp it out. He was not opposed to officers unburdening themselves about sensitive matters in unofficial letters, nor did he mind rotating officers from com-bat to noncombat duties. In fact, the Marine Corps' small size made the frequent cycling of officers from stateside to Pacific assignments and back absolutely necessary. Besides, doing so gave experienced officers a chance to rest and impart their knowledge to greenhorns back home. It also pro-vided stateside officers the opportunity to prove themselves in the Pacific. Nonetheless, Vandegrift believed that many of his commanders abused this system to rid themselves of officers they did not like, to the detriment of the Corps as a whole. He therefore made it clear that if commanders wanted to divest themselves of underperforming officers, they had to explain why on the record. He wrote, "I get rather fed up with these commanders who go around talking personally about officers under their command but say nothing officially one way or another. If he wants him relieved, have him put in an official letter saying why."[46] Once an officer's substandard conduct was officially noted, it was easier for Vandegrift to convene a retirement board to remove him from the Corps. Unfortunately, these efforts did not accomplish as much as Vandegrift had hoped. He continued to complain about the problem for the rest of the war.[47]

Perhaps Vandegrift's biggest accomplishment as commandant during the conflict was creating and maintaining sufficient combat units with which to fight the Japanese. Before the Pacific War, the Marines had never fielded anything larger than a division. Some officers, though, recognized from early on that playing a significant role in the conflict required the Marines to deploy not only divisions, but corps as well. Erskine had warned Vandegrift, "We got to have them. This is a big war, Vandy. It's not a little thing. Forget the regiment and start thinking now that this is a corps."[48] Holcomb and Vandegrift worked hard to establish divisions and corps under Marine control in the Navy-dominated Pacific Ocean Area. The 1st Marine Division's experience in MacArthur's Southwest Pacific Area theater showed the danger of surrendering Marine units to Army authority. Moreover, the Army opposed every augmentation to Marine Corps strength. The Corps would ultimately deploy six combat divisions to the Pacific organized into two corps, all led by Marine generals.

HQMC had increasing difficulty filling these units as Marine casualties skyrocketed in 1944 and 1945. HQMC took a number of steps to find sufficient manpower. It recruited 18,000 women for noncombat jobs to free up men for combat. It also persuaded thousands of seventeen-year-olds to enlist in the reserves, which made them eligible for active duty with the Marines instead of the Army or Navy when they turned eighteen. When HQMC learned that the Army did not include its sick and wounded as part of its official total strength, Vandegrift appealed all the way to the White House to permit the Marines to do the same. This enabled the Corps to increase its draft calls and bring in more men. Eliminating superfluous units, however, was the most important tactic HQMC adopted to maintain combat divisions. At the war's start, the White House and Navy strong-armed the Corps into establishing specialized units, such as raiders, paratroopers, defense battalions, and so on. Some of these outfits performed well, but even before Vandegrift took over as commandant a consensus had emerged at HQMC that they were not worth the investment because they removed quality personnel from the combat divisions that did most of the fighting. Thomas took the lead in securing King's permission to abolish most of them, which released around 20,000 men that HQMC used as the nucleus of new divisions. Despite these efforts, it was not enough. Had the United States invaded the Japanese Home Islands, the Marine Corps would have likely been forced to break up one of its divisions to flesh out the remainder. Fortunately for everyone, Japan's surrender rendered such a move unnecessary.[49]

KWAJALEIN

The Americans had begun preparing for their next campaign even before Operation Galvanic got under way. Nimitz's had set his sights on the Marshalls, a group of twenty-nine islands in two north–south chains covering 750,000 square miles of ocean just north of the equator and west of the International Date Line. The Japanese had seized them from Germany during World War I and considered them the outer ring of their empire that protected their more significant possessions in the Marianas and Carolines. The original U.S. plan, dubbed Flintlock, called for seizing the outer islands first before assailing Kwajalein, the most important atoll in the group. Galvanic, however, had taught Nimitz the virtue of simplicity, so he decided to bypass the outer islands and strike directly at Kwajalein. Spruance, Turner, and Holland Smith all objected because doing so would expose their forces to enemy attack from the other Japanese-held islands. Nimitz, though, believed that the increasing naval and air power of U.S. forces could neutralize that threat. When Turner continued to kvetch, Nimitz said, "This is it. If you don't want to do it, the Department will find someone else to do it. Do you want to do it, or not?"[50] Turner wanted the mission, but persuaded Nimitz to add the lightly defended island of Majuro, 250 miles southeast of Kwajalein, as an objective to better protect the Fifth Fleet's communications and supply lines. Nimitz issued his final orders on 12 December 1943, and Spruance, Turner, Holland Smith, and their staffs got busy adjusting their ideas to accommodate Nimitz's wishes. Although this back-and-forth pushed the operation back several weeks, until late January, Nimitz figured that the delay was worth it because it resulted in a better plan.

Kwajalein, the largest atoll in the Marshalls, lies 540 miles northwest of Tarawa and 2,100 miles from Honolulu. Triangular-shaped like Tarawa, Kwajalein consists of some ninety small islands totaling a little more than six square miles and encloses a giant lagoon covering 655 square miles. While the Army attacked Kwajalein proper at the atoll's base, the Marines' assignment was to assail two causeway-connected islands to the northwest collectively called Roi-Namur. A Japanese airfield took up most of Roi, whose terrain was open and clear. Namur, on the other hand, contained scrub brush and palm trees that concealed the Japanese. For these reasons American planners chose the operation codenames Camouflage and Burlesque for the attacks against dense Namur and the more exposed Roi, respectively. There were about eight thousand Japanese soldiers on the atoll, with approximately three thousand of them defending Roi-Namur.

The organization for Operation Flintlock was similar to that for Galvanic: Spruance commanded the Fifth Fleet, with Turner's V Amphibious Force responsible for transporting and supplying Smith's V Amphibious Corps. Although the Navy and Marines had tried to clearly delineate the lines of authority and responsibilities between the amphibious force and landing force commanders, it remained a work in progress, dependent in large measure on the personalities involved. Indeed, Turner and Smith still found plenty of issues on which to disagree, such as who would control the landing and shore parties, but familiarity and experience did much to alleviate most of these disputes. The assault troops for Flintlock consisted of the Army's 7th Division for Kwajalein proper, the 4th Marine Division for Roi-Namur, a battalion from the Army's 27th Division for Majuro, and Gen. Thomas Watson's unattached 22nd Marine Regiment as corps reserve.[51]

Smith was by now thoroughly familiar with most of the people who helped plan Flintlock, but he also had to deal with a few new faces, or more accurately, old faces filling new roles. The most obvious was the new commandant, Archibald Vandegrift. Like almost all the high-ranking Marine Corps officers, Smith and Vandegrift went way back. Smith had been unhappy with Holcomb recommending Vandegrift for the commandant's job because he was senior to Vandegrift. He should not have been

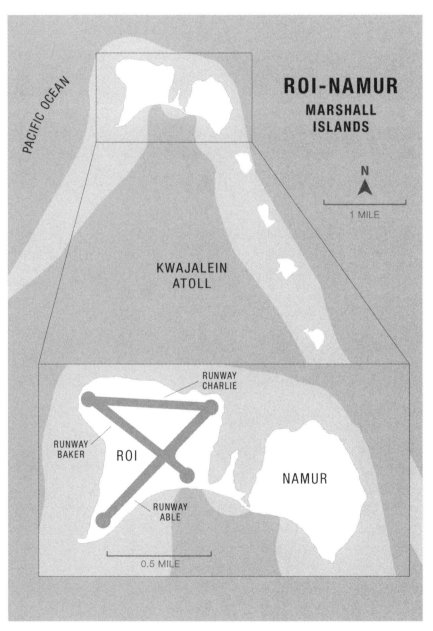

Map 6. Roi-Namur

surprised; Holcomb and Smith had never gotten along particularly well, whereas Vandegrift was Holcomb's protégé and the hero of Guadalcanal. Once word of Vandegrift's appointment leaked, Smith set aside whatever resentment he had and pledged his loyalty to Vandegrift. He also reassured Vandegrift that he had everything under control in the Pacific Ocean theater, including the thorny personnel and interservice issues that had generated so much friction. Even so, some sycophancy, doubts, and self-pity bled through. At one point Smith wrote to Vandegrift,

> Archer, out here we have problems in view, and we believe that you have the courage and good judgment to steer our ship through troubled waters; and I again reassure you that my loyalty and those who serve under me will continue. At times I feel discouraged over the tremendous odds against me. I am carrying a heavy load, and am frequently sniped at, not only by officers in the Army, but by certain individuals in Washington. God being my helper, I shall pursue the even tenor of my way, and give to my country the best that I have, regardless of whether I receive any credits for my efforts.[52]

Fortunately for Smith, Vandegrift respected his abilities and had no intention of removing him from his post.[53]

As Smith's letter to Vandegrift indicated, he faced continuing difficulties with Army officers in general and the Army's Central Pacific chief, Nellie Richardson, in particular. The differences were not personal—Smith and Richardson were invariably cordial with one another—but professional. As far as Richardson was concerned, Galvanic's confused command structure and the problems stemming from it had demonstrated that the Marines were incapable of leading large units, such as corps, into action. Richardson wanted to organize an Army corps led by an Army general to supplant the Marines in planning and implementing future amphibious operations. Marine divisions could of course participate, but their commanders would answer to the Army. Unfortunately for Richardson, the Navy dominated the Pacific Ocean Area, and naval officers preferred working with the Marines, over which they could more easily exert their authority, rather than with soldiers and their recalcitrant generals. King therefore rejected Richardson's proposal, to which Vandegrift added an adamant concurrence. Vandegrift opined to Smith that the best antidote to the Army's continuing efforts to usurp Marine prerogatives was continued battlefield success. However, he also warned Smith to keep on his guard and treat the Army carefully.

Vandegrift's advice no doubt explained Smith's uncharacteristic reticence in dealing with Gen. Charles Corlett, the flinty head of the Army's 7th Division. Although Corlett was subordinate to Smith, he had no intention of letting Smith boss him around. When Smith suggested to Corlett that he would accompany him to Kwajalein, and by implication take control of the landing, Corlett would have none of it. "I don't want you ashore until the fighting is done," exclaimed Corlett. "This is my battle. You may put some staff officers ashore as observers. If I find they have tried to issue any orders, I'll have them arrested."[54] Moreover, when Smith protested Corlett's insubordinate statements, Corlett repeated them. Such disharmony did not bode well for future interservice relations.[55]

Smith had less trouble with Gen. Harry Schmidt, commander of the new 4th Marine Division. Schmidt was one of the few high-ranking World War II Marine Corps combat commanders from west of the Mississippi River. The Nebraska-born Schmidt had attended Nebraska State Normal College before he gained a Marine Corps commission in 1909. He subsequently served in Guam, China, the Philippines, Veracruz, as a recruiter, and shipboard. He spent World War I on the battleship USS *Montana*, in Cuba, and at the Norfolk Navy Yard. In the 1920s he attended the Field Officers' course, instructed at the Marine Corps Schools, did a second stretch of recruiting, returned to China for another tour of duty, and fought in Nicaragua. After graduating from the Army's Command and General Staff College in 1932, Schmidt joined the Paymaster Department at HQMC before heading off to China for a third time. Holcomb brought him back to HQMC in 1938 as executive and personnel director of the Paymaster Department. He so impressed Holcomb in that position that in January 1942 Holcomb appointed him assistant commandant. A year and a half later, Holcomb assigned Schmidt to lead the 4th Marine Division.

Schmidt was a handsome man of medium height, with blue eyes and white hair. Unfortunately, there was somewhat less to Schmidt than met the eye. One person compared him to the stereotype of a stolid Dutch-man: careful, unimaginative, and thoroughly orthodox. As a stereotypical old-time Marine, Schmidt would follow instructions to the letter, but not go much beyond that. His conventionality led Turner to question his basic intelligence. Schmidt's personality did little to compensate for his character shortcomings. He possessed little warmth or charisma, was stingy with com-pliments, and was firmly convinced that rank had its privileges. After danc-ing the hula at a divisional party on Maui, for example, Schmidt ordered his assistant to seize and destroy any photographs of the occasion. He was so uncomfortable in public that one journalist, after listening to a nervous Schmidt's presentation, wondered if he had ever delivered a speech before. Small wonder Schmidt tended to sit silently through meetings, Buddha-like. Schmidt had his good points, however, among them determination and for-titude. Nonetheless, some credited his chief of staff, Col. Walter Rogers, for whatever World War II success he had. Schmidt, despite his limitations, fulfilled some of the Corps' toughest assignments in the conflict.[56]

Schmidt's appointment to lead the 4th Marine Division was the result of the usual Marine Corps combination of competence and connections. Holcomb was fond of Schmidt. In fact, after Schmidt left to assume com-mand of his division, Holcomb commented to several people that he missed Schmidt at HQMC. Holcomb also respected Schmidt enough to opine even before Schmidt saw action with his division that he would probably make a good corps commander. Holcomb's admiration was not, however, absolute. He had nixed Vandegrift's suggestion that Schmidt lead the 3rd Marine Division after Charles Barrett moved up to head the I Amphibious Corps because he thought Schmidt had been away from the troops for too long for such an immediate battlefield immersion. He also groused that Schmidt had engaged in nepotism by transferring his son and son-in-law to his division. Vandegrift and Holland Smith appreciated Schmidt's abilities as well. With such powerful backers and such a solid resume, Schmidt's advancement to division command made perfect sense.[57]

Although planning for Flintlock began before Tarawa revealed flaws in Marine amphibious doctrine, officers still had time to learn from their mistakes and make adjustments. One general remedy was to provide more of almost everything—men, landing craft, warships, ammunition, supplies, equipment, and so forth. Indeed, Turner's V Amphibious Force alone consisted of 297 vessels, including seven old battleships, eleven carriers of various sizes, twelve cruisers, seventy-five destroyers and destroyer escorts, forty-six transports, and twenty-seven cargo ships. In addition, the planners also gathered better intelligence about Kwajalein's beaches and offshore obstacles through submarine photography and reconnaissance missions by underwater demolition teams. This allowed them to develop and distribute accurate maps of the target. The Navy brought in specially designed command ships with dependable communications gear so generals could keep in touch with their commanders ashore and promised a longer, heavier, and more targeted preliminary bombardment with its warships. To deliver better fire support, the Marines decided to occupy several small islets near Roi-Namur the day before the invasion and establish artillery batteries on them that could fire accurately on the objective. Navy and Marine officers established Joint Assault Signal Companies to coordinate all this firepower. At Tarawa a good many Marines were killed wading from the coral reef across the lagoon to the beach. This time, the Marines secured more amtraks to deliver leathernecks directly onto the beach. They also filled landing craft with troops armed with rockets and machine guns to cover the assaulting Marines as they made their final approach to Roi-Namur.

On 20–21 January 1944, the Fifth Fleet departed Hawaiian waters for the Marshall Islands. Ten days later, Army and Marine parties secured islets off of Roi-Namur and Kwajalein proper and emplaced artillery batteries there to support the next morning's operations. At noon on 1 February Col. Louis Jones' 23rd Marine Regiment crashed onto Roi's southern shore. The momentum of the landing and Roi's flat terrain carried the leathernecks well inland. The officers on the ground, without much prompting from or even consultation with their commanders, immediately pushed northward, led by tanks and armored amphibious vehicles. The Japanese fought doggedly as usual, but the Navy's preliminary bombardment had stunned and disorganized them. Roi was in American hands by six o'clock in the evening.

To the east, Col. Franklin Hart's 24th Marine Regiment had a more difficult time overrunning rugged Namur. At around one o'clock, an hour after the Marine's came ashore, a leatherneck threw a satchel charge into a massive concrete building containing explosives. The resulting explosion showered debris throughout the island, killing twenty Marines and wounding another one hundred. One witness later wrote, "The whole of Namur Island disappeared from sight in a tremendous brown cloud of dust and sand." Another added, "Trunks of palm trees and chunks of concrete as large as packing crates were flying through the air like match sticks. . . . The hole left where the blockhouse stood was as large as a fair sized swimming pool."[58] The Marines did not finish occupying Namur until late the following afternoon.

The Army stormed Majuro and Kwajalein proper as the Marines landed on Roi-Namur. By the time Flintlock ended on 4 February, Marine and Army casualties numbered 815 and 966, respectively. The losses were considerably lower than those the Marines had sustained occupying Tarawa, even though there had been about twice as many Japanese on Kwajalein. These statistics indicated the extent to which the Americans had taken the lessons of Tarawa to heart. With a few exceptions, Flintlock had gone according to plan. Although the Japanese fleet again declined to engage its U.S. counterpart, the operation had brought the Americans another giant step closer to the Marianas and the China-Formosa-Luzon region. Indeed, the victory had been so lopsided that some wondered whether the Americans had committed disproportionate resources to the task. Turner was not one of them. "Maybe we had too many men and too many ships for the job," he said, "but I prefer to do things that way. It saved us a lot of lives."[59] Smith was full of praise for Schmidt, noting that he had gotten ashore on Namur even before the regimental commander. He was equally laudatory of the 4th Marine Division for demonstrating so much initiative and verve in its baptism of fire. As for Smith's reward for completing his mission so successfully, Vandegrift got King to endorse his promotion to lieutenant general, which came through in mid-March.[60]

Army-Marine relations resounded as Flintlock's one sour note. Because of Corlett's more methodical tactics, it took the 7th Division four days to overrun Kwajalein proper, or twice as long as the Marines' occupation of Roi-Namur. To Smith, this was more evidence that the Army was not up to the amphibious warfare job. He later wrote, "I fretted considerably at the slowness of the Army advance [at Kwajalein]. I could see no reasons

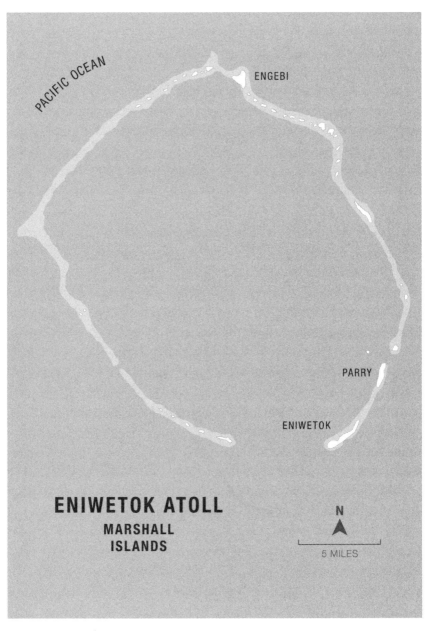

PACIFIC OCEAN

ENGEBI

PARRY

ENIWETOK

ENIWETOK ATOLL
MARSHALL
ISLANDS

N

5 MILES

Map 7. Eniwetok

why this division, with ample forces ashore, well covered by land-based artillery and receiving tremendous naval and air support, could not take the island quicker. Every hour the transports and other ships of the fleet had to remain in the vicinity of the action the greater was the danger from enemy air and submarine attack."[61] Although Smith would claim that he had kept his feelings to himself, this would have been completely out of character. In fact, at a press conference on Kwajalein after the battle, Smith so strongly inferred that the Army had been too slow in attaining its objectives that an irate Corlett interrupted and stated that Smith did not know what he was talking about. The Army's subsequent decision to organize its own corps in the Central Pacific Area was a warning shot that it did not intend to play second fiddle to the Marines forever.[62]

ENIWETOK

Flintlock was so successful that a consensus quickly emerged among Nimitz, Turner, and Smith that the V Amphibious Force should not return to Pearl Harbor, but instead immediately strike out for the next target: Eniwetok, 420 miles northwest of Kwajalein and 2,725 miles from Honolulu. In American hands, Eniwetok, the westernmost atoll in the Marshall Islands, would serve as a good forward base and anchorage for operations further west toward the Marianas. Eniwetok is circular atoll, about fifty miles in circumference, with less than six square miles of land. Its most important military feature was the airfield that the Japanese had constructed on the northern island of Engebi. There were about 1,200 Japanese soldiers there, as well as another 2,100 on Parry and Eniwetok islands on the southeastern part of the atoll. The Japanese could reinforce them at any time, so with that being the case, Nimitz decided to take advantage of Flintlock's success and move the Eniwetok operation from 1 May to 17 February. Because Flintlock had not required Smith to commit his reserves, he could use Gen. Thomas Watson's independent 22nd Marine Regiment and two battalions from the Army's 27th Division for the job.[63]

On 17 February, the V Amphibious Fleet steamed into Eniwetok's lagoon. While warships began the preliminary bombardment of the targeted islands, troops seized offshore islets and emplaced artillery on them.

The next morning two Marine battalions stormed Engebi and overran the island by evening, but the Army landing at Eniwetok proper the following day, 19 February, proved to be more difficult. The two Army battalions lacked sufficient amphibious training, so they came ashore disorganized. Within an hour Watson complained to the Army commander, Col. Russell Ayers, that he was advancing too slowly. To speed things up, Watson committed his reserves, the Marine battalion that had not fought at Engebi. The extra heft helped, but it also created coordination problems between soldiers and Marines unaccustomed to fighting together. Even so, the Americans secured Eniwetok on 21 February. Watson's final objective was Parry Island. He planned to use the Marines who assailed Engebi for the assault but decided to give them a short rest before he threw them at Parry on 22 February. The island fell after a bitter battle. The Eniwetok operation cost the Americans 348 killed and 866 wounded. The Japanese garrison of 3,300 men was practically wiped out.

The Americans had every right to be pleased with the Eniwetok operation. With only moderate losses and ahead of schedule, they had seized an important post for future operations. Much of the credit went to Watson for his aggressiveness and skill. Adm. Harry Hill, one of the amphibious force commanders, commended Watson to Vandegrift and recommended his promotion: "Watson handled this whole affair in a manner which was a credit to you and the Marine Corps. He knows his weapons, and has outstanding qualities of leadership, determination, and guts."[64] Holland Smith agreed. As with Kwajalein, though, Smith's griping about the Army's sluggishness on Eniwetok proper contaminated an otherwise harmonious enterprise and sowed more seeds of discord.[65]

SAIPAN

By June 1944 the war had clearly turned against the Axis. The previous summer the Soviet Red Army had defeated the German Wehrmacht in the epic Battle of Kursk. After that the Soviets had expelled the Germans from Ukraine and invaded Belarus and the Baltic states. The Germans suffered astronomical losses on the Eastern Front, and partisans harassed German troops across Eastern Europe and the Balkans. In the Atlantic, the German

U-boat campaign against Allied shipping had failed, enabling the Americans and British to more easily exert their power across the ocean. Although the Anglo-American strategic bombing campaign in Europe had not yielded the desired results, it was taking an increasing toll on Germany by destroying factories and diverting personnel, supplies, and equipment from the ground war. In the Mediterranean, U.S., British, and Free French forces had captured Sicily and pushed north into southern Italy. Rome's fall to the Allies on 4 June was overshadowed by the long-awaited Anglo-American D-Day landing in Normandy two days later that opened up yet another front for the Germans. It was too soon to say that Adolf Hitler's Third Reich was doomed, but Germany was obviously in serious trouble.

The Pacific War's fortunes had shifted dramatically after the Marines splashed ashore at Guadalcanal in August 1942. It had been a shoestring operation that required the bulk of available American resources in the Pacific, but by the summer of 1944, U.S. strength had grown so much that it could successfully wage war simultaneously against Germany and Japan. The U.S. submarine campaign was rapidly destroying Japan's merchant marine, and without reliable shipping, the Japanese were unable to supply their overseas garrisons, bring oil and other raw materials to their Home Islands, or transport troops from one place to another. In the Southwest Pacific, MacArthur's forces were streaking across New Guinea's northern coast toward the China-Formosa-Luzon area. Although the Navy had not yet engaged its Japanese counterpart in a decisive battle in the Central Pacific, it had seized the Gilberts and Marshalls. The Americans were not the only ones applying pressure on Japan. In Southeast Asia, an Anglo-Indian Army had defeated the Japanese at the Battle of Imphal, eliminating their threat to the Indian subcontinent. The unending war in China siphoned off a million Japanese soldiers who could have been deployed elsewhere. As with Germany, it was too early to say the writing was on the wall, but Japan's military fortunes were clearly fading.

For the U.S. Navy, capturing the Gilberts and Marshalls was preparatory to an offensive against the more strategically vital Marianas, a group of fifteen islands running 425 miles north–south about 3,850 miles west of Hawaii and 1,400 miles south of Japan. One of them, Guam, had belonged to the United States until the Japanese seized it right after attacking Pearl

Harbor. Japan had taken the remaining islands in the chain from Germany during World War I. In the Americans' hands, the Marianas would provide airfields from which the Army Air Forces could pound Japan with its new B-29 Superfortress bombers. That being the case, naval officers hoped that attacking the Marianas would tempt the Japanese fleet into a decisive engagement that would remove it from the strategic chessboard. Planning for Operation Forager began in December 1943 with a target date of 15 November 1944. As the U.S. counteroffensive across the Pacific accelerated, however, the Joint Chiefs of Staff advanced the operation's timetable to launch in mid-June. The Navy targeted three of the Marianas: Saipan, Tinian, and Guam. Because they lacked sufficient resources to attack all three simultaneously, naval officers opted to assail Saipan first, then Tinian, and finally Guam.

Saipan was different from any previous U.S. objective in the Central Pacific. At forty-five square miles, it dwarfs Betio, Roi-Namur, and Eniwetok. It is not an atoll, but a single island with a mountainous spine, hills and rolling plateaus in the north and east, and flat coastal plains in the south and west. There are also cliffs, jungles, and swamps along with the typical offshore coral reefs. Saipan's infrastructure was more developed than anything the Americans had so far encountered in the Central Pacific. Dense sugarcane fields, sugar refineries, small towns, two airfields, and even a railroad dotted Saipan. Finally, and ominously, the Japanese deployed 30,000 troops to defend Saipan, far more than the Americans had confronted in the Gilberts and Marshalls. One Marine medical officer explained to a group of leathernecks, "In the surf, beware of sharks, barracuda, sea snakes, anemones, razor sharp coral, polluted waters, poison fish, and giant clams that shut on a man like a bear trap. Ashore, there is leprosy, typhus, filariasis, yaws, typhoid, dengue fever, dysentery, saber grass, insects, snakes, and giant lizards. Eat nothing growing on the island, don't drink its waters, and don't approach the inhabitants." When he finished and asked for questions, one private raised his hand and exclaimed, "Sir, why don't we let the Japs keep the island?"[66]

Forager's organization was the familiar triumvirate of Spruance, Turner, and Holland Smith. This time, however, Smith had more authority than in previous operations. For one thing, he was now a lieutenant general, with

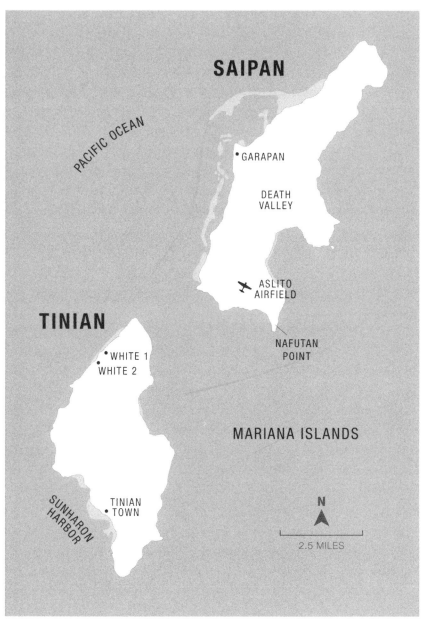

SAIPAN

PACIFIC OCEAN

• GARAPAN

DEATH
VALLEY

ASLITO
AIRFIELD

NAFUTAN
POINT

TINIAN

• WHITE 1
WHITE 2

MARIANA ISLANDS

SUNHARON
HARBOR

TINIAN
• TOWN

N

2.5 MILES

Map 8. *Saipan-Tinian*

all the perks and expectations that went with the rank. More important, Forager called for Smith to actually lead the troops invading Saipan. During the operations against the Gilberts and Marshalls, Smith's role had been largely supervisory—or more critically, superfluous—because the division commanders at Tarawa, Makin, Roi-Namur, and Kwajalein proper were perfectly capable of making the important tactical decisions. To take Saipan, the Americans planned to commit three divisions—two Marine and one Army. Smith and his V Amphibious Corps were necessary to direct these large units. Never before had a Marine general been responsible for so many troops in such a large undertaking. As Smith explained in his memoirs: "I cannot describe the exultation that swept through Marine ranks when it became known that for the first time we were to operate in the field as organic units instead of a joint command. We were a Marine field Army, commanded by a Marine General, going into action independently against the Japanese, and the opportunity to enhance the prestige of the Marine Corps was so great that it stirred every man in my command. . . . The Marine Corps had come of age."[67]

Smith's gung-ho attitude reflected that of most naval and Marine officers in the theater. There was a growing confidence among them in their mutual relationship and their ability to overcome any Japanese resistance.[68] There were, however, several issues nagging at Smith's optimism about his and his country's Pacific War prospects. Smith strongly and, as things turned out, quite rightly suspected that Forager would be more costly than previous Marine operations in the Central and South Pacific. Considering the bloodletting at Tarawa, this was enough to give this most stalwart of generals pause. In addition, the Army posed a continuing problem and threat. Although Smith worked hard to be cordial to Army officers like Richardson, discretion was not his forte. It was no secret that he was unhappy with the Army's performance in previous Central Pacific operations. He was reluctant to use the Army's 27th Division again because he felt it had been too cliquish and unaggressive at Makin and Eniwetok. His disparaging comments and attitude did not win him many friends among Army officers or those striving to promote interservice harmony. In fact, Richardson recommended limiting the V Amphibious Corps to administrative duties while the Army's new XXIV Corps led future Central Pacific campaigns.

Such advocacy was unlikely to work as long as Nimitz and the Navy continued to support Smith and the Marines, but the Army's role in the theater was likely to grow as the Americans pushed closer to Japan.[69]

The experienced 2nd and 4th Marine Divisions were allotted to Forager. The former had seen action at Guadalcanal and Tarawa, and the latter had its baptism by fire at Roi-Namur. General Schmidt still led the 4th, but the 2nd was under new management. Julian Smith had wanted and expected to take the 2nd to Saipan, but at a Pearl Harbor conference with a visiting Vandegrift, Smith noticed that the commandant had failed to mention the upcoming operation to him, even after he stated that his division was rested and ready to go. Somewhat suspicious, Smith asked Holland Smith whether anything was going on. Holland Smith replied that as far as he knew, Smith would still lead the 2nd Marine Division on Saipan. Smith returned to Camp Tarawa, on the Big Island of Hawaii, and tried to put the matter out of his mind, but spent the night tossing and turning. The next day he received a telegraph from Vandegrift removing him from command of the 2nd Marine Division and putting him in charge of something called the Marine Administrative Command, under Holland Smith's direct orders. Its responsibilities were mostly logistical.

Julian Smith was crushed to lose one of the Marine Corps' most important combat posts. He was also so disgusted with what he interpreted as the cold and duplicitous manner in which Vandegrift had made his decision that he sent the commandant an angry letter of protest. Smith's belligerent and hurt response startled Vandegrift. At a dinner party in Washington, Vandegrift told Smith's wife, "I just can't imagine why Julian is so upset over being reassigned. I was so surprised by his reaction. After all, it is a promotion. He is second in command over the Fleet Marine Force in the Pacific. I thought he would take it as a compliment and a vote of trust; it never occurred to me he would get so bent out of shape."[70] Vandegrift's protestations of innocence did little to assuage Smith's suspicions and concerns. Vandegrift could sugarcoat it however he wanted, but Smith still saw his assignment as a demotion. As things turned out, Smith's new job had even less authority than it appeared, perhaps because Holland Smith disliked Smith's negative attitude toward it. The upshot was that an embittered Smith never again led troops in action.[71]

Vandegrift replaced Julian Smith as 2nd Marine Division commander with Thomas Watson. It was a logical choice. Watson had successfully led the 22nd Marine Regiment at Eniwetok, making him the only available Marine officer without a division with that kind of independent experience. Indeed, his performance at Eniwetok had won praise from several witnesses who noted his aggressiveness and competence. Vandegrift had actually marked Watson for a division even before the Eniwetok battle. He had written to Holland Smith about Watson, "As you know, I am a great admirer of his, and would like some day to see him with a division."[72] Having moved Julian Smith up to Marine Administrative Command, Vandegrift took the opportunity to advance Watson as well.[73]

The Iowa-born Watson was one of only two high-ranking Marine combat commanders to enter the Corps as an enlisted man. In that capacity he had participated in the 1914 Veracruz occupation before attaining a commission two years later. He did not fight in France in World War I, but instead spent the conflict and the subsequent years in the Dominican Republic. For the remainder of the 1920s he recruited and trained Marines, garrisoned China, and was a student and an instructor for the Field Officers' course in Quantico. The early 1930s found him back in the Dominican Republic, this time as naval attaché. From there he worked at HQMC, served in Nicaragua, commanded a battalion, and became chief of the War Plans Division for the Fleet Marine Force. Watson graduated from the Army War College in 1938, ran the War Plans Section at HQMC, and ascended to executive officer for the Plans and Policies Division. After World War II broke out, he sailed to Samoa with the 3rd Marine Brigade as Barrett's chief of staff. Holcomb later sent him to the V Amphibious Corps to lead the Marine attack on Eniwetok with the 22nd Marine Regiment.

Watson was nicknamed "Terrible Tommy" for his diminutive size and stormy personality. He was sarcastic, opinionated, emphatic, and intolerant of failure. One officer remembered, "He would not tolerate for one minute stupidity, laziness, professional incompetence, or failure in leadership. . . . His temper in correcting these failings could be fiery and monumental."[74] He often treated his staff officers poorly and did not seem to care about his troops. In the middle of one battle, Watson hollered over the phone at one of his battalion commanders, "There's not a goddamned thing up on that hill but some Japs with machine guns and mortars. Now get the hell up there and get 'em."[75] Considering his attitude, it was unsurprising that many officers and men disliked him. Fortunately for Watson, Vandegrift and Holland Smith were not among them. Indeed, Vandegrift and Watson were old friends. Vandegrift valued Watson for his imagination, knowledge, and loyalty. Watson hindered the relationship, however, with his intense dislike of many of Vandegrift's other friends. Holland Smith respected Watson for his performance in seizing Eniwetok and with Vandegrift's support marked him for greater things.[76]

By the end of May, the giant American armada necessary to implement Operation Forager was ready. It consisted of around eight hundred vessels of varying sizes and types, including 110 transports carrying 71,000 Marines and soldiers slated for the battle. The Marines assembled in Eniwetok, while Ralph Smith's 27th Division gathered at Kwajalein. The leading elements of the fleet got under way on 25 May. Twenty-one days later, on 14 June, the Navy began its preliminary bombardment of Saipan in earnest. The next morning the two Marine divisions landed on the island's southwestern shore, the 2nd Marine Division to the north and the 4th Marine Division to the south. Both outfits encountered heavy opposition. Although amphibious craft lashed the coast with rockets and machine guns, Japanese fire torched amtraks as they headed toward the beach. Once ashore, the leathernecks pushed inland, running into Japanese defenders. One Marine remembered, "All around us was the chaotic debris of bitter combat: Jap and Marine bodies lying in mangled and grotesque positions; blasted and burnt-out pillboxes; the burning wrecks of LVTs [Landing Vehicles, Tracked] that had been knocked out by Jap high velocity fire; the acrid smell of high explosives; the shattered trees; and the churned-up sand littered with discarded equipment."[77] By early afternoon more than a third of Col. James Riseley's 6th Marine Regiment had been killed or wounded, and at the end of the day Marine casualties had reached two thousand. Even so, the leathernecks succeeded in carving out a foothold. Watson and Schmidt arrived to establish their command posts. Schmidt and his staff initially disembarked in the middle of a Japanese supply dump full of bangalore torpedoes. They hurriedly vacated the premises and found a safer spot from which to start the campaign.[78]

Things did not get any easier for the Marines in the following days. They brought in reinforcements and supplies, secured the beachhead, and started clearing the southern part of the island of Japanese troops. Smith's methodical plans were upset by larger events. The day after the landings, Spruance informed Holland Smith that the main Japanese fleet was on its way to confront its U.S. counterpart. That being the case, Spruance wanted to clear the decks before engaging the Japanese in the climactic battle the Navy had been actively seeking for the past six months. This included getting the transports out of range. Although most of the Marines were already ashore, the Army's 27th Division was still on board. Smith did not want to lose the division's services, so with Spruance's permission he ordered it landed as soon as possible. Its first elements disembarked on the night of 16–17 June, and Smith assigned it the task of seizing Aslito Airfield. The soldiers did so on 18 June, but then got bogged down trying to pry the Japanese out of Nafutan Point, on Saipan's southern tip. While the Army struggled there, Schmidt's 4th Marine Division cut across to Saipan's east coast and turned northward to align itself with the 2nd Marine Division. By 22 June, most of the southern part of the island was in American hands. Before undertaking the hard work necessary to conquer the remainder, Smith ordered most of the 27th Division northward to join his Marines, leaving behind one battalion to finish the job at Nafutan Point.

Although the Marines had suffered heavy casualties in their first week of combat on Saipan—2,500 killed and wounded for the 2nd Marine Division and 3,600 for the 4th Marine Division—Holland Smith was in an optimistic mood as he redeployed his forces for the drive northward. He complained that Schmidt was too orthodox in his tactics, and that Watson had not maintained a large enough reserve, but on the whole he was pleased with their performances. In a letter to Vandegrift, he rated Schmidt as the slightly better commander. As for Ralph Smith's 27th Division, Smith noted that it had so far done everything he had asked of it, but admitted that it had not yet played a major role in the operation. Smith kept the 2nd Marine Division on the west coast, moved the 4th Marine Division to the eastern shore, and directed the 27th Division to take up positions between the two. When the V Amphibious Corps attacked northward on 23 June, the two Marine divisions made good progress, but the 27th Division got stuck in the aptly named Death Valley. Japanese troops ensconced in the overlooking mountains and ridges made it almost impossible for the soldiers to advance. Meanwhile, the Army battalion at Nafutan Point also gained little ground.[79]

Smith was frustrated with the 27th Division's inability to achieve its objectives. He had harbored doubts about the unit's effectiveness after it assailed Makin six months earlier. As far as he was concerned, it was slow and unaggressive. Smith liked the division's commander, Ralph Smith, personally and respected his professionalism, but had also concluded that Ralph Smith was not pushing his men hard enough. Smith felt that Ralph Smith's lethargy was jeopardizing the operation and costing Marine lives. On the afternoon of 23 June, Smith consulted Gen. Sanderford Jarman, the Army officer slated to run Saipan once it was secured. After hearing Smith's concerns, Jarman volunteered to talk with Ralph Smith and try to light a fire under him. Ralph Smith admitted to Jarman that he too was unsatisfied with his division's performance and promised it would do better the next day. In fact, Jarman later stated that Ralph Smith had said that he should be relieved if he failed to deliver on his pledge. Unfortunately, the 27th Division did not meet either of the Smith's expectations on 24 June. For Holland Smith, its failure was the last straw. He and his chief of staff, Erskine, motored to *Rocky Mount* and explained the situation to Turner, who heard them out and then took them to see Spruance on board his flagship, the heavy cruiser USS *Indianapolis*. Spruance was enmeshed in his own controversy over his incomplete victory over the main Japanese fleet in the Battle of the Philippine Sea. Spruance listened to Smith and asked what he recommended. Smith responded that he wanted Spruance's blessing to relieve Ralph Smith and replace him with Jarman. Spruance agreed, and Smith issued the necessary orders that afternoon. Smith later claimed that he knew that removing Ralph Smith would cause an interservice ruckus, but was convinced it was the right thing to do. He explained to a journalist, "Ralph Smith is my friend, but, good God, I've got a duty to my country. I've lost 7,000 Marines. Can I afford to lose back what they have gained? To let my Marines die in vain? I know I'm sticking my neck out—the National Guard will try to chop it off—but my conscience is clear. I did my duty. When Ralph Smith issued an order to hold after I had told him to attack, I had no other choice but to relieve him."[80]

Smith's decision to remove Ralph Smith from his command had consequences all around. For now, however, Smith focused on winning the battle and conquering Saipan. Despite all the personnel drama, Forager's outcome was no longer in serious doubt. Spruance's Fifth Fleet had defeated its Japanese counterpart at the Battle of the Philippine Sea, thus ending any hope of rescue and reinforcement for Saipan's Japanese garrison. It became all but inevitable that the superior materiel and firepower of the V Amphibious Corps would destroy the Japanese in light of their finite and dwindling numbers and resources. Victory was, in short, a question of time and casualties. Smith wanted to keep both to a minimum, but it was a difficult scale to balance. Blasting the resolute and well-positioned Japanese defenders out of their mountainous strongholds was grinding work for the increasingly tired Americans. Soldiers overran Nafutan Point on 27 June. Three days later, the rest of the 27th Division, with Marine assistance, occupied Death Valley in an operation that won Schmidt's praise. On 1 July, the 2nd Marine Division seized Garapan, Saipan's largest town, without much opposition. Six days later, the Japanese launched their biggest banzai charge of the war. The 27th Division's 105th Regiment bore the brunt of the assault in a chaotic engagement that generated still more controversy about the division's effectiveness. Nonetheless, the result was the expenditure of the last Japanese reserves. Turner declared the island secured on 9 July, twenty-four days after the Marines first came ashore, though mopping up continued. The price had been steep. Forager cost the Americans the equivalent of an entire division: 3,225 killed, 13,061 wounded, and 326 missing.[81]

The Smith versus Smith controversy marred what was in fact an important U.S. victory. To be sure, Holland Smith exaggerated when he called the battle for Saipan the Pacific War's most decisive, but occupying Saipan gave the Americans a foothold in the Marianas that they quickly exploited and provoked the Japanese fleet into an engagement that led to a substantial, though not definitive, U.S. naval victory. Marine officers may have denigrated the Army's performance, but they were full of praise for their own. Vandegrift lauded the tactical prowess that Smith, Schmidt, and Watson had displayed. Smith was also happy with Schmidt and Watson. Indeed, all three men had demonstrated considerable relentlessness and aggressiveness in handling their units. On the other hand, there was room for criticism that extended beyond poor interservice relations. In the big scheme of things, U.S. victory was certain once the Marines established a beachhead, though doing that was an accomplishment that should not be overlooked. The continuous pressure that Smith, Schmidt, and Watson put on the enemy exemplified their forcefulness, but not necessarily their tactical wisdom. Some regimental commanders complained that Smith's demand for constant action sometimes placed their outfits on untenable ground, and his insistence on dawn attacks prevented them from undertaking proper reconnaissance that might have saved lives. One wrote, "Progress through heavy canefields, through dense underbrush, and over extremely rough terrain, such as was encountered, cannot be made at 'book speed.'"[82] Finally, the heavy casualties the Marines suffered on Saipan may have been necessary to bring the operation to a speedy and successful conclusion, but in the long run the Corps lacked the manpower to wage many such costly battles.[83]

CONTROVERSY AND REORGANIZATION

Nellie Richardson was a frustrated general in the summer of 1944. On paper he had a plum assignment as the top Army officer in the Central Pacific, but in truth there was rather less to it than met the eye. Although Richardson was responsible for administering, training, and supplying the growing Army contingent in the theater, he had no authority to actually lead soldiers in combat. Nimitz had given that job to Holland Smith's V Amphibious Corps. Nimitz did so partly because the Marines were the amphibious warfare experts and partly because the Marines were more subject to Navy control. For Richardson, it felt akin to a cuckold in an unconsummated marriage. Moreover, Richardson disliked the Navy and Marine way of doing things. He did not think that Marine officers understood Army doctrine or possessed sufficient skill to undertake large-scale operations. As a result, they tended to misuse and unfairly criticize the soldiers under their command. He also resented the publicity that the Marines accrued at the Army's expense. His attempts to rectify these and other problems by calling Nimitz's attention to them met with little success. Richardson did, however, organize an Army unit, the XXIV Corps, in Hawaii for use in future operations should it become necessary.[84]

Richardson was predictably outraged when he learned that Holland Smith had relieved Ralph Smith as commander of the 27th Division. On 12 July, he flew to Saipan without informing Holland Smith. Smith was busy entertaining Spruance when Richardson arrived, so Richardson cooled his heels by inspecting soldiers and distributing decorations. When Smith and Schmidt visited Richardson in his quarters later to pay their respects, Richardson immediately lit into them. He did not dwell on Ralph Smith's discomfiture, probably because he saw it more as a symptom than a cause, but instead focused on the Marine Corps' overall conduct in the theater. His voice rising, Richardson listed his grievances and added that the Marines could no longer push the Army around. He emphasized that the Marines simply were not competent to handle the kind of complicated operations called for by the Pacific War. "Marines are just beach runners and are not qualified to conduct land operations!" he shouted. Richardson repeatedly threatened to report everything he had witnessed to George Marshall, the Army's chief of staff, and promised to initiate an investigation into Ralph Smith's removal. Smith held his temper because Spruance had asked him to, but defended the Corps by stating that Marines were well trained in Army doctrine. He added that he welcomed an inquiry into his actions in regard to Ralph Smith as long as he could cross-examine witnesses. Smith keeping cool in the face of Richardson's accusations may have been a minor miracle, but no such phenomenon prevented Turner from giving Richardson both barrels when they met to discuss the issues that had brought Richardson halfway across the Pacific.[85]

The controversy did not end with Richardson's irate visit. Indeed, his anger echoed throughout the Army. For example, Gen. George Griner, Jarman's replacement as head of the 27th Division, complained that Smith was so prejudiced against the Army and so obsessed with publicity for the Marine Corps that no Army unit could get impartial treatment under his command. Moreover, the dispute spilled over into the press and simmered there for the remainder of the year. Richardson kept his word and initiated an inquiry into Ralph Smith's relief. The Buckner Board, chaired by the Army's Gen. Simon Buckner, was hardly unbiased. It took testimony from Army officers only, depriving Navy and Marine officers of the opportunity to tell their side of the story. Smith, not surprisingly, resented charges by

Army officers and journalists that he had an axe to grind against the Army and felt that they were being unfair. Fortunately for Smith, he retained Vandegrift's support and sympathy. Vandegrift was furious with the Army in general and Richardson in particular for, as he saw it, creating this hullabaloo for their own selfish bureaucratic purposes. As far as Vandegrift was concerned, Smith had had every right to relieve Ralph Smith. Vandegrift wrote Smith, "Let me say right here that I think you showed more forbearance than I could possibly have shown under similar circumstances for I think I would have relieved him summarily myself, but I am glad that you did not and that you had Spruance do it. I have read your last letter over several times and every time I do I get madder than before. There is no earthly excuse for Richards[ons]' actions and I want you to know that this headquarters and I myself will back you up in everything that you have done."[86]

As things turned out, this interservice dispute did not get out of hand because high-ranking Army and Navy officers, including Nimitz, focused instead on winning the war. Nimitz wanted to keep any Army-Marine disagreements within his theater and was dismayed when Richardson got the Joint Chiefs involved. His seemingly bland impartiality frustrated outraged Army and Marine officers seeking justice for Holland Smith or Ralph Smith, but Nimitz knew full well that he needed both the Marine Corps and the Army to successfully prosecute his part of the conflict. As for the Buckner Board, Buckner took his cues from Nimitz. Buckner wanted a prominent combat command, and as a good bureaucratic operator he knew that pouring oil on troubled waters was a good way to win Nimitz's approval and support. He kept his investigation as low key as possible and worked hard to produce an anodyne report. Ultimately, Bruckner's inquiry found that Holland Smith had the right to relieve Ralph Smith, but added that Ralph Smith's removal was "not justified by the facts" because Holland Smith was ignorant of the 27th Division's conditions and circumstances. King and Marshall came to a tacit agreement to put the controversy behind them and get on with the war. Marshall, however, informed King that it would be best for interservice relations if Holland Smith never again led Army soldiers into battle.[87]

There is little doubt that the Smith versus Smith controversy, as journalists dubbed it, was an unfortunate distraction, but it was also an anomaly.

Thereafter Army and Marine units fought side by side in the Pacific without the kinds of problems that manifested themselves on Saipan. There was plenty of blame on both sides of the imbroglio. Holland Smith was correct in assessing the 27th Division as a problematic unit. It was one of only two National Guard divisions that the Army had failed to overhaul and purge of the cliques and favoritism that infested such outfits before the war. Because of these difficulties, its regiments responded insufficiently to Ralph Smith's orders and did not always fight as aggressively as needed. Moreover, Army officers often expressed little understanding of or sympathy for the limitations under which the Navy and Marine Corps labored in amphibious operations.[88]

On the other hand, Holland Smith shared some of the blame. He did not recognize that Army divisions were different from their Marine counterparts. The Army had its own doctrine and tactics along with personnel from a larger and less select cross-section of American society. To expect the 27th Division to fight like the more experienced 2nd and 4th Marine Divisions was unrealistic. Moreover, Smith was clearly biased against the 27th Division because of what he had seen as its substandard performances at Makin and Eniwetok, which inclined him to think the worst of it. Smith was not the most tactful man to begin with, and he infected his staff officers with his negative attitude toward the 27th Division. They in turn conveyed it throughout the V Amphibious Corps, to the detriment of morale and interservice relations. His failure to sufficiently encourage and cultivate the outfit played no small role in the controversy.

Finally, it is important to remember that Saipan was Smith's first battle as a combat commander. In the Gilberts and Marshalls his role had been primarily supervisory, but at Saipan he actually directed his three divisions in action. It was therefore unsurprising that he made rookie mistakes, some of which affected his handling of the 27th Division. He split up the division and threw it into battle before it was ready, underestimated Japanese opposition at Nafutan Point and Death Valley, gave Ralph Smith unclear and sometimes contradictory orders, and did little to gain a firsthand understanding of the difficulties the division faced. If he was not exactly looking for an opportunity to relieve Ralph Smith and condemn his division, he was certainly receptive to one. A more considerate and appreciative attitude by Holland Smith would have yielded better results.[89]

Major organizational changes were in the works even before Forager and the Smith versus Smith controversy, changes that intersected with the interservice difficulties that plagued American efforts to secure Saipan. Vandegrift had been convinced for some time of the need for one Marine general to oversee all the leathernecks in the Pacific War. He envisioned a Fleet Marine Force commander to take care of Marine administration, training, and logistics throughout the Pacific. The biggest obstacle to his plan was King, who stood dead set against an additional bureaucratic layer cluttering the chain of command. It took time, but Vandegrift eventually prevailed. Once he did, he had to select a general for this important assignment.

Holland Smith was the obvious choice for the new post. He was the most senior officer in the Pacific and was already fulfilling many of the responsibilities Vandegrift envisioned for the job. Moreover, Vandegrift respected him for his loyalty, commitment, and determination. Smith, however, was not entirely happy to get the position. He wrote later, "I feared that now I would become a highly paid administrator, coordinator and supervisor little better than Richardson."[90] Even so, Smith recognized the logic of such a post, and as usual, duty came first. Besides, Smith hoped that if he played his cards right, his Fleet Marine Force might morph into a field army that would enable him to take both the Pacific War's amphibious corps into battle, making him the first leatherneck to lead troops at that level. He assumed his new detail on 12 July, taking with him his indomitable chief of staff, Erskine, and leaving the rest of his staff behind. In September, Smith traveled to the States and spent five days in Washington. The reception he received pleased him, especially a dinner Vandegrift threw in his honor. He was thankful that he retained the support of and saw eye-to-eye with his commandant. He looked forward to getting back to work in his new position.[91]

Smith's ascension to Fleet Marine Force commander opened up a slot as the head of the V Amphibious Corps. Vandegrift gave the job to Harry Schmidt. Vandegrift believed that Schmidt had done fine work with the 4th Marine Division at Roi-Namur, and his subsequent performance on Saipan did nothing to change Vandegrift's mind. Smith approved too. On 7 June, even before the Saipan operation, Smith wrote to Vandegrift, "The selection for Commanding General, V Amphibious Corps [Schmidt] finds me in full agreement. It has been obvious to me that he is the best qualified."[92] There had been other candidates with combat leadership experience whom Vandegrift passed over for various reasons. For instance, Julian Smith would have jumped at the opportunity to lead the V Amphibious Corps, but Vandegrift had already slated Smith for the Marine Administrative Command, and moving him over to the V Amphibious Corps would have seemed like a demotion. Allen Turnage was another option. He had successfully taken his 3rd Marine Division through the Bougainville operation, but Vandegrift harbored doubts about Turnage's leadership skills. Although Turnage had done well on Bougainville, he had not seen the kind of ferocious combat that Schmidt faced at Roi-Namur. Besides, the 3rd Marine Division was just then preparing to invade Guam, and replacing Turnage at such a crucial juncture would have been unwise. Finally, there was William Rupertus, who had gone through both Guadalcanal and Cape Gloucester with the 1st Marine Division. He and Vandegrift were tight, but his uncertain health had already interfered with the performance of his duties. Considering these alternatives, Vandegrift's selection of Schmidt made perfect sense.[93]

TINIAN

The occupation of Saipan did not end the V Amphibious Corps' operations. Indeed, taking Saipan was in many respects a prerequisite for seizing a more precious objective just three miles off Saipan's southern shore: Tinian. At thirty-nine square miles, Tinian is smaller than Saipan. Much of its prewar population of 18,000 grew sugarcane on tiny rectangular-shaped farms. Tinian derived its military value from its flat terrain, having none of Saipan's forbidding mountains and cliffs. With Tinian in American hands, Army Air Force aviation engineers could construct as many airfields as necessary for the new B-29 Superfortress bombers to undertake the strategic bombing campaign designed to burn up the Japanese Home Islands. The only thing preventing the Americans from implementing this apocalyptic scenario was Tinian's garrison of 8,900 Japanese troops.

In terms of terrain and Japanese defenses, Tinian certainly seemed like a weaker nut to crack than Saipan. Moreover, the Americans had their usual advantages of air and naval supremacy and all the firepower that came with it. In addition, much of Tinian was within range of artillery batteries emplaced on southern Saipan. On the other hand, Gen. Holland Smith had to conduct the invasion with the forces he had on Saipan. His three divisions had all suffered heavily from the fighting there, and some continued to mop up die-hard Japanese soldiers. His troops were tired and replacements few. Indeed, some battalions stood at half strength, which made Smith open to using every possible advantage to make Tinian's occupation easier and quicker. There were only a few beaches on Tinian suitable for amphibious assault. The original plan called for landing at Sunharon Harbor, near Tinian Town. The problem was that it was the most obvious place to come ashore, so the Japanese had deployed their forces there in strength. The more Smith and his planning staff studied Tinian, the more convinced they became of coming ashore at two small beaches, collectively dubbed the White Beach, on Tinian's northwest tip. Each beach was less than two hundred yards wide, well short of the five hundred yards a single battalion usually required for such an amphibious assault, let alone two regiments. Landing there, however, had the advantages of surprise and proximity. In fact, the Marines could motor over from Saipan, a less risky proposition than a ship-to-shore assault. Although tricky, it seemed doable.

Securing Turner's support for the idea proved difficult. As far as Turner was concerned, White Beach was too small and the hydrography too uncertain for the suggested undertaking. At a meeting on *Rocky Mount*, Turner poured Smith a drink and came to the point. "Holland," he said, "you are not going to land on the White Beaches. I won't land you there." Smith roared back, "Oh yes you will. You'll land me any goddamned place I tell you to. I'm the one who makes the tactical plans around here. All you have to do is tell me whether or not you can put my troops ashore there." After Turner explained his reasoning, Smith asked about the validity of his information. Turner replied that it was based on aerial reconnaissance. Smith snorted, "Aw, you can't tell a goddamned thing from those photographs, Kelly." Smith decided to deploy his own reconnaissance team, which after a firsthand look confirmed the feasibility of coming ashore at the beaches. As matters stood, Smith and Turner could, and did, argue all they wanted, but Spruance had the final say. He liked the boldness of an attack on the White Beach and called a conference with the principals to get their views. Smith,

Schmidt, and Watson supported a White Beach landing. All eyes turned to Turner, who, persuaded by the evidence, quietly assented.[94]

Schmidt's elevation to V Amphibious Corps commander meant that the 4th Marine Division needed a new leader. Vandegrift had made his choice even before Operation Forager began: Gen. Clifton Cates, one of three World War II Marine Corps division commanders who would rise to become commandant. Born in Tennessee in 1893, Cates attended the Missouri Military Academy before graduating from the University of Tennessee with a law degree. He accepted a Marine Corps commission after the United States entered World War I and fought valiantly in France at Belleau Wood, Soissons, St. Mihiel, and in the Argonne. The cachet he gained within the Marine officer corps for his courage helped compensate for the serious injuries he sustained. In fact, he was wounded often enough to earn the nickname "Lucky." After the conflict he became an aide to Commandant George Barnett. He fulfilled a wide variety of assignments in the 1920s: company commander, recruiter, and member of the American Battlefields Monument Commission. From 1929 to 1932 he served in Shanghai before coming home to attend the Army Industrial College. He then returned to Shanghai, this time at the head of a battalion. After graduating from the Army War College in 1940, he became director of the Basic School in Philadelphia. From there he took over the 1st Marine Regiment in 1942. His impressive performance at Guadalcanal prompted Holcomb to bring him home to run the Marine Corps Schools at Quantico. He was still there when, in June 1944, Vandegrift tapped him to lead the 4th Marine Division.

Cates was among the most well-regarded and well-liked men in the Marine Corps. Fair, considerate, and versatile, one officer referred to him as a "crackerjack commander." His relaxed and low-key leadership style allowed him to get along with and to get the most out of everyone who worked for him. At Guadalcanal he used his pistol to shoot toward Marines who refused to stay in their foxholes during Japanese air raids. He backed his subordinates and refused to engage in petty intrigue. His admirers included both Holcomb and his close friend Vandegrift. Well dressed, wearing shiny boots, and sporting a cigarette holder, Cates "looked as if he'd stepped out of a bandbox." Summing him up, another officer said, "A quiet man, [with]

a great sense of humor, [he] operated with the attitude that was imperturb-
able, and a lot of people didn't understand how a man . . . who operated so
quietly and kept such an even temper all the time could really be as big a
man as he was. And he was a tremendous man."[95]

Although Cates was surprised by Vandegrift's decision to appoint him
to lead the 4th Marine Division, he should not have been. Vandegrift had
been impressed with Cates' performance as a regimental commander on
Guadalcanal and in running the Marine Corps Schools. Moreover, he had
been stateside for more than a year conveying his hard-won combat wisdom to other leathernecks, so it was time for him to return to the Pacific.
Holland Smith had known that the 4th Marine Division would need a
new boss when Schmidt moved up to lead the V Amphibious Corps, but
he made no recommendations and was content to leave the selection in
Vandegrift's hands. There were other combat-hardened regimental chiefs
available, but none of them possessed Cates' combination of connections,
stateside and overseas experience, and likeability.[96]

On the morning of 24 July, elements of Watson's 2nd Marine Division
appeared off the coast of Tinian Town and prepared for what appeared to
be a major amphibious assault. The maneuver was a diversion, however,
to distract Japanese attention from the actual landing by Cates' 4th Marine
Division regiments at White Beach. The two regiments—Col. Frank Hart's
24th and Col. Merton Batchelder's 25th—crossed over from Saipan, scattered the few surprised Japanese defenders, and established a beachhead.
That night the Japanese launched a major counterattack that not only
failed, but also destroyed their reserves. Indeed, more than 1,200 Japanese
died in the unsuccessful attack. The next day the 2nd Marine Division
arrived to reinforce the 4th Marine Division, and the two outfits pushed
southward, the 4th along the west coast and the 2nd along the eastern
shore. Cates emphasized the need to move fast to keep Japanese opposition
from gelling. By way of motivation, he added that the sooner the division
wrapped up the operation, the sooner it could return to the comforts of
Maui. The Marines made steady progress against sporadic, and occasionally
determined, Japanese resistance. The island's flat terrain, declining number of defenders, and overwhelming U.S. firepower from land, sea, and air
made it impossible for the Japanese to organize a coherent defense. The 4th

Marine Division occupied Tinian Town on 30 July. Two days later Turner declared Tinian secure, though mopping up continued. The operation cost the 2nd Marine Division 105 dead and 653 wounded. The 4th Marine Division suffered 212 dead and 897 wounded. Though not inconsiderable losses, they paled in comparison to those sustained on Saipan. In the larger scheme of things, it was a small price to pay for such a strategically valuable prize.[97]

Indeed, the Marines had every reason to be satisfied and proud of the conquest of Tinian. The small size of the island had limited the Marines' tactical options, and the units employed in the invasion were tired and at half strength from having fought on Saipan. To gain an advantage, Marine and naval officers made use of their one chance at tactical surprise and innovation by landing at White Beach. This caught the Japanese so flat-footed that they never regained sufficient equilibrium to effectively contest the Americans' advance. Again, as had become the case, the Japanese had almost no chance of winning the battle, but they could by fighting delay the U.S. timetable and inflict heavy casualties. Schmidt, Watson, and Cates fought so skillfully, deftly, and aggressively, however, that the island fell in only a week. Small wonder Cates bragged to Vandegrift that it was a "model operation."[98]

GUAM

The conquests of Saipan and Tinian represented only one part of the Marianas campaign. The liberation of Guam, 136 miles southwest of Saipan, was the other component. Unlike the case with Saipan, Tinian, and most other Pacific island battlegrounds, the Americans were thoroughly familiar with Guam. It had been a U.S. possession before the conflict, one of the spoils of the Spanish-American War of 1898. The Japanese had occupied it without serious opposition days after their attack on Pearl Harbor. At 212 square miles, Guam is the largest island in the Marianas' chain. Its northern half consists of a limestone plateau rimmed with formidable cliffs and is covered with jungle, hardwood trees, and sword grass. The southern half is flat and fertile. A low mountain range runs along the southwestern coast. To defend the island, the Japanese deployed 18,500 troops.

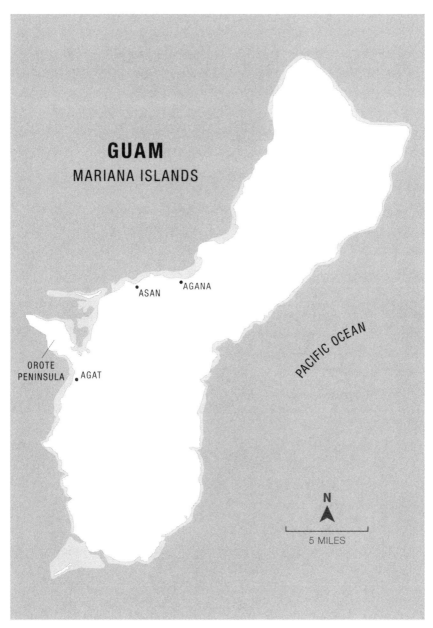

GUAM
MARIANA ISLANDS

ASAN

AGANA

OROTE
PENINSULA

AGAT

PACIFIC OCEAN

N

5 MILES

Map 9. Guam

The command structure for the Guam operation was more multilayered than usual. Holland Smith was technically in charge, but he delegated most of his authority to Adm. Richard Conolly and to Gen. Roy Geiger, who had been cooling his heels in Guadalcanal since the end of Operation Cartwheel and the neutralization of Rabaul. Although Geiger appeared outwardly to be his usual phlegmatic, inscrutable, and stalwart self, he was inwardly concerned about his status. He enjoyed running a corps, but felt there was not much point to it unless he could lead it in battle. He was therefore pleased with Nimitz's orders to assail Guam. The change in venue included a change in nomenclature. On 15 April, Geiger's I Amphibious Corps became the III Amphibious Corps. Nimitz had originally slated the invasion of Guam for 18 June—three days after Smith's V Amphibious Corps landed on Saipan—but overrunning Saipan required more time and resources than expected, including the commitment of the entire 27th Division. Nimitz therefore postponed attacking Guam until the situation on Saipan stabilized. Doing so meant leaving the Marines on board their transports and finding new troops to replace the 27th Division as Geiger's reserve. After witnessing the bitter fighting and high casualties on Saipan, Geiger and Conolly decided to use the delay to their advantage to conduct a longer, heavier, and more systematic preliminary naval bombardment than had preceded previous U.S. amphibious assaults. Hopefully all this additional firepower would make liberating Guam a less costly proposition than occupying Saipan.[99]

To storm Guam, Geiger had at his disposal three major combat units. The first was Allen Turnage's 3rd Marine Division, veterans of Bougainville. Although the 3rd Marine Division had impressed observers with its snap and discipline, it had not seen the kind of heavy and sustained combat that characterized other Marine operations. Turnage seemed solid enough, but he was not a hard-driving commander who frequently got out into the field. There were also questions about the quality of his staff. To replace the 27th Division as Geiger's reserve, Nimitz authorized using another Army outfit, Gen. Andrew Bruce's untested 77th Division in Hawaii. Securing the vessels to transport the division to the Marianas took time, delaying the invasion. Geiger also had the 1st Provisional Marine Brigade at his disposal. Organized on 22 March, it consisted of Col. Merlin Schneider's 22nd Regiment and Col. Alan Shapley's 4th Regiment. The former had spearheaded the attack on Eniwetok, and the latter were largely former raiders with combat experience in the Solomons. The brigade was only two-thirds the size of a division, but it made up in quality what it lacked in quantity.[100]

Vandegrift assigned Gen. Lemuel "Lem" Shepherd to lead the 1st Provisional Marine Brigade. Shepherd, born in Norfolk, Virginia, in 1896, graduated from the Virginia Military Institute and procured a Marine Corps commission right after the United States entered World War I. He fought valiantly in France during the conflict and was wounded three times—twice at Belleau Wood and once at Blanc Mont. After the war, Commandant John Lejeune tapped him as his aide, always a sure sign of an officer with high prospects. From there he went to sea, commanded the Sea School, did a tour of duty in China, and attended the Field Officers' course. In the 1930s he served in Haiti, graduated from the Naval War College, and ran a battalion. When World War II began in Europe, he was teaching at the Marine Corps Schools. Shepherd pleaded with Holcomb to send him overseas, but Holcomb insisted that he was needed at home. Holcomb eventually gave him the 9th Marine Regiment, which Shepherd took to Guadalcanal as part of the 3rd Marine Division. Shepherd's wish to lead the outfit in battle ended when Holcomb selected him as the 1st Marine Division's assistant commander. Because he had not seen service on Guadalcanal, Shepherd initially had a hard time gaining the respect of the division's officers during the Cape Gloucester operation, but eventually they came around.[101]

Intelligent, competitive, spit and polish, and thoroughly professional, Shepherd impressed everyone who met him. Indeed, one officer remembered that Shepherd's reputation was exceeded only by the reality of the man. Shepherd also possessed a fatalistic religious streak, once stating that in combat only God could help a Marine. Observers marked him as a future commandant long before it became a fact. One wartime correspondent wrote accurately enough, "His friends believed that Shepherd's uniformly high standard of performance, plus his general popularity, marked him as a likely candidate for Marine Corps Commandant."[102] On the other hand, some felt that Shepherd was so ambitious that he sometimes put his own career ahead of the good of the Corps.[103]

Although Shepherd had seen action at Cape Gloucester, his Pacific War combat record was no better than that of some other high-ranking officers.

He owed his rise to brigade command primarily to his connections and prewar resume. Holcomb had identified him as a potential division chief at the war's start, and Vandegrift and Holland Smith were both big boosters. Indeed, Vandegrift had originally slated Shepherd to take over the 1st Marine Division until he calculated that the Corps had enough men to create the 1st Provisional Marine Brigade. He opted to leave Rupertus with the division and gave the brigade to Shepherd. Shepherd was disappointed to lose the chance to lead the now-fabled 1st Marine Division. He referred to the 1st Provisional Marine Brigade as a "bobtail division," and, moreover, had a difficult time organizing it. He had so much trouble finding quality officers that he eventually flew from Guadalcanal to Pearl Harbor to wheedle some out of Smith. The brigade contained good men, but their primary loyalty was to their regiments, so Shepherd had to work hard to persuade them to cooperate and transfer their allegiance to the brigade. Despite these problems, Shepherd got results. He trained the brigade well, emphasizing tank-infantry tactics to overcome Japanese machine gun emplacements, and by summer 1944 he had it ready to go.[104]

There were pros and cons to postponing the Guam operation. On the one hand, it gave the island's Japanese defenders more time to brace themselves for the U.S. attack. It also meant that the Marines slated to assail Guam had to remain on board their hot and cramped transports for about fifty days. Indeed, they did not leave the Eniwetok area for Guam until 11 July. On the other hand, the delay enabled Conolly to undertake the most thorough, systematic, and effective preliminary naval bombardment of the Pacific War. Starting on 8 July, his warships pounded troop concentrations, bridges, supply dumps, and gun emplacements across the island. By the time the U.S. armada of 275 vessels and 55,000 troops regrouped on Guam's west coast on 20 July, the island's Japanese garrison was weary and stunned. Geiger's plan called for assaulting Guam's western coast in two places. To the north, the 3rd Marine Division's three regiments would come ashore at Asan, just to the west of Guam's capital, Agana. Five miles farther south, across the rocky Orote Peninsula, Shepherd's 1st Provisional Marine Brigade would land at Agat.

Despite Conolly's thorough preliminary bombardment, the Marines still encountered heavy Japanese fire when they stormed Guam's beaches on the morning on 21 July. The 3rd Marine Division got ashore around Asan, and Turnage established his command post there in the early evening. Although the beaches to the south were generally better, Japanese resistance was also fiercer. Here, too, the leathernecks managed to carve out a beachhead. The next day a regiment from the 77th Division arrived to reinforce Shepherd's brigade, but continuing Japanese opposition and a lack of amtraks gave the outfit almost as much trouble as the Marines had faced the previous day. Persistent nighttime counterattacks swelled the number of casualties, but also cost the Japanese their remaining reserves. While the 3rd Marine Division struggled to secure the heights overlooking its beaches and elements of the 77th Division fanned out across southern Guam, the 1st Marine Provisional Brigade sealed off and destroyed the Japanese defenders on the Oroto Peninsula.

Geiger was ashore by then. There was later some criticism that his staff had not ventured to the front often enough, but this certainly did not apply to Geiger. He kept close tabs on the fighting, visiting battalions and even companies in action. One day he and several colleagues left their jeep and driver behind so they could more safely find and confer with Turnage. When they returned, they discovered that mortar fire had killed the driver. Geiger was pleased with his progress, and especially with his good relationship with Bruce and his 77th Division. Indeed, the rookie 77th performed so well that Marines referred to it as the "77th Marine Division." This Army-Marine rapport stood in stark contrast to the animosity between the two services on Saipan. After a short break, on 31 July Geiger ordered an offensive northward, with the 3rd Marine Division pushing up the west coast and the 77th operating on the eastern shore. Agana fell within a few hours. Both units made steady headway and reached Guam's northern tip on 10 August, when Geiger declared the island secure. Doing so had not been cheap. In the twenty-one days of fighting, the Marines suffered 1,567 dead and 5,308 wounded. Army losses totaled 177 dead and 662 wounded.[105]

Guam's liberation completed the Mariana trifecta. Seizing the island involved good planning, thorough preparation, fine interservice cooperation, and ruthless implementation. Geiger, Turnage, and Shepherd handled their responsibilities with aplomb and skill. Small wonder Geiger wrote, "It is my considered opinion that the Guam operation is the best executed of any in which I ever participated, or of which I have personal knowledge."[106] Geiger of course had a proprietary interest in painting the operation in the brightest possible colors, but others shared his view, Vandegrift being the most important. Vandegrift was pleased that Geiger had performed on Guam with the same professionalism he had demonstrated on Bougainville and Guadalcanal. Vandegrift was also so impressed with Shepherd's handling of his brigade that he determined to elevate him to divisional command at the first opportunity.

All this backslapping, however, obscured some deflating facts. For one thing, the operation succeeded despite, not because of, the convoluted command structure. Also, the Americans were thoroughly familiar with the place, and the population was sympathetic. In addition, the long delay caused by the fighting on Saipan gave the Navy plenty of the most precious commodity, time, to work over the island. Future operations were unlikely to possess this advantage. One admiral warned, "I think it is a grave error to set up the Guam operation as the standard for the future. It is erroneous to lead the Marines or other troops to expect any such support prior to landing. It never happened anywhere else and probably never will again."[107]

PELELIU

Operation Forager did not spell an end to the Central Pacific offensive. There was one remaining operation for the Marines, a sour, costly, and forgotten one of questionable strategic value presciently codenamed Stalemate II. The Palau Islands stood as the last major obstacle between the Americans and their goal of reaching the China-Formosa-Luzon area. Located about five hundred miles north of New Guinea and east of Mindanao, the Palaus are a collection of islands that ran northeast–southwest for approximately one hundred miles. In the Americans' hands, they would project the Navy's power northward and provide airfields and anchorages to protect MacArthur's right flank when he assailed the Philippines. The original plan called for a major offensive against the islands with Geiger's III Amphibious Corps and the Army's XXIV Corps, but in August it was scaled back because of continued U.S. successes. In late August and early September, William Halsey's Third Fleet conducted a series of air raids in the region that met almost no opposition. The Japanese were husbanding their remaining resources for a showdown with the U.S. fleet covering the next major amphibious assault. Halsey incorrectly concluded, however, that Japanese strength in the area was weak. That being the case, he recommended accelerating the timetable for invading the Philippines. The Joint Chiefs of Staff agreed. In the reshuffling, Nimitz and MacArthur decided to use the XXIV Corps against the central Philippine island of Leyte and send the III Amphibious Corps to seize three objectives in the Palaus: Ulithi, Angaur, and Peleliu.

Peleliu, one of the southernmost islands in the Palau chain, derived its military significance from its airfield, which allowed Japanese planes to threaten MacArthur's invasion of the Philippines. Five miles square and surrounded by a coral reef, Peleliu's shape reminded some of a lobster claw. Its southern half, site of the airfield, is relatively flat, but the northern part is full of coral ridges with deep narrow valleys. Stifling humidity and heat engulf the entire island. At the time Peleliu suffered a chronic lack of easily accessible water, and with much of it being heavily forested, it provided plenty of options for the ten thousand Japanese defenders there to hole up in caves and crags.

The organizational structure for Stalemate II was convoluted even by Pacific Ocean Area standards. With Holland Smith and Geiger focusing their attention on the Marianas, Nimitz concluded that no one was providing the Palau operation with the necessary attention and leadership. He therefore asked Julian Smith to assume that responsibility. Smith was serving as Holland Smith's head of Marine Administrative Command, an important post involving Marine logistics. Vandegrift had assigned him the position as a reward for his good work with the 2nd Marine Division at Tarawa. Smith, however, had interpreted the appointment more as a punishment than a prize. He saw himself first and foremost as a combat commander and therefore found riding a desk at Pearl Harbor difficult, confining, and uninteresting. Moreover, he lacked authority because Holland Smith did not have complete confidence in him. He explained to a friend, "Archer [Vandegrift] might have considered this a promotion, but I am nothing more than an administrator; all they have done is hand me a gun with no ammunition. I am not in command of anything."[108] Now, however, Smith

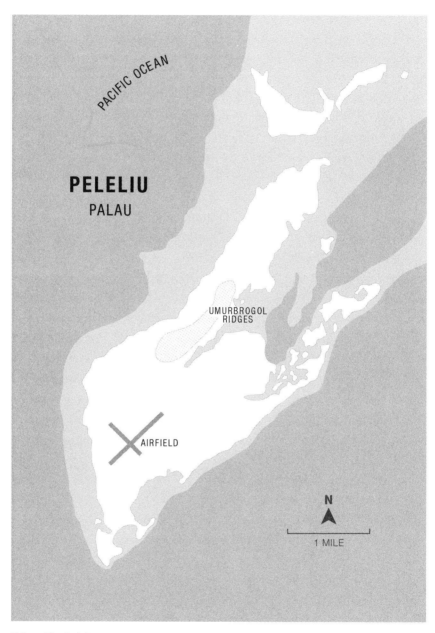

Map 10. Peleliu

had what appeared to be an opportunity to return to a more active role in the war, so he undertook the preliminary planning for Stalemate II with gusto. Unhappily for Smith, his bad luck resurfaced. Once the III Amphibious Corps had wrapped up Guam's liberation, Nimitz selected Geiger to command Operation Stalemate II. Although Smith retained a supervisory role, he would not get to lead leathernecks into battle. Smith swallowed his deep disappointment and graciously permitted Geiger and his staff to carry out Stalemate II's detailed planning.[109]

Nimitz assigned the Army's rookie 81st Division and Rupertus' veteran 1st Marine Division to implement Stalemate II. Julian Smith gave the combat-hardened Marines the more difficult mission of seizing Peleliu, and left Angaur's and Ulithi's occupations to the Army. In May 1944, after the Cape Gloucester invasion, the Navy sent the 1st Marine Division to recuperate on Pavuvu, a tiny island in the central Solomons. There the leathernecks established a squalid camp amid rotten coconuts, omnipresent rats and crabs, and plenty of mud. Rupertus did not share his men's discomfort. For one thing, his quarters were so noticeably luxurious by Pavuvu standards that people commented on it. For another, Vandegrift ordered him home in May for a long leave. While there, he traveled to Washington for consultations. Vandegrift noted that Halsey had specifically requested him for the Peleliu assault but promised to transfer him back to the States for new duty after Stalemate II. This was fine with Rupertus, who hoped to take over the Marine Corps Schools. When Rupertus returned to Pavuvu in mid-June, he was pleased with his division's condition and assessed it ready to go. Having no love for the Army, he was happy to be back under Navy command. As for the upcoming operation, Rupertus was openly optimistic that it would be quick. He wrote to Vandegrift, "There is no doubt in my mind as to the outcome—short and swift, without too many casualties."[110] He was wrong.[111]

Soon after he returned to Pavuvu, Rupertus fractured his ankle while observing a training exercise; the handhold of the amphibious tractor he was boarding broke on him as he was leaving the beach, and he fell backward onto some coral rocks. When Vandegrift visited Pavuvu shortly after the accident, he found Rupertus tired, hobbling on crutches, and headquarters-bound, but with no intention of surrendering his command.

Rupertus assured Vandegrift that he would recover in plenty of time to take his leathernecks onto Peleliu and added that the only problem he currently faced was his inability to get around to inspect his men. Fortunately, he continued, his staff and assistant division commander, Gen. Oliver Smith, were fully capable of assuming that role and making up for any of his temporary health-related shortcomings. Oliver Smith, however, was not so sure. He was so concerned about Rupertus' ability to function effectively that he sought out a doctor and asked him whether Rupertus was physically capable of leading the operation. The doctor replied that he probably could but would need a cane to ambulate. Rupertus intended to compensate for his immobility by exercising his authority by remote control. At a preinvasion conference, he informed his subordinates that he might not get ashore until the day after the landing, and until then he expected them to follow his plan regardless of circumstances.[112]

Oliver Smith was not the only high-ranking Marine worried about Peleliu and Rupertus. Geiger had concerns as well. Geiger did not believe that the two days the Navy had allotted for the preliminary bombardment of Peleliu was long and thorough enough. Although he persuaded the Navy to add an additional day, this fell far short of the standard set at Guam. Geiger was also uncomfortable with Rupertus' decision to keep only one battalion in reserve and very unhappy to learn the true extent of his injury. During late August rehearsals at Cape Esperance, Oliver Smith led the leathernecks ashore and established the division's command post because Rupertus could not get out of his boat. Geiger arrived and asked Smith for Rupertus' whereabouts. When Smith told him, Geiger said, "If I had known I'd have relieved him." There was not much love lost between the two men, so Geiger, unlike Vandegrift, had little sympathy for Rupertus' plight. However, he concluded that it was too late to make such a significant change, so Rupertus retained his command.[113]

There was one final factor about Peleliu that would have given the Marines pause had they known about it. The Japanese military, like its U.S. counterpart, was also learning from its experiences to fight more effectively. After analyzing previous Pacific War engagements, the Japanese recognized the futility of assailing the Americans at the water's edge in uncoordinated charges. Such efforts not only invariably failed because of overwhelming

U.S. firepower, but also cost the Japanese so many casualties that the battle's outcome became a foregone conclusion. In mid-1944 the Japanese adopted new tactics that they would introduce on Peleliu. Rather than waste manpower trying to overrun the Americans at their beachheads, the Japanese embraced a defense in depth that called for carefully husbanding their limited resources. Doing so made it easier for the Americans to get ashore, but their subsequent efforts to advance inland would bog down in the face of well-prepared Japanese defenders taking full advantage of the terrain. Overcoming such defenses would hopefully cost the Americans dearly in lives and time. It was a shrewd plan that caught the Marines storming Peleliu by surprise, and one that would bedevil the Americans for the remainder of the conflict.

On the morning of 15 September, the Marines encountered punishing fire when they came ashore on Peleliu's southwestern coast. Soon wrecked and blasted landing craft littered the waterline. Despite these losses, the veteran leathernecks pushed inland against increasingly stiff opposition that included tanks. On the northernmost beaches, Col. Lewis "Chesty" Puller's 1st Marine Regiment suffered especially high casualties. In the late morning, Oliver Smith arrived to set up an advanced command post with Col. Harold Harris' 5th Marine Regiment in the center of the division's shallow beachhead. Two hours later, as Japanese mortar shells fell around him, Smith looked up and saw Geiger approach. Smith told him he had no business being there, but Geiger replied that he wanted to know what was going on. Smith said that if Geiger wished to see the airfield, he could climb to the other side of their ditch. When Geiger lifted his head to take a look, Japanese rifle and machine gun fire peppered the area. Geiger and Smith then visited the 5th and 7th Marine Regiments' command posts, but were unable to get to Puller's 1st. Offshore, on the command ship *Mount McKinley*, Rupertus fretted about the unexpectedly ferocious Japanese resistance. He was especially unhappy to learn that Geiger had already reached the island, and radioed Smith to see if he should join them. Both Smith and Rupertus' staff officers insisted that bringing him ashore would require landing craft desperately needed for ammunition and supplies. Rupertus grudgingly accepted their logic and did not land until the next morning to finish establishing the division command post in Smith's ditch near the airfield.[114]

From that point Peleliu degenerated into a prolonged and gruesome battle of attrition for the Marines. They made some initial progress but suffered heavy casualties. The 5th Marine Regiment overran the airfield while Col. Herman Henneken's 7th Marine Regiment secured the southern part of the island. The problem was rooting the Japanese out of their stronghold in the Umurbrogol ridges in the north. These deep, wooded, and coral-covered ridges were tailor-made for defense. It was almost impossible to spot the snipers and infiltrators making life miserable for the leathernecks. The terrain offered no secure footing and no place to dig in. Exploding artillery and mortar shells turned the omnipresent coral into deadly shrapnel. Meanwhile, the heat was appalling, and water and ammunition grew scarce. One officer recalled,

> [T]he terrain was against us. The weather was against us. We were on the tail end of a typhoon. We ran short of rations. Food was being flown in by airplane every day. The terrain was abominable. It was the most horrible terrain I've ever encountered. It was as though several submerged reefs had been forced up out of the water with their jagged sharp edges and made several ridges that were up to 200–300 feet high and maybe 400 feet coming to a sharp ridge just like the ridge of a house. The sharp coral would cut up the shoes and clothing of the Marines. Then the island had been mined for many years for phosphate deposits. So there were many tunnels running through those ridges. And in addition many caves and tunnels had been dug by the defending forces.[115]

Puller's 1st Marine Regiment suffered especially heavy losses attempting to bull its way through the ridges. Puller resorted to dragooning noncombat personnel and feeding them into his depleted rifle companies. By 22 September, after a week of combat, the Marines had sustained 3,946 casualties, with no victory in sight.

Peleliu was hard on everyone involved, including those at the top of the 1st Marine Division's hierarchy. Although Rupertus' living conditions were not as spartan as those of the typical leatherneck, he was burdened with the responsibilities of his command. In addition, his injury prevented him from getting around as much as a division commander should. He had believed, and promised, that his Marines would secure Peleliu quickly. As September turned into October and the Marines continued battering the Umurbrogol ridges without much success, Rupertus began to unravel psychologically. He remained publicly optimistic, but privately he had no idea how to win the battle anytime soon. Although he received a letter from Vandegrift congratulating him on his fine job on Peleliu and promising to appoint him head of the Marine Corps Schools after the operation, Vandegrift had written assuming that everything was going according to plan. The commandant might view things differently once he learned the truth—and act accordingly. At one point Rupertus put his head in his hands and said to a staff officer, "This thing just about got me beat." When Harris, commander of the 5th Marine Regiment, visited division headquarters on 5 October, he found Rupertus in tears. "Harris," said Rupertus, "I'm at the end of my rope. Two of my fine regiments are in ruins."[116]

Unlike Rupertus, Geiger toured the front frequently to assess the battle and keep his subordinates on their toes. Although he became increasingly concerned with the 1st Marine Division's casualties and lack of progress, he hesitated to interfere with Rupertus' prerogatives as commander. On 21 September, Geiger visited Puller at the 1st Marine Regiment's rudimentary command post. No one doubted Puller's fearlessness and aggressiveness, but he often simply threw his leathernecks at the Japanese defenses without much tactical finesse or fire support. Moreover, he suffered from obvious exhaustion and struggled to explain the current situation coherently. Puller was, however, adamant that he did not need any assistance to achieve his objectives. A skeptical Geiger then drove to the 1st Marine Division's headquarters and examined Puller's casualty reports. He learned that the regiment had sustained 1,672 dead and wounded on Peleliu. Indeed, one of its battalions had lost 71 percent of its strength. Geiger informed Rupertus that Puller's outfit was "finished" and insisted on its relief and replacement by one of the regiments from the Army's 81st Division, which had recently overrun Angaur. Rupertus strongly disagreed. Given his distaste for the Army, he abhorred the thought of its soldiers ending a job that the Marines had started. He insisted that the Marines could wrap up the operation in a day or two. Not persuaded, Geiger issued the necessary orders. On 23 September, what was left of the 1st Marine Regiment pulled out and made way in the line for the Army's 321st Regiment.[117]

With the help of fresh Army troops, the Americans renewed their efforts to secure Peleliu. The 321st Regiment drove up Peleliu's west coast, opening the door for the 5th Marine Regiment to overrun the northern half of the island. Together the soldiers and Marines gradually isolated the remaining Japanese troops into what became known as the Umurbrogol Pocket. There was nothing easy about it. Although the Japanese were surrounded, hungry, and tired, they continued to fight skillfully from their stronghold. Marine officers complained that Rupertus was exerting too much pressure on their tired leathernecks. By 29 September, the 1st Marine Division counted 843 dead, 3,845 wounded, and 356 missing, for a total of 5,044 casualties. Morale declined, and the Marines no longer pushed their attacks with the aggressiveness and proficiency that characterized their early efforts. Fortunately for the Marines, Nimitz concluded that the operation was almost over, so he ordered Geiger and Rupertus to turn the battle over to the 81st Division and bring the 1st Marine Division back to Pavuvu. On 20 October, Geiger and Rupertus left the island, but the last elements of the division remained until mid-November. In the meantime, the 81st Division officially took over the operation. Heavy rains hindered Army efforts to reduce the pocket, which did not fall until late November, more than two months after the Marines first splashed ashore.

Unlike Guadalcanal, Tarawa, and Iwo Jima, Peleliu quickly disappeared from the Marine Corps' shared consciousness. There were good reasons for this collective amnesia. For one thing, many questioned the operation's strategic value. They argued that the Americans could have safely bypassed Peleliu without endangering MacArthur's right flank. Moreover, the Marines were unable to complete the operation without the Army's help. Indeed, the 1st Marine Division had left the island by the time the Army's 81st Division finally reduced the Umurbrogol Pocket. Although Marine Corps amphibious doctrine never expected leathernecks to fight for a long time, it was hardly surprising that for many Marines pride trumped dogma. Finally, the price for this Pyrrhic victory was steep. The battle cost the 1st Marine Division 1,124 dead, 5,024 wounded, and 117 missing, for a total of 6,265 casualties. The division suffered so much damage that it took months to rebuild it. Small wonder that one Marine officer said, "[S]omebody forgot to give the orders to call off Peleliu. That's one place nobody wants to remember."[118]

Although high-ranking Marine officers could not be held accountable for Peleliu's selection, they bore considerable responsibility for the battle conducted. As 1st Marine Division commander, Rupertus deserved censure for underestimating the operation's difficulties, undertaking an assignment for which he was not physically fit, and using and tolerating Puller's unimaginative tactics. If reports of Rupertus' performance on the island soured Vandegrift on his old comrade, he did not say so to anyone. As for Rupertus himself, he was happy to escape Peleliu—in a letter to Vandegrift he called it that "Godforsaken island"—and assume his new duties stateside. After he returned home, however, doctors detected high blood pressure and sent him to Bethesda Naval Hospital for a cardiograph that revealed heart disease. A medical board concluded that he was unfit for duty and should be retired. Rupertus seemed surprisingly resigned to his fate when he broke the news to Vandegrift. Although Vandegrift could not forestall Rupertus' retirement, he offered to recall him to duty at the Marine Corps Schools because of his experience and knowledge. However, on 25 March 1945, Rupertus suffered a fatal heart attack while eating dinner at a restaurant. For all the controversy Rupertus generated, Vandegrift still valued him. He wrote to Holland Smith, "We of the Marine Corps have lost one of our outstanding generals, and I myself have lost one of my closest friends."[119]

Peleliu also terminated Julian Smith's role in the Pacific War. Smith had been unhappy ever since Vandegrift kicked him upstairs after Tarawa to head the Marine Administrative Command at Pearl Harbor. He had hoped that Stalemate II would be his ticket back to a more active part in the conflict, but Nimitz relegated Smith to a glorified coordinator when he gave Geiger the job of leading the III Amphibious Corps in the operation. Small wonder he complained to Vandegrift that his assignment had become superfluous. In October Smith secured a thirty-day leave to return to the States to see his family. When it was over, out of the blue Vandegrift appointed him commander of the Department of the Pacific, headquartered in San Francisco. It was an important and prestigious post, but one that took him even farther from the action. The shocked and surprised Smith was deeply disappointed with his new job. He concluded that he never should have left Hawaii and complained to his wife, "It's all over for me. All the noise and the thunder of the Pacific has ended as far as I'm concerned."[120] He would have been even more angered and hurt if he had known that one of Vandegrift's motives for transferring him to San Francisco had been to ensure that Geiger serve as the number two Marine in the Pacific and that Holland Smith agreed with that logic. Regardless, Smith was determined to fulfill his new mission. He took comfort in Nimitz's promise to keep him in mind if a combat slot commensurate with his rank opened up. However, in February 1945 a medical board diagnosed Smith with hypertension and reported him unfit for overseas duty. Smith spent the remainder of the conflict fighting the finding. For Smith, it was an unfortunate conclusion to a frustrating war.[121]

Although Marine officers could not see it, Peleliu was an unhappy harbinger of things to come. The Marines had encountered thousands of Japanese soldiers defending the outer ramparts of their oceanic empire in the Solomon, Gilbert, and Marshall Islands, but the size of the Japanese garrisons would increase to tens of thousands as the U.S. counteroffensive approached Japan's Home Islands. Moreover, new tactics that eschewed fruitless banzai charges meant that the Japanese were fighting more effectively. On top of that, Japanese fanaticism and determination would surge in proportion to the fight's proximity to their homeland. Marine casualties were therefore likely to increase dramatically, as would the time necessary to secure objectives. Neither factor boded well for a relatively small force like the Marine Corps. The Army's assistance was one antidote to this troubling contingency. If Geiger and Rupertus had brought in the 81st Division to Peleliu sooner, the operation might have ended in a less costly and more timely manner, and perhaps without wrecking the 1st Marine Division. The problem, as Rupertus and other Marine officers recognized, was that the more Army help they needed, the more control the Army could assume over the Corps. The Marines had fought throughout the war to avoid that but, as Peleliu demonstrated, continuing to do so meant more casualties than the Marine Corps could easily afford.

CONCLUSIONS

Despite the Marines' difficulties on Peleliu, they could take pride in their collective performance in the Central Pacific offensive. In less than a year, they played the key role in storming Tarawa, Roi-Namur, Eniwetok, Saipan, Tinian, Guam, and Peleliu. By securing these islands, they had provided the Army Air Forces with airfields from which to launch the strategic bombing of Japan, covered MacArthur's concurrent campaign across New Guinea's northern coast, and killed large numbers of Japanese troops. Along the way the Marines learned a great deal about amphibious warfare. Tarawa may have been touch and go, but by the time the leathernecks assailed Peleliu, landing operations had become, if not exactly routine, then certainly manageable. Once the Marines established themselves ashore, victory became a matter of time. The Marines' organization, planning, logistics, training, and tactics deserved much of the credit for this inevitability, playing as large a role as combat prowess in the Marines' success in seizing their objectives.

Holland Smith and Roy Geiger were the Marine generals most responsible for overseeing the high-level preparations for amphibious operations in the Central Pacific. Smith supervised the attacks on the Gilberts, Marshalls, and Saipan-Tinian. He demonstrated an ability to learn from his mistakes and take advantage of the cornucopia of resources increasingly at his disposal. His major shortcoming was interservice relationships. He established a good rapport with the Navy because he respected the branch in general, and Turner in particular. On the other hand, his dealings with the Army were much more contentious. Smith mistrusted the Army's motives and its amphibious warfare competency. He worried that Richardson would persuade Nimitz to give the Army control over amphibious operations and Marine divisions. This would not only strip the Marine Corps of its raison d'être, but also place leathernecks under the command of Army generals whose competence Smith doubted. These suspicions went a long way in explaining the Smith versus Smith controversy on Saipan. As for Geiger, he deserved kudos for designing the assaults on Guam and Peleliu. His biggest sin was in underestimating Japanese opposition on Peleliu. On the whole, though, both generals did fine jobs of paving the way for their division and regimental commanders to fulfill their missions.

Nine Marine generals took part in the Central Pacific offensive's six major operations at the corps, division, and brigade levels: Cates, Geiger, Rupertus, Schmidt, Shepherd, Holland Smith, Julian Smith, Turnage, and Watson. Most of them saw action only once. Although Holland Smith oversaw Marine operations in the Gilberts, Marshall, and Marianas, he actually led his corps in combat only on Saipan. Similarly, Julian Smith (Tarawa), Turnage (Guam), Cates (Tinian), Rupertus (Peleliu), and Shepherd (Guam) each participated in a single engagement. On the other hand, Geiger commanded his III Amphibious Corps on both Guam and Peleliu. Schmidt fought his 4th Marine Division on Roi-Namur and Saipan, and then succeeded Holland Smith at the head of the V Amphibious Corps for the invasion of Tinian. Watson presented a bit of an anomaly. Only a regimental chief at Eniwetok, he assailed the island in an independent capacity. His performance there secured him command of the 2nd Marine Division for the assaults on Saipan and Tinian.

The wide distribution of generals indicated a good use of the Marine Corps' limited personnel resources. With the exception of Rupertus at Peleliu, all of the generals showed considerable tactical competency. Geographic constrictions certainly limited their opportunities to display the kind of tactical finesse that some contemporary Army generals demonstrated in North Africa, Sicily, and northwestern Europe, but these Marine generals fought persistently, aggressively, and skillfully. The upshot was that Vandegrift had at his disposal a stable of thoroughly capable and experienced corps and division chiefs available for the Pacific War's final battles.

═══ ★ F O U R ★ ═══

CLOSING IN
ON JAPAN

B y early 1945 time was clearly running out for the Axis powers. On Germany's Eastern Front, the Soviet Red Army stood at Berlin's doorstep, having overrun most of the Baltics, Poland, and East Prussia. To the south, the Soviets had driven into the Balkans and Hungary, forcing the Germans to evacuate most of Greece and Yugoslavia. After seizing Rome in June 1944, Anglo-American forces had advanced to the top of the Italian peninsula. That same month, Anglo-American armies also landed in Normandy and from there moved on to liberate France and Belgium and push toward Germany's western border until outrunning their supply lines. Although Germany's December 1944 counteroffensive through Belgium's Ardennes Forest had thrown the Anglo-Americans off balance, by January they had recouped their losses and were heading toward the Rhine River. Germany's U-boat campaign against Allied shipping had clearly failed, and the Anglo-American strategic bombing offensive was finally yielding results by targeting Germany's vulnerable oil industry.

While the Allied coalition continued to hold firm despite strains over the fate of Poland and Eastern Europe, Germany could not rely on its allies for salvation or even assistance. Its European friends—Italy, Bulgaria, Hungary, Finland, and Romania—had all surrendered or been conquered. The Nazi

143

empire, which in Europe had once stretched from France to the outskirts of Moscow, was now limited to northern Italy, parts of the Balkans, chunks of Austria and Czechoslovakia, the northern Netherlands, Denmark and Norway, various surrounded enclaves, and the German heartland. By any objective and reasonable assessment, Hitler's Germany was doomed.

At first glance, Japan's situation in early 1945 seemed more promising, or more accurately less dire, than Germany's. After three years of world war, the Japanese retained control over their Home Islands, Korea, Manchuria, much of eastern China, Formosa, Malaysia and Singapore, Indochina, the Dutch East Indies, and innumerable island strongholds scattered across the Pacific. U.S. strategic bombing efforts against Japan's Home Islands had so far proven ineffective, and Japanese morale appeared as strong and resolute as ever. A closer look, however, belied such an optimistic analysis. The U.S. Dual Drive Offensive had relentlessly ground its way across the Pacific, bypassing or obliterating Japanese-held island fortresses in its path. Contrary to the laws of entropy, it had gained momentum, power, and violence as it progressed westward. The U.S. submarine campaign had sunk much of Japan's merchant marine, making it increasingly difficult for the Japanese to import raw materials, resupply and reinforce its overseas garrisons, and take the strategic initiative. The Americans had also destroyed much of Japan's surface fleet at the Battle of Leyte Gulf in late October 1944. At the Tehran Conference in November 1943, the Soviets had promised to declare war on Japan three months after Germany's eventual capitulation, which would give the Japanese another formidable enemy to fight. In addition, Germany's surrender would free up an enormous amount of U.S. and British resources for deployment in the Pacific against Japan. Finally, unbeknownst to the Japanese, the Americans had almost completed building atomic bombs, whose destructive power exceeded all previous weapons. Although many high-level Japanese policymakers realized that their country's armed forces would not prevail, they did not know how to end the war short of the unconditional surrender the Allies were demanding.

By September 1944 the U.S. Dual Drive Offensive across the Pacific from Hawaii and Australia had reached the China-Formosa-Luzon region. Although many naval officers wanted to next assail Formosa, MacArthur persuaded the Joint Chiefs of Staff to instead authorize a campaign to liberate the Philippines. He cinched his case by stating that he would be ready to invade the archipelago in October, whereas the Navy could not for logistical reasons attack Formosa until the following March. As things stood, many naval strategists had at any rate come to question the logic of seizing Formosa. While MacArthur invested his time, energy, and resources to storming first Leyte and then Luzon, the Navy decided to use its forces to position itself for a final assault on Japan. This included occupying one of the Bonin Islands. Doing so would provide emergency landing strips and protection for the B-29 Superfortress bombers raiding Japan. It would also remove a site from which the Japanese could issue early warnings to their colleagues on the Home Islands of incoming bomber missions. The Joint Chiefs signed off on the operation in October, and shortly thereafter Adm. Chester Nimitz and his planners zeroed in on Iwo Jima as the target of Operation Detachment.

IWO JIMA

Located about 660 miles south of Tokyo, pork chop–shaped Iwo Jima consists of eight square miles of land. Japan had formally claimed the island in 1891, and when the Pacific War began about 1,100 inhabitants eked out livelihoods there by fishing and farming. Iwo Jima was a gloomy and forbidding place. It offered no shelter for ships, and heavy surf made bringing supplies ashore difficult. Dormant Mount Suribachi, at the island's southwestern tip, overlooked the three airfields that gave the place its strategic value. Its barren landscape reminded more than one person of the moon's surface. Soft black volcanic sand with the consistency of dust covered Iwo Jima's southern half, making it difficult to walk through and impossible to dig into. A series of bleak rising plateaus marked the landscape of the northern part of the island. There were no streams or lakes on Iwo Jima, so the locals used cisterns to collect rain for fresh water. The entire island reeked of sulfur from volcanic vents. One person compared Iwo Jima to something out of Dante's *Inferno*. Another remarked, "After God got through making the world, he must've took all the dirty ash and rubble left over and made Iwo Jima."[1] It was an ominous location for a battle even before 21,000 Japanese soldiers turned it into a fortress.

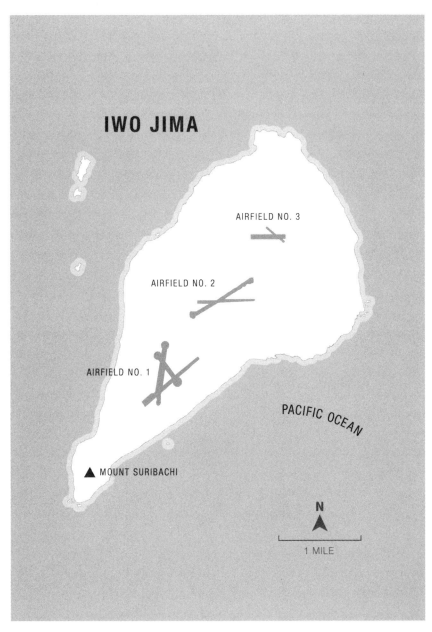

IWO JIMA

AIRFIELD NO. 3

AIRFIELD NO. 2

AIRFIELD NO. 1

PACIFIC OCEAN

▲ MOUNT SURIBACHI

N
▲

1 MILE

Map 11. Iwo Jima

Nimitz assigned Spruance's Fifth Fleet the job of conducting the Iwo Jima operation. Kelly Turner's V Amphibious Force was responsible for transporting and supporting Harry Schmidt's V Amphibious Corps. This arrangement was reasonable enough, but Spruance and Turner insisted that Holland Smith, now commander of the Pacific Fleet Marine Force, accompany the invasion fleet. Neither Smith nor Schmidt liked the idea. Schmidt did not want Smith cramping his style and looking over his shoulder during the upcoming battle, and Smith believed that his presence on Iwo Jima would be embarrassing, distracting, and superfluous. Vandegrift agreed. He felt that Spruance and Turner were repeating the same mistake Nimitz had made in assigning Julian Smith as well as Geiger to oversee Stalemate II in the Palaus. With Vandegrift's consent, Smith strongly protested the decision all the way to Nimitz, but to no avail. Spruance and Turner told him that they had no doubts about Detachment's success as long as he was there. The implication, of course, was that they lacked such confidence in the inarticulate Schmidt. After the war, however, Turner explained his thinking in a letter to Schmidt: "The reason I wanted him [Holland Smith] along was not at all because of any lack of confidence in you, but was solely because, for one thing, I wanted to keep him in the picture in case we should go into China, in which case we might have raised two small field armies, one composed mostly of Marines and the other of Army elements, the whole under MacArthur. A secondary, though important reason was a recognition that if we did *not* go into China, then Iwo would be Smith's last chance for active field service."[2] Whatever the truth, the decision needlessly complicated the command structure.[3]

Schmidt's V Amphibious Corps would deploy three divisions for the Iwo Jima invasion: the 3rd Marine, the 4th Marine, and the 5th Marine. The 3rd Marine Division was busy mopping up remaining Japanese resistance on Guam. Allen Turnage had commanded the outfit since September 1943, leading it through Bougainville and Guam. Vandegrift liked to rotate his high-ranking combat generals to keep them fresh, and Turnage had been in the Pacific for well over a year. Moreover, although Vandegrift considered Turnage a friend, he had always harbored doubts about his decisiveness and initiative. Once the III Amphibious Corps secured Guam, Vandegrift ordered Turnage home to take over the Personnel Department at HQMC and replaced him with another Pacific theater mainstay: Bobby Erskine.

Erskine was Holland Smith's long-suffering and efficient chief of staff, and in that capacity he had impressed almost everyone with whom he came into contact, including Nimitz, Spruance, Turner, and many Army generals. In spring 1944 Vandegrift traveled to the Pacific for an inspection that included a conference with Smith and Erskine. There Erskine asked Vandegrift for a combat command, justifying his request by explaining that he had put in more than enough time on staff duty. Vandegrift was sympathetic. He greatly respected Erskine and knew that he could not rise to the top of the Marine Corps' hierarchy without leading troops into battle. At the same time, however, he did not want to deprive Smith of Erskine's valuable services as chief of staff. Fortunately for Erskine, Smith did not want to retard Erskine's career by keeping him on. When Vandegrift returned to the Pacific after the Tinian operation, he and Smith informed Erskine that they planned to recommend his promotion to major general and assign him the 3rd Marine Division. Despite their often rocky relationship, Smith was quite fond of Erskine and was sorry to lose his services for both professional and personal reasons. Indeed, he refused to accompany Erskine to the airport when Erskine left for Guam because he feared he would not be able to control his emotions when he said goodbye.[4]

Erskine had come to the Marine Corps in a roundabout way. He enlisted in the Louisiana National Guard in 1912 while attending Louisiana State University and was sent to the Mexican border to help deal with Pancho Villa and his bandits. When the United States entered World War I, Erskine attained a Marine Corps commission. He saw considerable action in France and was wounded at Belleau Wood and St. Mihiel. He opted to remain in the Corps after the conflict ended. In the 1920s he worked as a recruiter and quartermaster, did sea duty, served in Haiti and the Dominican Republic, attended the Army's Infantry School, instructed at the Marine Corps Schools, and was in charge of the honor guard that returned the remains of the Unknown Soldier to the States. The turn of the decade found him in Nicaragua chasing Augusto Sandino and protecting the Nicaraguan president. He later graduated from the Army's Command and General Staff College, taught again at the Marine Corps Schools, and went to China. When

World War II broke out in Europe, he was chief of staff for the Atlantic Fleet's amphibious force and in September 1942 assumed the same job with its Pacific counterpart.

Tall and muscular, the well-dressed Erskine had a soft voice, cold blue-green eyes, and a reputation as one of the toughest and most proficient officers in the Marine Corps. Vandegrift referred to Erskine as a "paragon of efficiency" and noted that he could spot a piece of wayward lint on a rifle from five hundred yards. His high standards, abruptness, perfectionism, total commitment to the Corps and its mission, and spit-and-polish attitude made him a hard man to like. He once complained about a young officer who was reading the *Saturday Evening Post* while off duty because he was not using his spare time to brush up on training manuals. One officer, however, asserted, "You know, he had a terrific reputation for being hardnosed. I'm sure some people felt he was unfair. But I'll say this on the record: I never worked with a finer professional, and a fair man, a man that taught you."[5] Not surprisingly, Erskine's obvious competency, raw intelligence, and organizational skills made him a first-rate chief of staff. "The Big E" also impressed as a combat leader. On the battlefield he was ruthless, aggressive, and impatient. Although some officers criticized him for grandstanding and refusing to worry about his flanks, others rated him as one of the Marine Corps' best World War II division commanders.[6]

The 3rd Marine Division was not in the best shape when Erskine arrived in Guam in October 1944 to take charge. HQMC had not yet made good on replacing the losses it had sustained in seizing the island, and the surviving leathernecks were living in primitive, rain-soaked camps. Constant patrolling to hunt down Japanese stragglers had exhausted the men and undermined their morale. Moreover, Erskine quickly concluded that some of the staff officers were overrated, and that excessive decentralization of support units to the regimental level had made the division unresponsive. Hard charging as ever, Erskine immediately began working to right these deficiencies. He got out into the field frequently so the troops could see him. He initiated a rotation policy, cleaned up the camps, and concentrated supporting units under division control. He also made a virtue of necessity by using mopping up missions to train his Marines. It was hard work, but Erskine relished the opportunity to run such a large organization, telling a friend, "I am in glory with this division."[7] Within a short time he was confident enough to tell his 6th Marine Division counterpart, Lem Shepherd, in a letter that the 3rd was "a damn fine division. I am proud of it, they are proud of themselves."[8]

While the 3rd Marine Division's leathernecks trudged through Guam's jungles in search of errant Japanese, Clifton Cates' 4th Marine Division had returned to its camp on Maui to rest and recuperate from its ordeal on Saipan and Tinian. It was a veteran outfit now, with a cocksure attitude to prove it. Cates, though, was not one to let any unit rest on its laurels, so he quickly got his men into a rigorous training regimen. In a few months, Cates was pleased enough to write, "My division is in excellent shape, everyone is in good physical condition, it is well trained and, most important of all, it has had the advantages of having been in three operations. All the training in the world doesn't compare with actual combat on the field of battle."[9] Cates of course had a proprietary interest in painting his division in the brightest possible colors, but more objective observers agreed with his assessment. Both Holland Smith and Schmidt lauded the division after their inspections, with Smith commenting that it looked like a million dollars. As it was, the 4th Marine Division was in better shape than its commander, at least at first. Cates had fought a bad back on and off since before the Tinian operation and afterwards suffered from stomach problems severe enough to put him on the sick list. His physical breakdown depressed Cates, but he concluded that vigorous exercise would be as beneficial to him as to his men. For this, tennis was his weapon of choice. Fit as a fiddle by January, Cates said his only complaint was the stress of waiting for the next operation.[10]

The scale of the Pacific War forced the Marine Corps to organize and field not only regiments, but divisions and corps as well. Because securing the men to fill these units affected national conscription policy, the Corps needed the approval of both the Navy and the Army to augment its strength. As the war intensified, Holcomb concluded that the Corps required a fifth division, and in August 1943, he asked King, Chief of Naval Operations, for one. King agreed on the condition that Holcomb build it out of the Corps' current authorized strength. Even so, King felt obligated to secure the Joint Chiefs of Staff's consent. The Army's redoubtable chief of staff, George Marshall, was dead set against additional Marine divisions. He was not a big Marine Corps fan to begin with and had fought hard against the creation of the 3rd and 4th Marine Divisions because every increase in the Corps' numbers meant a smaller manpower pool from which the Army could draw for its needs. Marshall grudgingly went along with King's request on the condition that it be the last division the Marines requested. Vandegrift later wrote that King got the division "practically over General Marshall's dead body."[11] In November 1943 Holcomb informally activated the 5th Marine Division at Camp Pendleton, California.[12]

To lead the new 5th Marine Division, Holcomb turned to Gen. Keller Rockey. The Indiana-born Rockey graduated from Gettysburg College, studied forestry at Yale, and in 1913 accepted a Marine Corps commission. Of the twenty-one second lieutenants in his Norfolk, Virginia, officer training class, he was one of eight who became a World War II general. Rockey served in France in World War I, mostly in staff positions, but saw considerable action at Chateau-Thierry and elsewhere. After the conflict, he fought Caco bandits in Haiti, but spent most of the 1920s either teaching or as a student, including a stint at the Army's Command and General Staff College. At the end of the decade, he led a Marine battalion in Nicaragua against Augusto Sandino. In the mid-1930s he became the first director of the War Plans Division before working in the Office of the Chief of Naval Operations from 1939 to 1941. When the Japanese attacked Pearl Harbor, he was chief of staff for the 2nd Marine Division. From there Holcomb appointed him first head of the Plans and Policies Division and then assistant commandant. In February 1944 Vandegrift assigned him to command the new 5th Marine Division.

Rockey was a sturdy, large man with rugged features. There was nothing brilliant about him. He was, instead, one of those solid and competent generals who peppered the ranks of World War II division and corps leaders. His subordinates appreciated him for his honesty and fairness. Battalion and regimental commanders noted that he supported their efforts, protected them from undue pressure from higher-ups, and did not scapegoat. Holcomb and Holland Smith liked him, as did Vandegrift, though he sometimes complained that Rockey was insufficiently direct and forceful. Turner, on the other hand, had small use for Rockey—the feeling was mutual—and saw him as just about the least effective Marine division commander with whom he worked.[13]

Holcomb had had Rocky in mind for division command for some time. Indeed, since the war's start he had carefully managed Rocky's assignments to prepare him for the job. To give him more administrative experience, Holcomb appointed Rocky first as director of the Plans and Policies Division and then assistant commandant. Vandegrift agreed with Holcomb's assessment of Rocky's potential. He called Rocky their "ace in the hole," ready to take over a division if anything happened to its current chief. When Holcomb placed Rocky in charge of the 5th Marine Division, he let Rocky organize and train the outfit without much supervision. The assignment pleased Rocky, who found building the division interesting. Being happy with the results, he looked forward to leading it into combat. The fact that a good many of the 5th Marine Division's leathernecks possessed combat experience certainly helped. Rocky's positive opinion about the division was undoubtedly biased, but Schmidt felt the same way when he inspected it on Maui in October 1944.[14]

Although two commanders, Erskine and Rocky, had not led their outfits into battle, all three of the divisions Nimitz assigned to the Iwo Jima invasion were in fine shape and full of veterans. Schmidt, head of the V Amphibious Corps, was also an experienced combat leader with a first-rate record, and most of the Fifth Fleet's high-ranking officers were proven and skilled leaders. The consensus among these men was that Operation Detachment would be rough but fast. Cates guessed that overrunning the island would require one or two weeks at most, while Schmidt estimated ten days. The big doubter was Holland Smith, who focused his disgruntlement on the Navy's preliminary bombardment. Spruance had allotted only three days for it, far short of the ten days Smith thought necessary. Smith's dispute with the Navy over this issue was symptomatic of greater concerns, however. He concluded that securing Iwo Jima would be so prohibitively expensive for the Marines that it was not worth the effort. In a letter to Vandegrift, Smith wrote, "We have done all we could to get ready for the next operation, and I believe it will be successful, but the thought of the probable casualties causes me extreme unhappiness. . . . Would to God that something might happen to cancel the operation altogether."[15] Smith could be brutally persuasive when convinced of the righteousness of his cause, but in this case his influence was muted. For one thing, as Fleet Marine Force chief he no longer played an integral role in planning. That was Schmidt's job, but Schmidt lacked Smith's forcefulness and determination. For another, in November Smith was hospitalized with a hernia and acute cystitis. He recovered in less than a month, but his illness took something out of him and made it difficult for him to press his case. Small wonder he choked up during a preinvasion press conference on Turner's flagship just before the leathernecks assailed Iwo Jima's beaches.[16]

Vandegrift and Smith's concerns about heavy Marine losses on Iwo Jima were practical as well as humanitarian. The uncomfortable reality was that the Marine Corps was running out of men. The previous July, Vandegrift had warned Smith that the Corps would be in serious trouble if the casualties in the next operation equaled those sustained in the Marianas, especially among junior officers. Three months later, Vandegrift informed Smith that the Corps' kitty was as flush as it was going to get. He explained that the Secretary of the Navy was in no mood to lobby for an increase in strength and that there was already growing public pressure to demobilize now that the war against Germany was ending. Vandegrift hoped to return to the Pacific some of the leathernecks who had been rotated home and to free up manpower by eliminating superfluous units, but the fact remained that the Marines had to finish the war with their current strength. As Vandegrift explained to Schmidt, "We cannot get any additional men and we have got to fight this war out with the number we now have."[17] As of 1 January 1945, the Marine Corps had 421,065 leathernecks, barely enough to man the Navy's warships, fulfill stateside responsibilities, perform innumerable logistical duties, and fill the combat divisions that did almost all of the fighting and dying.[18]

By 1945 massive assemblages of U.S. ships were not unusual. Even so, the huge fleet of 550 vessels that gathered off of Iwo Jima in mid-February impressed observers. On the morning of 19 February, the Navy intensified its three-day preliminary bombardment as everything from battleships to landing craft lashed the island with shells, rockets, and machine-gun fire. Indeed, the Navy threw ten thousand rockets alone at Iwo Jima that day. Aircraft roared overhead to drop ordnance and strafe targets of opportunity. Marines watching this awesome display of naval strength from their transports, command ships, and landing craft fervently hoped that the overwhelming firepower would render the Japanese defenders helpless, but most knew from hard experience how unlikely that would be. Just before nine o'clock, 482 amtraks carrying eight battalions from the 4th and 5th Marine Divisions headed for Iwo Jima's southern shore. Opposition on the beaches was comparatively sporadic, so the leathernecks sorted themselves out and pushed inland. As they did so, Japanese resistance increased dramatically, dashing all hopes of easy victory. One journalist wrote about the first night, "[It] can only be described as a nightmare in hell. About the beach in the morning lay the dead. They died with the greatest possible violence. Nowhere in the Pacific have I seen such badly mangled bodies. Many were cut squarely in half. Legs and arms lay 50 feet away from any body. All through the bitter night, the Japs rained heavy mortars and rockets and artillery on the entire area between the beach and the airfield. Twice they hit casualty stations on the beach. Many men who had been only wounded were killed."[19]

To the Marine Corps participants, the battle for Iwo Jima quickly assumed two defining characteristics: the island's geography and brilliant Japanese tactics. The island's unforgiving geography was unlike anything they had encountered in the Pacific War. Iwo Jima was almost completely barren, devoid of trees, shrubs, or vegetation of any kind behind which to take cover. Moreover, the fine, powdery volcanic ash that covered the island's southern half made it impossible to dig foxholes. This left the Marines constantly exposed to fire from Japanese troops concealed in caves, pillboxes, bunkers, and dugouts almost impervious to U.S. artillery and aircraft. One regimental commander recalled, "It was just like shooting fish in a barrel, and you were the fish."[20] The island was too small for the Marines to maneuver on, which limited their tactics to direct frontal charges backed by as much armor, air, naval, and artillery support that could be mustered. Such assaults were usually costly, however, and yielded minimal gains. Schmidt later wrote, "There was no way around so the battle developed into a hammer and tongs uphill frontal attack with men, tanks, artillery, naval gunfire and air attacks thrown against successive positions."[21]

There was nothing new or unusual about dogged Japanese defenders, but on Iwo Jima Japanese troops displayed a tenacity and skill the Marines had never encountered. The Japanese commander, General Tadamichi Kuribayashi, had opted to embrace and refine the tactics his colleagues had adopted on Peleliu. Kuribayashi, aware that he could not defeat the Americans, hoped to drag out the battle for as long as possible to buy time for his countrymen in the Home Islands to prepare for the anticipated U.S. invasion. He opted to forgo the fruitless and expensive banzai charges that the Japanese had employed in previous Pacific engagements and instead to carefully husband his limited resources. To this end, Kuribayashi had his men dig in deep, using the island's caves and caverns to escape U.S. firepower. He also ordered them to wait patiently for Marine attacks, inflict as many casualties as possible, fight for their positions until the last minute, and then retreat to the next line of defense to repeat the process. The Japanese also employed small infiltration teams and snipers to harass the leathernecks, and huge 320-mm spigot mortars that inflicted disproportionate losses on the Marines. Such tactics won the respect of the Marine generals. Holland Smith wrote to Vandegrift, "The Japanese General in command of this island impresses me as a smart one. He makes few counter attacks and only local ones because, in my opinion, he realizes he can cause us more casualties by making us come to him rather than counter attacking us."[22]

Iwo Jima's geography and skilled Japanese opposition explain why Operation Detachment degenerated into a brutal and costly battle of attrition that took the Marines five weeks to win. Marine losses were substantial. Although the Marines declared the island secure on 26 March, heavy fighting continued for weeks afterwards. Marine casualties topped 26,000 killed and wounded. Almost the entire Japanese garrison perished. One battalion commander recalled that he went through two complete sets of platoon leaders and that at the end of the engagement sergeants led half-strength companies. To fill the holes in the ranks, the Marines rushed in painfully young and barely trained replacements who were often killed the day they entered the lines. Tossed into combat before they were adequately prepared and unfamiliar with their comrades and surroundings, it was hardly surprising that they did not last long. The manpower crisis became so acute that on 9 March Rockey sent personnel from supporting outfits to reinforce his depleted rifle companies. Morale, aggressiveness, and teamwork all declined as unit cohesion deteriorated. Officers lost their nerve. One journalist described the severity of the losses in the 5th Marine Division: "D Day produced 849 casualties, and the next three days 557, 534, and 467 more. For the next few days losses dropped to an average of 250, but by D plus 11 and 12, when the reports came in from that bloody rock called Hill 362, the division casualties shot up again, to 394 and 494. As late as D plus 23, two days before Iwo was declared secure, the Fifth lost 327 men. And there were more than 500 casualties after the island was declared ours, from D plus 26 to D plus 35."[23]

Iwo Jima was hard on the generals too though for different reasons. Holland Smith, for example, had little to do because he wanted to stay out of Schmidt's way. He refrained from visiting the island frequently and tried to keep his tactical suggestions to a minimum. As things stood anyway, he thought Schmidt was doing a good job under the circumstances. Smith's redundancy, however, made him feel useless, bored, bitter, and depressed. He worried that people would blame him for Iwo Jima's high casualty figures. He complained about King, Nimitz, Richardson, Vandegrift, Turner, and Spruance. The stress took a toll on both his mental and physical health. Indeed, he returned to Honolulu, exhausted and demoralized, even before the battle ended.[24]

The battle was also difficult for the corps and division commanders. Schmidt landed on Iwo Jima on 24 February. He had hoped and expected the Japanese to launch an unsuccessful counterattack on the first night of the battle that would expend their reserves. He was disappointed when this failed to materialize and displeased to learn that the Navy's preliminary bombardment had had minimal impact on Japanese defenses. The situation left him with no choice but direct frontal assaults, even though such attacks would swell the casualty lists. Although Smith refrained from overly interfering, Schmidt still resented him looking over his shoulder. Despite these problems, Schmidt was proud of his generalship, of his division commanders, and of his leading the largest number of Marines ever committed to one engagement. Indeed, he later referred to Iwo Jima as the highlight of his career.[25]

The three division commanders on Iwo Jima responded to the battle according to their circumstances, personalities, and characters. Schmidt deployed Erskine's 3rd Marine Division at the center of the U.S. line, which consisted of only two regiments because Turner and Smith held the third back as a reserve. Some felt that Erskine gained a disproportionate and unfair share of the credit for winning the engagement. Vandegrift and Smith's partiality explained part of this, but Erskine's knack for self-promotion also played a role. Leathernecks who had grumbled about Erskine's rigorous training regimen appreciated his exacting standards once they encountered the Japanese on the island. Erskine fought in an aggressive and self-contained manner, pushing his men hard to achieve their objectives with minimal outside help. He tried to do so without utilizing air support because he was so exasperated with its shortcomings. Erskine's frustrations extended beyond the skies. He considered Cates' 4th Marine Division too slow and thought Rockey's 5th Marine Division failed to pull its weight. As for Schmidt, Erskine complained that he did not concentrate his artillery effectively. All of these men were old friends, so Erskine muted his criticisms. Indeed, even Erskine's own body let him down. He fell ill with pneumonia but refused to be evacuated. His chief of staff ran the division for several days until Erskine recovered sufficiently. The skill that Japanese soldiers demonstrated impressed Erskine, and as the days turned into weeks, he became increasingly concerned about the declining quality of his division due to heavy casualties and the infusion of poorly trained replacements. Nonetheless, he felt that his division had done well.[26]

Cates' 4th Marine Division anchored the southern part of the U.S. line across Iwo Jima. Although Cates knew from the start that seizing the island would be difficult, the first day of the engagement convinced him that the Corps faced its toughest challenge of the war. Fortunately, the 4th Marine Division was a veteran outfit, with plenty of combat experience at Roi-Namur, Saipan, and Tinian. Cates took full advantage of the assets at his disposal, including air power. Throughout the battle, he remained dapper and clean-shaven. He may have been generally more unassuming than his friend Erskine, but the two men shared a good many traits that exhibited themselves on Iwo Jima. One was aggressiveness. Cates summed up his tactics, "Well, we'll keep on hitting them. They can't take it forever. We've got to keep pressing 'em until they break. Don't let up."[27] Like Erskine, Cates respected the fighting prowess of Iwo Jima's Japanese defenders. He also had health problems. In Cates' case, it was an inflamed right eye caused by the island's volcanic dust. Cates also had as much pride in his 4th Marine Division as Erskine took in his 3rd Marine Division.[28]

Schmidt deployed Rockey's 5th Marine Division on the northern end of the U.S. line across the island. Rockey was the least experienced of the division commanders on Iwo Jima, so unsurprisingly, some saw him as less capable than Erskine and Cates. On the other hand, many of his regimental and battalion leaders appreciated his efforts to insulate them from outside pressure and praised his integrity. Rockey's accomplishments were by no means unimpressive. He pointed out later that the 5th Marine Division captured more territory, had a smaller percentage of personnel evacuated for illness and combat fatigue, and was in contact with the enemy as long or longer than Cates' or Erskine's outfits.[29]

One of the biggest controversies surrounding Iwo Jima involved Col. James Stuart's 3rd Marine Regiment. Although the unit was part of Erskine's 3rd Marine Division, Turner and Holland Smith had decided to hold it back from Iwo Jima as their reserve. As Marine casualties mounted and progress remained glacial, it seemed reasonable to commit the 3rd Marine Regiment to the battle, so on 28 February Schmidt and Erskine asked for the outfit. They argued that a fresh, combat-hardened regiment would help break the back of Japanese resistance and end the operation more quickly. Turner and Smith denied the request, believing that there was not enough room on the island for an additional regiment. Smith explained, "Hell, there are 58,000 troops ashore now. Where are you going to put them? . . . Why, I'd have to pull regiments off to put more men on and the garrison troops are coming soon, and we can't land airplanes on that [air]field until we've knocked out that gun that's still firing on it."[30] When Schmidt and Erskine persisted, Smith said that he would secure Turner's permission only if Schmidt stated that he could not capture the island without the 3rd Marine Regiment's assistance. Schmidt would not do that. He knew that victory was all but inevitable with or without the unit, but deploying the regiment would help in seizing the island sooner rather than later and with fewer killed and wounded. Such logic went over Smith's head. As a result, Schmidt had to finish the engagement with the exhausted leathernecks on hand. Marine officers then and later insisted that the 3rd Marine Regiment could have made a major difference in the time required and the resulting losses to finish the fight.[31]

By 11 March, the Marines had confined the Japanese to three separate pockets. Tired and reluctant to close with the enemy, the leathernecks blasted the Japanese out with flame-throwing tanks, bulldozers, and demolition teams. An amazed Cates counted eight hundred Japanese corpses in his sector alone. There was nothing easy about the process, and their tactics continued to cost the Marines substantial casualties. Although Schmidt declared the island secure on 26 March, heavy fighting continued for weeks afterwards. Indeed, the Army's 147th Regiment killed 1,602 die-hard Japanese defenders after it arrived on Iwo Jima on 20 March to serve as its garrison.[32]

There was no denying that the Marine Corps covered itself in glory at Iwo Jima, but the price was exorbitant. Of the Corps' 26,000 casualties on the island, nearly seven thousand were killed. These losses made Iwo Jima the bloodiest fight in Marine Corps history. It was also the only engagement in the U.S. counteroffensive across the Pacific in which more Americans fell than Japanese. Holland Smith was not the only person who questioned Iwo Jima's utility. The battle wrecked three of the Corps' six combat divisions. It would take months to bring them back up to strength for the anticipated assault on the Japanese Home Islands. Moreover, Iwo Jima never became a major base for either the Navy or Army Air Forces. Although the operation's supporters noted that the airfields there provided refuge for 2,451 B-29 Superfortress bombers carrying around 27,000 crewmen, most of those planes landed there to refuel, not because they were damaged.

Despite the casualties sustained and controversy generated, Vandegrift expressed no regrets about the necessity of assailing Iwo Jima. He was shocked by the heavy Marine losses, which he attributed to the island's peculiar terrain, but he saw the engagement as part and parcel of the kind of warfare necessary to defeat Japan. Indeed, he was proud of his leathernecks for winning such a horrific battle. "There is nothing that anyone could have done to have lessened the cost," he assured Holland Smith, "and it was a magnificently executed operation by very courageous men."[33] Vandegrift had nothing but praise for his combat commanders. Upon reading Smith's admittedly biased reports, he was inclined to rate Erskine as Schmidt's most capable division chief, followed by Cates and then Rockey. He also complimented Smith and Schmidt for their contributions to victory. Even so, he worried that the Marines could not afford another Iwo Jima and still expect to play a major role in the anticipated invasion of Japan.[34]

OKINAWA

Seizing Iwo Jima may have made the strategic bombing of Japan easier, safer, and more effective for the Army Air Forces, but it did not provide the Americans with the base they needed for the final assault on the Japanese Home Islands. To do this, on 3 October 1944, the Joint Chiefs of Staff authorized Operation Iceberg, which called for the occupation of the island of Okinawa sometime in the following spring. Okinawa, located in the Ryukyu chain, sits 350 miles south of the southern Japanese island of Kyushu. The Japanese annexed it in 1879, but its population remained linguistically and culturally distinct. Okinawa is sixty miles long but with a maximum width of only eighteen miles. With 466 square miles of territory, it was big enough to accommodate all the weapons, supplies, equipment, and personnel the Americans needed for their invasion of Japan. The northern two-thirds of the island, heavily forested and mountainous, was sparsely populated. Most of Okinawa's half million inhabitants lived in the flatter and more open southern region, which included the island's only town, Naha, where they made a living farming sugarcane and sweet potatoes in the temperate climate. To defend the island, the Japanese deployed approximately 130,000 troops, making it the most formidable force the Americans in the Pacific Ocean Area had yet encountered.

Although U.S. intelligence underestimated Japanese strength on Okinawa, it was still clear that seizing the island necessitated a larger force than deployed thus far in the Pacific Ocean Area. Nimitz had at his disposal two corps: Geiger's III Amphibious Corps and the Army's XXIV Corps. Leading both units required a field army and a field army commander. Holland Smith wanted the assignment. As he saw things, he had earned the post by successfully overseeing the troops that conquered the Gilberts, Marshalls, and Marianas. He felt that he had more experience than anyone else in working with the Army and Navy, training and organizing soldiers and Marines for amphibious assaults, and leading men in combat. Spruance and Turner agreed, probably because they were familiar with Smith and figured that as a Marine, he would be more susceptible to Navy influence than a soldier. Nimitz, however, gave the job to an Army general, Gen. Simon Buckner, and his new Tenth Army. He undoubtedly did so because

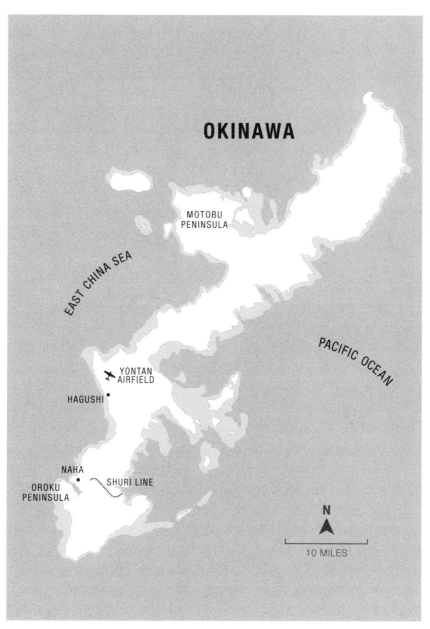

OKINAWA

MOTOBU
PENINSULA

EAST CHINA SEA

PACIFIC OCEAN

YONTAN
AIRFIELD

HAGUSHI

NAHA

OROKU
PENINSULA

SHURI LINE

N

10 MILES

Map 12. Okinawa

he knew that the Army's chief of staff, George Marshall, would not consent to placing a unit as large as a corps under a Marine general, let alone
the one who had supposedly mistreated and disrespected the 27th Division on Saipan. Unlike Smith, Buckner had proven that he could pour oil
over troubled interservice waters by skillfully finessing the Army's report on
Ralph Smith's relief on Saipan.

Holland Smith was of course deeply disappointed with Nimitz's decision.
To add insult to injury, in his quarterly efficiency report for April–July 1944,
Nimitz had labeled Smith excellent in all categories except cooperation,
in which he assessed him as "good." This less-than-perfect rating greatly
offended Smith. He concluded that Nimitz was punishing him for his role
in the Smith versus Smith controversy. As far as Smith was concerned, he
was the victim in that hullabaloo because the Army had unfairly maligned
him for doing his duty on Saipan by relieving Ralph Smith. He felt unap-
preciated and slighted. He wrote Vandegrift that he was just about ready to
tell everyone off and return home. One admiral recalled, "He was a different
man—bitter, dejected, and morose. . . . His bitterness was outspoken. I don't
know what discussions he had with Nimitz after Saipan, but he seemed to
be mad at everyone: General Richardson . . . Nimitz, Turner, Spruance, and
many others. He was so depressed I feared he might try to harm himself."[35]
Vandegrift sympathized with Smith's plight but urged him to make the best
of the bad situation, difficult advice for someone with Smith's temperament to heed. The more Smith studied Iceberg, the more convinced and
concerned he became that American losses would be prohibitively heavy.
Indeed, he estimated that occupying Okinawa would cost 50,000 casualties.
Small wonder he was so glum and despondent during and after Iwo Jima.[36]

Geiger's attitude and prospects were brighter than Holland Smith's. He
and his III Amphibious Corps staff officers took a month-long leave stateside during October–November 1944 to see their families and recharge
their batteries. They returned to their Guadalcanal headquarters ready to
undertake their new assignment. Geiger's relationship with the Army was
much better than Smith's. Geiger and Buckner were old friends. They had
attended the Command and General Staff College together in the 1920s
and kept in touch afterwards. In addition, Geiger and the XXIV Corps
commander, Gen. John Hodge, got along well. Because Buckner and most

of his Tenth Army staff had no World War II combat experience, their war-hardened III Amphibious Corps counterparts were inclined to dismiss them as greenhorns. Buckner, though, appreciated Geiger and his III Amphibious Corps, and his example helped generate mutual respect between the two staffs. As a result, planning for Iceberg proceeded smoothly. Indeed, Buckner was so impressed with Geiger that he designated him his Tenth Army successor in case anything happened to him on Okinawa. Richardson put the kibosh on that, however, by stating that Buckner had overstepped his authority, but the incident demonstrated Geiger's stature within Tenth Army headquarters. The only fly in Geiger's career ointment was concerns about his health. In March 1945 Vandegrift had asked Holland Smith to investigate reports that Geiger's heart was giving out. The rumors were accurate, but Vandegrift either did not know or did not care about the truth enough to take action against Geiger. Unruffled as ever, Geiger organized and trained his corps to prepare it for the ordeal it would soon face. A naval officer on his way to Okinawa, right before the invasion, discovered Geiger in his stateroom in his underwear reading a detective novel. When the officer commented that Geiger did not seem very worried about the upcoming operation, Geiger responded, "Oh, nothing to it. [The Navy] will put us ashore and then we'll lick 'em. In the meantime I don't have anything to do."[37]

Geiger's III Amphibious Corps consisted of three divisions, including the 1st Marine Division, which had returned to Pavuvu after its ordeal at Peleliu to rest and refit. It had a new commander: Gen. Pedro del Valle. Del Valle was born in 1893 in Spanish-speaking Puerto Rico and grew up there. His father was mayor of San Juan, and the senior del Valle's decision to support U.S. control of the island after the Spanish-American War paid off when his son received an appointment to the Naval Academy. After graduating in 1915, young del Valle accepted a Marine Corps commission. Duty in Haiti and the Dominican Republic followed. He did not get to France during World War I, but instead spent the conflict on board the battleship USS *Texas*. Afterwards he worked as a regimental adjunct and as an aide to Gen. Joseph Pendleton, attended the Field Officers course, and served in Haiti and Nicaragua. In the mid-1930s he went to Rome as assistant naval attaché, during which he observed the Italian invasion of

Ethiopia. He returned home to attend the Army War College and then went to HQMC to oversee training operations. In April 1941 Commandant Holcomb assigned del Valle to lead the 11th Marines, an artillery regiment. His outspokenness led to conflict with the 1st Marine Division commander, Gen. Philip Torrey. To make things worse, an allegation circulated that at a party del Valle had made disparaging remarks about President Franklin Roosevelt and his foreign policy. Holcomb eventually dispatched an officer to investigate the charges, but nothing came of it. Fortunately for del Valle, Holcomb replaced Torrey with the friendlier Vandegrift. Del Valle skillfully ran his regiment during the Guadalcanal campaign but ended up going home for a while due to injuries he sustained in a plane accident. He returned to the Pacific in 1944 as head of the III Amphibious Corps' artillery during the Guam operation.

Del Valle's character and personality were as unusual in the early twentieth-century Marine Corps as was his Puerto Rican background. On the one hand, he was well regarded by his fellow officers for his competence, professionalism, and courage. In particular, they respected his skills as an artillerist. His competitiveness contributed to his effectiveness as a trainer. On the other hand, his extreme political opinions, which included large dollops of anti-communism and anti-Semitism, came across as irrational and led some to question his efficiency as an officer. Most people liked him as a person, however, and were inclined to dismiss his bigotry as a peculiar and harmless idiosyncrasy. As one officer put it, "If you just sort of discounted a lot of that talk, he really didn't mean what he was saying. It's like so many people [who] are so rabid about something, they're rabid about it but when it gets down to maybe acting on it, they don't act. They talk."[38] Another called him a "delightful, likeable fellow."[39] Whatever his political views, there was no doubt about his commitment to the Marines under his command. When his regiment was en route to New Zealand in 1942, the crew of the transport ship carrying it shut down the chow line before all the Marines had eaten, citing union regulations. The next day del Valle threatened the union representative with summary execution by shipboard firing squad unless the galley stayed open until every leatherneck was fed. Whatever his prejudices, del Valle was grateful that his health, God, and circumstances had all cooperated to give him a chance to defend his country and ply his trade.[40]

Del Valle owed his appointment to lead the 1st Marine Division to his war record and his relationship with Vandegrift. The two had served together on Guadalcanal. Del Valle had so impressed Vandegrift with his capable handling of the division's artillery that he recommended del Valle's promotion to brigadier general. Vandegrift's appreciation was not transitory; the following year he assured del Valle that he would keep him in mind for future important assignments. In the summer of 1944 del Valle contributed to the comparatively easy conquest of Guam as the III Amphibious Corps' artillery chief. When Vandegrift visited Guam, del Valle boldly told the commandant that he expected Vandegrift to assign him to command the 1st Marine Division. Vandegrift did not say anything one way or another in response, but del Valle was encouraged by his knowing smile. In fact, del Valle was an obvious choice to take over the 1st Marine Division. He was familiar with the outfit, had fought with it in two successful operations, and was well regarded in the Corps.

The 1st Marine Division was in poor condition when del Valle took it over on Pavuvu Island in October 1944. It was still recovering from its Peleliu ordeal, and approximately 5,800 of its leathernecks had been overseas for almost thirty months. Impetuous as ever, del Valle immediately got to work refitting the division for Iceberg. He built a close-knit staff and gave its officers plenty of authority to do their jobs. He also instituted a rigorous training program, even though there was not much room for the exercises on Pavuvu. In addition, he secured replacements so those veterans who had gone through both Guadalcanal and Cape Gloucester could rotate home. One Marine officer remembered, "General del Valle came, and the spirit of that division as you know changed overnight. What a wonderful leader! The best leader in the Marine Corps that I've ever seen."[41] When Buckner inspected the division in late January 1945, he too was impressed with del Valle's accomplishments.[42]

The 1st Marine Division was not the only Marine division training on Guadalcanal in late 1944 and early 1945. The 6th Marine Division was also there. As commandant, Holcomb had envisioned a Marine Corps comprised of six divisions divided into two corps. He felt that this would give the Corps sufficient strength to play a major role in the Pacific War. Vandegrift agreed with his predecessor's goal. The obstacles in turning this dream

into reality were securing Admiral King's permission and finding enough
manpower for the new outfit. When King had authorized the creation of
the 5th Marine Division, he got the Army's chief of staff, Marshall, to go
along with the plan only on the condition that the 5th would be the last
Marine division deployed for the conflict. King was a hard-nosed man, but
even he hesitated to renegotiate the issue with the formidable Marshall.
Vandegrift, though, was persistent and persuasive. After hearing Vandegrift
out, King resorted to subterfuge to acquire another Marine division. King
told Vandegrift that if he could convince Nimitz to request another Marine
division, King would consent to it without raising the matter with the Joint
Chiefs of Staff. The catch was that Vandegrift would have to form the unit
out of the Corps' current strength. During a subsequent inspection trip to
the Pacific after the Marianas operation, Vandegrift broached the idea with
Nimitz, who unsurprisingly was amenable to an additional Marine division
with which to conduct his operations. He was happy to ask King for it, and
King okayed his application forthwith. Now that he had King's approval,
Vandegrift had to find the manpower for the division. Fortunately, the ker-
nel for it already existed. Shepherd's 1st Provisional Marine Brigade contained two regiments, the 4th and 22nd. To bring it up to divisional size,
Vandegrift built the 29th Regiment out of stateside recruiting depots and
formed the brigade's artillery batteries into the 15th Artillery Regiment.
When combined, he had enough for the 6th Marine Division.[43]

To command the 6th Marine Division, Vandegrift followed the path of
least resistance and simply elevated Shepherd. He was, after all, already leading the 1st Provisional Marine Brigade, whose leathernecks made up more
than half of the new division. There was more, however, to Vandegrift's
selection of Shepherd than mere convenience. Shepherd had impressed
Holcomb and Vandegrift from the war's start, and he had justified their
confidence with his solid performance at the head of the 1st Provisional
Marine Brigade on Guam. Shepherd's new assignment of course pleased
him. Before Shepherd could assume command, though, Vandegrift ordered
him stateside for a rest in October 1944. When Shepherd returned to
Guadalcanal, he immediately launched a rigorous training regimen for his
division. It was not a simple job. For one thing, roughly 1,500 leathernecks
in the 22nd Regiment had been overseas for nearly two and a half years,

and many were tired and wanted to go home. Shepherd told Vandegrift that he preferred to go into battle without them. He was also unhappy with Col. Victor Bleasdale, commander of the 29th Regiment. Shepherd perceived Bleasdale as a good trainer but did not think he could coordinate and control his unit. Despite such reservations, Shepherd opted to keep Bleasdale at his job for the time being. Another issue Shepherd faced involved persuading his Marines to transfer their loyalties from their regiments to their new division. None of these problems dissuaded him. As far as he was concerned, his men needed to prepare themselves for the brutal ordeal he knew to be ahead. He said, "You've got to instill in your men the will to kill the enemy to the point—perhaps because they are heathens, so to speak—that killing a Jap was like killing a rattlesnake."[44] Shepherd was content with his young and energetic staff and was convinced that his division was the best-prepared in the Marine Corps. He did not stand alone in his assessment; Buckner had been equally impressed during his late January visit.[45]

Implementing Iceberg required the Navy to organize another massive invasion force. Nimitz once again gave the job to Spruance and his Fifth Fleet. Spruance, in turn, assigned Turner the task of transporting Buckner's Tenth Army to Okinawa and then supplying it. The U.S. armada consisted of 318 combat and 1,139 auxiliary vessels to carry 548,000 soldiers, sailors, and Marines. It departed from the lagoon of the Ulithi atoll during 25–27 March and gradually gathered off Okinawa several days later. The typically complicated landing plan required the Army to secure various anchorages on offshore islets before the main assault. The Marine contribution called for putting the 1st Marine and 6th Marine Divisions ashore with two XXIV Corps divisions on Hagushi beaches, on Okinawa's west coast, while Gen. Tom Watson's 2nd Marine Division conducted a feint off the island's southeastern shore. Geiger gave del Valle's and Shepherd's divisions the starring roles because they had trained so closely with each other and with the III Amphibious Corps headquarters in the Solomons. Watson's division, on the other hand, had prepared on distant Saipan and was not as well known to Geiger's officers. The Navy began its preliminary bombardment on 25 March to soften up the Japanese defenses on Okinawa. The consensus among American planners was that the Japanese would severely contest the Tenth Army every step of the way.[46]

On 1 April, an Easter Sunday, 10 battleships, 9 cruisers, 23 destroyers, and 177 gunboats pounded Hagushi beaches. At around seven o'clock in the morning, troops from four Tenth Army divisions—from north to south, the 6th Marine Division, 1st Marine Division, 7th Division, and 96th Division—came ashore. Landing conditions were ideal: calm seas, intermittently clear skies, and moderate winds. To everyone's surprise and amazement, the soldiers and Marines encountered almost no resistance at the waterline and inland. Indeed, the 6th Marine Division's 4th Regiment occupied Yontan airfield in midmorning. By nightfall around 50,000 American troops were on Okinawa, at a cost of twenty-eight killed, 104 wounded, and twenty-seven missing. Until then, the Japanese had strongly contested almost every major amphibious operation in the Central Pacific. Their atypical docility on Okinawa was mystifying but welcome. Shepherd said, "There was a lot of glory on Iwo, but I'll take it this way."[47] When Vandegrift heard the news, he hoped that the unopposed landing was a harbinger of things to come, one that would enable the Marine Corps to maintain six combat divisions for the invasion of the Japanese Home Islands. He should have known better.[48]

Buckner's plan called for the Army's XXIV Corps to push southward from Hagushi beaches while Geiger's III Amphibious Corps cleared the northern part of Okinawa. Although Shepherd's 6th Marine Division fought hard to overrun the Motobu Peninsula, for most of the remaining Marines their mission had been relatively safe. Indeed, waging war in northern Okinawa was unlike previous Marine operations in the steamy South Pacific or on the Central Pacific's windswept atolls. Okinawa's cooler temperatures required heavier clothing than elsewhere. The leathernecks marched through pine trees instead of palm trees. They camped in wide open spaces, from which they could see miles of surrounding countryside. The earth was soft and loamy. Civilians huddled in their huts, and livestock roamed the fields. Combat was mostly limited to sporadic encounters with roving bands of Japanese soldiers. Although Marines could die in northern Okinawa as surely as in any combat zone, their situation was preferable to the ordeal their XXIV Corps comrades were experiencing after running into the main line of Japanese resistance. Geiger declared an end to organized resistance on 20 April, freeing up his two divisions to participate in the nightmare in progress in the south.

The Japanese commander on Okinawa, General Mitsuru Ushijima, had prepared carefully for the U.S. invasion. Like his colleagues on Peleliu and Iwo Jima, Ushijima did not believe that he could beat the Americans. Instead, he hoped to delay and bleed them to buy his compatriots in the Home Islands time to prepare for a U.S. assault. To that end, he decided to concentrate his forces on the southern part of the island and make his stand there. He also chose not to expose his troops to the Americans' firepower by contesting their landing. Turning southern Okinawa into a fortress, however, was just one arrow in the Japanese quiver. Kamikazes were another. The Japanese planned to use suicide plane attacks to decimate the U.S. fleet deployed off Okinawa to support operations on land. When Hodge's XXIV Corps moved southward, it ran into a Japanese buzzsaw. Just clearing the outposts that fronted the Shuri Line took everything the corps had. The Japanese resisted fiercely and skillfully from their all-but-invulnerable strongpoints located on the high ground. Meanwhile, coordinated kamikaze attacks offshore took an increasing and alarming toll on the Navy's ships. Indeed, kamikazes sank or damaged more than 125 vessels of various types in April alone. It was obvious to everyone that the Marines had their work cut out for them when Geiger gradually deployed his III Amphibious Corps alongside the beleaguered XXIV Corps in early May.

With the Navy suffering such heavy losses to Japanese kamikazes off Okinawa, Nimitz urged Buckner to do whatever he could to win the battle as soon as possible. Some officers concluded that undertaking an amphibious assault behind Japanese lines on the island was the best shortcut to victory. Doing so would take advantage of their mobility and amphibious expertise. Del Valle and Shepherd supported the idea, as did Turner and the commander of the Army's 77th Division, Gen. Andrew Bruce. When Vandegrift flew to Okinawa on 21 April for an inspection, he raised the issue of an amphibious assault at a conference at Geiger's headquarters with Buckner, Geiger, Turner, and Nimitz's chief of staff, Adm. Forrest Sherman. Vandegrift suggested using Watson's 2nd Marine Division, then killing time on Saipan, to land on Okinawa's southeastern beaches behind the Shuri Line. He assured the participants that the division could be under way in six hours. Buckner and Sherman were skeptical. For one thing, they hoped to use the 2nd Marine Division in a subsequent operation further up the

Ryukyu chain. Moreover, they worried that supplying troops over a second beachhead would be too difficult logistically. Although Geiger said little at the meeting, perhaps out of fear of contradicting his boss, he agreed with Buckner. Geiger told one officer that he learned the hard way on Guam to avoid dividing his men between two unconnected beaches. Vandegrift might be the Marine Corps commandant, but Buckner had the final say, and he rejected the proposal. The Tenth Army would instead continue to grind down Japanese resistance from the north through brutal attrition.[49]

The Okinawa campaign lasted until the Tenth Army snuffed out the last organized Japanese resistance on 21 June, though mopping up die-hard survivors continued until the end of the war. Overcoming the ferocious Japanese opposition required soldiers and Marines to engage in fierce battles for locales with innocuous-sounding names like Sugar Loaf Hill, Conical Hill, Chocolate Drop, Strawberry Hill, and Dakeshi Ridge. Despite pressure from naval officers, Buckner opted to go about his operations methodically. He deployed maximum firepower in a marginally successful effort to keep American casualties as low as possible. He referred to his tactics as "cork-screw and blowtorch," meaning using demolitions to crack open Japanese fortifications and flamethrowers to roast their occupants. It was a heartless and savage form of warfare that cost a good many Marines and soldiers—let alone Japanese—their lives in the process. In late May, torrential rains trans-formed the southern Okinawa battleground into a morass reminiscent of World War I's Western Front. The constant downpours turned the ground into a muddy mess that made living conditions abominable. The omnipres-ent detritus and corpses became even more repulsive. Worse yet, the weather provided the approximately 30,000 Japanese troops still manning the Shuri Line with the opportunity to escape unscathed to Okinawa's southern tip to make their last stand. When the skies finally cleared on 5 June, the Tenth Army advanced southward and, after more hard fighting, finally burned the Japanese out of their remaining strongholds.

Shepherd's 6th Marine Division and del Valle's 1st Marine Division maintained a rivalry throughout the campaign. Its origins went back to Guadalcanal, where the two units had trained together. Much of the com-petitiveness grew out of their commanders' personalities. Shepherd pushed his subordinates hard to achieve their objectives and was not always forgiving

of failure. For example, he relieved Victor Bleasdale, chief of the 29th Regiment, for not moving fast enough on the Motobu Peninsula. Shepherd
regularly roamed the frontlines to keep an eye on things. He broke an arm
when an aide jumped on top of him during a Japanese mortar attack. Later
a leatherneck accidentally injured Shepherd's knee with his rifle butt. Shepherd believed that his Marines could overcome Japanese defenses at a reasonable cost through the skillful use of tank-infantry teams, but this often
worked better in theory than reality. The aggressive attitude that Shepherd
worked to inculcate may have paid dividends on the battlefield, but Buckner
for one complained about the wanton destruction that the division left in
its wake. Observers commented that the 6th Marine Division as an organization was cockier, flashier, pushier, and more sensitive to slights than its 1st
Marine Division counterpart.[50]

Del Valle was every bit as competitive as Shepherd, but his 1st Marine
Division had less to prove than the 6th. One officer commented that
although del Valle's unit lacked the 6th Marine Division's flash, it demonstrated on Okinawa the reliability and sturdiness that had characterized its
performances at Guadalcanal, Cape Gloucester, and Peleliu. When engineers from the 6th Marine Division proudly erected a sign identifying one
of their bridges as the longest one ever constructed by a Marine Corps
engineering battalion, del Valle responded by labeling one of his division's
bridges as the shortest ever built by a Marine Corps engineering battalion,
much to Shepherd's annoyance. Del Valle also got crossways with Bruce,
commander of the Army's 77th Division. The 77th was supposed to seize
Shuri Castle, but del Valle's men got there first and then added insult to
injury for northern-born soldiers by raising the Stars and Bars over the battered remnants. Del Valle's tendency to overstep boundaries did not prevent
others from noting the skill and determination he displayed on Okinawa.
Buckner may have complained on occasion that del Valle was not moving
fast enough to suit his tastes, but on the whole he was pleased with the 1st
Marine Division's actions.[51]

As usual, Geiger insisted on staying dangerously close to the front. At
one point, he displaced a battalion headquarters so he could establish his
corps command post on the site, even though the Japanese were shooting at
the position from 1,400 yards away. Another time, Geiger was approaching

an observation post when the Japanese opened fire on him. He continued walking forward after a nearby Marine saw him and exclaimed, "Get down you old bastard before you get your fuckin' head shot off!" Geiger finally took cover when the Marine was killed seconds later. Geiger wrote to Vandegrift that his leathernecks accepted their ordeal without complaint, fulfilled their missions, and showed plenty of initiative. He also continued to get along well with Buckner and Tenth Army headquarters. Indeed, he had only two grievances against them. One was over tombs on Okinawa. Buckner wanted the troops to avoid them out of respect for the dead, but the Marines and soldiers disregarded the orders because the tombs were ideal for headquarters. When an Army inspector general made a big deal about it during a visit, Geiger chewed him out and sent him on his way. The other was over publicity. As far as Geiger was concerned, the Army deliberately slighted the Marine contribution to the campaign.[52]

On 18 June, Buckner was killed by Japanese mortar fire while visiting the front held by the 1st Marine Division. When Geiger and Hodge got the bad news, they huddled at Tenth Army headquarters with Gen. Fred Wallace, the Army general responsible for developing Okinawa's infrastructure, to discuss who would replace Buckner. Before the campaign, Buckner had tried to designate Geiger as his successor, but Richardson thwarted the effort. Now Wallace put himself forward, asserting that as the senior officer present, he should take over. Hodge and Geiger countered that amphibious warfare doctrine superseded the regulations Wallace was citing to stake his claim. That being the case, they believed that Geiger should temporarily run the Tenth Army. Wallace persisted, but Geiger, with Hodge's support, impatiently dismissed him. As a result, the next day Geiger became the only Marine officer to lead a field army during World War II. To no one's surprise, his tenure was brief. Geiger may have been well respected throughout the Pacific, but there was no chance the Army chief of staff, Marshall, would permit a Marine to run a field army composed mostly of soldiers. He quickly appointed Gen. Joseph Stilwell to head the Tenth Army. Stilwell arrived on Okinawa on the morning of 23 June, and under his leadership the Tenth Army finished mopping up the remaining Japanese resistance.[53]

Okinawa was the bloodiest operation of the Pacific War. U.S. casualties topped 50,000 by sea, land, and air. The Navy alone had thirty-four ships sunk, an astonishing 368 damaged, and nearly five thousand personnel killed, mostly due to kamikazes. The Marines suffered 14,200 dead and wounded, almost a combat division. The campaign lasted for three months and consumed the efforts of two corps and a half dozen divisions, including two Marine divisions. Although it is hard to be precise, more than 100,000 Japanese soldiers died on the island, with approximately 10,000 captured. About a fourth of the Okinawan population, 100,000 or so, succumbed as well. In exchange for all this bloodshed, the Americans seized the base they needed from which to launch their planned invasion of the Japanese Home Islands.

The Marines could hold their heads high for their performance on Okinawa. They committed no major tactical blunders, and they consistently fought doggedly and aggressively against some of the strongest Japanese defenses of the war. They rapidly secured the northern part of the island before joining their Army colleagues in the south for the grueling combat necessary to destroy the Japanese troops there. There was nothing new about leathernecks battling courageously, but on Okinawa they also worked well with the Army and managed to avoid the controversies that had plagued interservice operations on the Gilberts, Marshalls, and Marianas. Buckner was largely responsible for the positive relations. He respected the Marines, welcomed their officers into his Tenth Army staff, and in particular got along with Geiger. Although he occasionally groused about Marine actions, for the most part he was pleased with and grateful for their contribution to the campaign. Because the Army and Marine Corps would wage war side by side in an invasion of Japan, their ability to cooperate on Okinawa was a good omen. As for Vandegrift, he was happy that Iceberg vindicated his selection of del Valle and Shepherd as division commanders. He also praised Geiger for so competently handling his troops on the island and rewarded him by recommending his promotion to lieutenant general.[54]

WAR'S END SHUFFLES THE DECK

By any objective measurement, Japan was prostrate by the summer of 1945. The U.S. counteroffensive across the Pacific had reached its doorstep, and American military planners were preparing for a final assault on the Home Islands. The Japanese army remained large and formidable, but hundreds of thousands of troops were stuck on the Asian mainland or on bypassed Pacific islands, and therefore of little use defensively. The Allies had destroyed most of Japan's surface fleet and merchant marine, making it almost impossible for the Japanese to import the foodstuffs and raw materials upon which their war effort depended. The strategic bombing campaign of the Army Air Forces had begun obliterating Japanese cities one by one, destroying factories and driving the population into the countryside. A bombing raid on Tokyo in March 1945 killed 85,000 people and incinerated almost sixteen square miles of the city. Japanese morale plummeted as fast as industrial production. Japan's diplomatic situation was just as dire. Germany had capitulated the previous spring, freeing up substantial U.S. and British resources for redeployment to the Pacific. Moreover, the Soviet Union was preparing to enter the war and attack Japanese forces in Manchuria. Many Japanese policymakers recognized defeat but were willing to submit only if the Allies guaranteed the emperor's preservation. Their effort to open negotiations on this basis ran aground on the Allied demand for unconditional surrender.

Although some American military planners believed that U.S. air and naval power would compel Japan's capitulation without a bloody invasion, most thought that one would be necessary. The Joint Chiefs of Staff reorganized the Pacific War's command structure in preparation for this eventuality. It put naval assets under Nimitz's control and gave MacArthur authority over ground forces, which of course included the Marines. Operation Downfall was the codename selected for the climactic assault on the Japanese Home Islands. It consisted of two parts. The first, Operation Olympic, called for Gen. Walter Krueger's Sixth Army to assail the southern Japanese island of Kyushu in November 1945. The V Amphibious Corps (2nd Marine Division, 3rd Marine Division, and 5th Marine Division) would be the Marines' contribution to Olympic. The second component was Operation Coronet. For this campaign, MacArthur assigned Gen. Courtney Hodges' First Army and Gen. Robert Eichelberger's Eighth Army the task of landing on the main Japanese island of Honshu near Tokyo in March 1946. MacArthur expected the Marines to provide their III Amphibious Corps (1st Marine Division, 4th Marine Division, and 6th Marine Division). The Marine Corps, however, had a problem: It did not have the personnel to fulfill its role in Downfall. To be sure, on 30 June 1945, it had 476,709 leathernecks, but that was not enough to fill and support six combat divisions. Even before Iwo Jima and Okinawa, the Corps had been scraping the bottom of its manpower barrel, and those engagements cost it 40,000 casualties. It is quite possible that it would have been necessary to cannibalize one of the divisions to bring the remainder up to snuff for Downfall.[55]

Before the Okinawa campaign ended, Vandegrift had begun reorganizing the Marine Corps' command structure in the Pacific to prepare for Downfall. He started at the very top. Gen. Holland Smith had been the Pacific's Fleet Marine Force commander since July 1944. During an inspection trip to the Pacific in April 1945, Vandegrift had stopped at Pearl Harbor to see Smith and found him tired, bitter, and overwrought. Smith complained that Nimitz in particular was needling him and denigrating the Marines' contribution to the Pacific War. This accusation seemed odd because it contradicted Nimitz's genial and gracious reputation. The more Vandegrift thought about it, the more convinced he became that it was time to bring Smith home. After all, he had been in the Pacific for two years, during which time he had had much responsibility and little rest. No longer a young man, Smith's health was uncertain. Moreover, he had alienated enough people to call into question his ability to do his job well. Neither King nor Nimitz objected to the idea. Vandegrift said to Smith, "I think you'd better come home for a little rest." Surprisingly, Smith did not put up much of a fight. Indeed, he seemed resigned to his fate and ready for a less strenuous job. Vandegrift assigned him to San Diego to take over the Marine Training and Replacement Command.[56]

On 5 July, Smith arrived at San Francisco's Hamilton Airfield from Pearl Harbor on board a B-24 Liberator bomber after a twelve-hour flight across the Pacific. He inhaled the cool, moist air and compared it favorably to Hawaii's blistering heat. Smith knew that his active role in the Pacific War was over, but he accepted his transfer with uncharacteristic acquiescence and grace. No Marine general had played a longer or more important part in the conflict than Smith. The operations in the Gilberts, Marshalls, and Marianas all bore his imprint. He took pride in his actions and felt that he had done his duty. Even so, the war had been frustrating for him because, except for Saipan, he never had the opportunity to actually direct troops in battle. He spent most of his time as a trainer, organizer, and planner—crucial jobs that he did well, but not exactly what he had sought. Ironically, the man who greeted him at Hamilton Airfield was another disgruntled Marine general whose Pacific War ambitions had not panned out: Julian Smith.[57]

Finding a new Fleet Marine Force chief was not difficult. Vandegrift gave the job to Geiger, the obvious choice. Geiger had an exemplary, though not perfect, combat leadership record. He had run the air war on Guadalcanal and then commanded the III Amphibious Corps at Guam, Peleliu, and Okinawa. Although his hands-off approach probably prolonged the Peleliu operation, Vandegrift was unaware of the difficulties this caused. In addition to Geiger's proven combat and administrative experience, Vandegrift also hoped that his taciturn and phlegmatic personality would bring more interservice harmony to the Pacific War than the tempestuous Holland Smith had been able to provide. Geiger's only competition for the post had been Harry Schmidt, who had led the V Amphibious Corps at Tinian and Iwo Jima. Schmidt, however, possessed neither Geiger's seniority nor his close personal relationship with the commandant. King and Nimitz approved of Geiger's selection, and Geiger was pleased with his promotion, though sorry to leave his III Amphibious Corps. Geiger's regrets deepened when he realized that his new job would mostly be administrative. He soon grew restless operating out of a Pearl Harbor office far from the impending action. That aside, his health was deteriorating. One officer noticed that he had stopped smoking his dozen fine cigars a day. Geiger claimed that he did so because his habit had become too expensive, but in all likelihood he was starting to suffer from the lung cancer that would kill him less than two years after the war ended.[58]

Geiger's ascension to run Fleet Marine Force opened a slot at the head of the III Amphibious Corps. Fortunately for Vandegrift, there were several capable division leaders eligible for the job, including del Valle, Watson, Erskine, Cates, and Shepherd. It was therefore surprising that Vandegrift gave the post to the 5th Marine Division's Rockey, who had not been overseas as long as his colleagues and had seen less combat than they had. Although Rockey's one operation, at Iwo Jima, was a baptism by total immersion, Vandegrift had concluded that Erskine and Cates had fought better. Nonetheless, Rockey had a few things going for him that convinced Vandegrift to elevate him over his more experienced and talented competitors. For starters, he was senior to them, and seniority mattered to Vandegrift. Also, there is some evidence that Vandegrift believed that Rockey would make a better corps than division commander, even though corps commanders did less of the administrative work that Rockey had performed at HQMC. In addition, Vandegrift probably reckoned that Rockey was fresher than his more battle-weary divisional competitors, all of whom had been in the Pacific for quite some time. Whatever Vandegrift's reasoning, Rockey got the assignment and assumed his new post on 30 June. To replace him at the top of the 5th Marine Division, Vandegrift appointed a hard-bitten artillery general with plenty of Pacific War combat experience named Thomas "Gene" Bourke.[59]

Vandegrift also made a number of changes at the divisional level. He did so partly to bring overworked divisional commanders home for rest and important stateside jobs and partly to give worthy generals a shot at leading a division in combat before the war ended. Watson, for instance, had run the 2nd Marine Division since April 1944. He fought well at Saipan-Tinian but did not get the opportunity to play much of a role at Okinawa, much to his frustration. Vandegrift ordered him home to run HQMC's Personnel Division and assigned Gen. Leroy Hunt to replace him. Although Hunt and Vandegrift were close personal friends, Vandegrift had relieved Hunt as a regimental commander on Guadalcanal for inefficiency. Vandegrift wanted to give Hunt an opportunity to redeem himself, so in 1944 he had assigned Hunt as Watson's assistant division chief; in that capacity Hunt participated in mopping up operations in the Marianas. He did well enough there that Vandegrift thought he deserved a shot at the division's top spot. Hunt took over in June 1945.[60]

Vandegrift also ordered del Valle home to become the Corps' inspector general. Vandegrift did so not only because he wanted to give the assistant commandant, Gen. Dewitt Peck, the opportunity to run a division, but also because he believed del Valle would perform well at the newly created post. Holcomb agreed, writing tongue-in-cheek to Vandegrift that del Valle would do a good job because he had plenty of experience being investigated. Del Valle was surprised and shocked to learn of his transfer. He liked leading the 1st Marine Division and believed he had done well on Okinawa. He wondered whether his angry protests about Nimitz's decision to keep the 1st Marine Division on Okinawa to refit, instead of sending it to Hawaii, had prompted his relief. Geiger, though, assured del Valle that there was no subterfuge involved. Geiger told Vandegrift that del Valle could be hard to handle, but added that he had fought well. Even so, Peck assumed command of the division in August 1945.[61]

Vandegrift contemplated bringing Shepherd, head of the 6th Marine Division, home for two months. Shepherd had appeared tired during Vandegrift's trip to Okinawa, and Vandegrift did not want to wear him down to the bone. Vandegrift greatly valued Shepherd's abilities—referring to him as a "whaling good division commander"—and wanted to save him for the invasion of Japan. Geiger agreed, and assured Vandegrift that Shepherd would be ready for the next operation. He noted that because Shepherd took things seriously, worked hard, and was nursing his injured arm, he had appeared more exhausted than was actually the case. Shepherd liked the idea of seeing his family, but he did not want to leave his division. As things turned out, events soon overtook Shepherd's furlough and rendered moot Vandegrift's personnel plans for Downfall.[62]

Although Marine generals like Shepherd viewed Downfall as a career opportunity, almost no one relished the idea of assailing Japan. After all, if the Japanese were willing to fight so fiercely and effectively for tiny Pacific atolls and islands such as Tarawa and Iwo Jima, then their determination to defend their Home Islands would be fanatical. Invading Japan might not only cost tens of thousands of American lives, but could lead to the extinction of Japanese civilization. On 6 August, however, a B-29 Superfortress bomber flying out of a Tinian airfield dropped an atomic bomb on the Japanese city of Hiroshima, killing an estimated 70,000 people that day alone. Three days later, another B-29 subjected Nagasaki to the same treatment, resulting in an additional 40,000 Japanese deaths. The bombings, as well as the Soviet Union's entry into the conflict on 8 August, ultimately convinced the Japanese to surrender. With that, the Marine Corps' mission changed to occupying Japan and eastern China.

CONCLUSIONS

Iwo Jima and Okinawa were the two bloodiest Marine Corps battles of the Pacific War. Approximately 40,000 leathernecks were killed and wounded on the islands, enough personnel for nearly three combat divisions. Fortunately for the Marines, they could wage these campaigns with their best slate of corps and division leaders of the conflict. It included Schmidt (V Amphibious Corps), Erskine (3rd Marine Division), Cates (4th Marine Division), and Rockey (5th Marine Division) at Iwo Jima, and Geiger (III Amphibious Corps), del Valle (1st Marine Division), and Shepherd (6th Marine Division) at Okinawa. Both operations generated controversy. At Iwo Jima, people criticized the Navy's short preliminary bombardment and Turner and Holland Smith's failure to commit one of the regiments of the 3rd Marine Division to the battle. At Okinawa, many questioned Buckner's rejection of an amphibious assault behind Japanese lines. The Marine Corps' corps and division commanders at Iwo Jima and Okinawa were not, however, responsible for these decisions. Indeed, none of them made any major mistakes that affected the outcome of their engagements. They all fought professionally, persistently, and competently.

By this stage of the war, Vandegrift had plenty of combat-hardened officers from which to select his division and corps commanders. He chose them based on their previous combat records in the conflict and his personal knowledge of their characters and personalities. The ones who fought at Iwo Jima and Okinawa were almost all veterans whom Vandegrift knew fairly well. Geiger had led his corps at Guam and Peleliu; Schmidt saw a division through Roi-Namur and Saipan; and Cates, del Valle, and Shepherd had headed regiments in previous operations. Iwo Jima was Erskine's first opportunity to take men into battle, but he had served as Holland Smith's chief of staff, and therefore was thoroughly familiar with many of the Pacific War's challenges. Indeed, Rockey was the only rookie of the group, which undoubtedly contributed to the consensus that he had been the least effective division chief on Iwo Jima. With the possible exception of Rockey, it is hard to see how Vandegrift could have selected better Marines for these jobs.

CONCLUSION

Gaining and Losing Combat Command

The Marine Corps of World War II stands as a unique military organization. It was designed to undertake one specific and difficult military mission: amphibious warfare. Its officers spent their prewar years studying, organizing, and training for amphibious operations before getting the opportunity to put their theories into practice against the Japanese in the Pacific. Although Marines contributed to unsuccessful efforts to stop the initial Japanese onslaught during 1941–42 in the Philippines and on Wake Island, their main role in the conflict would be spearheading the U.S. counteroffensive up the Solomon Islands and across the Central Pacific. The Marines participated in twelve major and distinct engagements: Guadalcanal, Bougainville, Cape Gloucester, Tarawa, Roi-Namur, Eniwetok, Saipan, Tinian, Guam, Peleliu, Iwo Jima, and Okinawa. These battles differed in various ways: Sometimes the Marines fought side-by-side with the Army, but in other cases they operated alone. Some of the islands they assailed were large jungle-covered masses, others small, barren atolls. Japanese opposition on the beaches ranged from nonexistent to ferocious, and Marine casualties from moderate to heavy. Some of the confrontations lasted only days, some weeks, and others months. With the possible exception of the battle for Peleliu, however, there was one common denominator for all twelve operations: When the smoke cleared, the Marines emerged the victors.

Plenty of reasons account for the Marines successes during the U.S. counteroffensive across the Pacific. Some resulted from factors above and beyond the Marine Corps, such as U.S. economic power and the Navy's ability to isolate Japanese island garrisons by seizing control of the surrounding waters. Similarly, the Marines benefited from Japanese strategic and tactical blunders that often left their troops vulnerable and exposed to attack. Regardless, the Marine Corps still deserved credit for manufacturing its victories. Marine officers developed a flexible, thoughtful, and realistic amphibious doctrine and drafted solid and thorough plans that took full advantage of U.S. firepower and materiel. Marine weapons, tactics, and training were superior to those of the Japanese, and leathernecks almost always fought courageously. It is impossible to overlook the importance of Marine leadership at the corps and division levels. After all, a combat unit tends to be no better than the individual at the top. The officers who ran Marine divisions and corps were responsible for training and organizing their outfits, selecting their staff officers and subordinate commanders, and of course leading their men into battle. Without good leadership, the Marines would have never attained their superlative record in the Pacific War.

The Marine Corps consisted of almost a half million men and women during World War II, enabling it to field two corps and six divisions. It fell to the commandant to appoint the leaders of these units, but unfortunately, the pool from which to choose was rather shallow. In July 1941 the Marine Corps had only thirteen generals and seventy colonels. From this list the commandant had to choose not only division and corps chiefs, but also assign officers to fill high-level slots at HQMC, various Marine posts, Marine air, and so forth. During the Pacific War, sixteen men served overseas for a substantial amount of time as Marine corps and division commanders: Charles Barrett, Clifton Cates, Pedro del Valle, Graves Erskine, Roy Geiger, John Marston, Keller Rockey, William Rupertus, Harry Schmidt, Lemuel Shepherd, Holland Smith, Julian Smith, Allen Turnage, Archibald Vandegrift, Clayton Vogel, and Thomas Watson.

Both World War II commandants, Thomas Holcomb and Alexander Vandegrift, relied on similar criteria in choosing their corps and division commanders. The first and most important was personal connection. Although the small size of the prewar officer corps limited Holcomb's and Vandegrift's options, it also meant that both men knew almost every high-ranking officer personally or by reputation. They were familiar with their strengths and weaknesses, personalities, idiosyncrasies, histories, and character. This also provided Holcomb and Vandegrift insight beyond personnel files. Such knowledge, however, was sometimes a double-edged sword. On the one hand, it enabled them to make some astute appointments. For instance, on paper Roy Geiger was unqualified to run a corps. He had plenty of military education, but no practical experience leading troops in ground combat. Geiger was first and foremost an airman. Both Holcomb and Vandegrift knew Geiger well enough to recognize that his abilities transcended air power and that made them comfortable selecting him to direct a corps. Geiger justified their confidence by ably leading his corps from Guam to Okinawa. On the other hand, familiarity sometimes blinded Holcomb and Vandegrift to an officer's true mettle. In the most obvious case, Vandegrift's unrealistically high opinion of his friend Rupertus contributed to the 1st Marine Division's difficulties on Peleliu. On the whole, however, personal knowledge of the officer corps played a large and mostly beneficial role in almost every important personnel decision Holcomb and Vandegrift made during the conflict.

Both Holcomb and Vandegrift took into account an officer's age and health when selecting their corps and division chiefs. As far as they were concerned, the two were interrelated; younger officers were more likely to be physically fit than older ones. Both commandants wanted comparatively youthful and virile men—meaning officers in their fifties—leading these large and important outfits. Linking health and age put senior officers at a disadvantage in the quest for combat posts. Holcomb, for example, refused to consider Marine officers over sixty-four years of age for active duty. Thus, of the thirteen Marine Corps major generals and brigadier generals in mid-1941, only five—Marston, Holland Smith, Julian Smith, Vandegrift, and Vogel—took combat units overseas. In Holcomb and Vandegrift's eyes, the remaining officers were too old or otherwise unqualified for such strenuous and important combat posts. At the war's start, all the Corps' division and corps commanders were under sixty, with their average age around fifty-three. Holland Smith and Barney Vogel were, at fifty-nine, the oldest, and forty-four-year-old Erskine the youngest. In addition to age, Holcomb's and Vandegrift's ongoing interest in the health of Geiger, Rupertus, Shepherd, Holland Smith, and Julian Smith showed that they paid close attention to this factor.

Holcomb and Vandegrift examined an officer's combat leadership record when selecting division and corps leaders to take troops into battle. Before the Marines began fighting in the Pacific, however, this did not impact Holcomb's appointments. Rather, he had had other reasons for choosing Barrett, Marston, Holland Smith, Julian Smith, Turnage, Vandegrift, and Vogel. As the conflict progressed, though, those who had led lower-level units into action earlier in the war had a better chance of rising to run divisions and corps than those who had not. In particular, officers who served under and impressed Vandegrift on Guadalcanal secured an edge over all others, causing some to identify a Guadalcanal Gang, which gained so much power and influence that its members ran the postwar Corps. Geiger, Cates, Rupertus, and del Valle owed their ascent to division and corps command at least in part to their time under Vandegrift at Guadalcanal. Shepherd and Watson could also thank their elevations to lead divisions to previous combat leadership experience at the head of regiments and brigades. Among the exceptions, Schmidt and Rockey took over divisions without putting in time at the regimental level. They did so because the commandant—Holcomb in Schmidt's case and Vandegrift in Rockey's—based their assignments on other criteria. As for Erskine, he had impressed Holland Smith and Vandegrift with his performance as Smith's chief of staff. The small size of the prewar Marine Corps' officer corps meant that many Marine officers ran regiments, but for the few who reached the next rung of the ladder, overseeing a regiment was usually a ticket that they needed to punch.

On the other hand, there were some factors that Holcomb and Vandegrift might have used as criterion in appointing their division and corps commanders but did not. One was an officer's socioeconomic background. The Corps' institutionalized racism and sexism limited the officer corps to white males, but within that particular group there was no discrimination based on an officer's class, education, and birthplace before entering the

Marine Corps. As far as most officers were concerned, the Corps' mono-chromatic and all-encompassing institutional culture erased those sorts of distinctions. The best example of this was Pedro del Valle, born and raised in Puerto Rico. Del Valle's Hispanic ethnicity did not prevent Vandegrift from selecting him as 1st Marine Division commander. There was also no career penalty for the means by which someone attained a Marine Corps commission. Geiger and Watson, for instance, started out as enlisted men before becoming officers, but Holcomb and Vandegrift did not care about that. What mattered was a man's performance after his commissioning.

No evidence exists that Holcomb or Vandegrift gave officers extra points for having served in France in World War I. To be sure, most of the Corps' World War II division and corps commanders saw action on the Western Front, but a large minority—Marston, Rupertus, Schmidt, Julian Smith, Turnage, and Vandegrift—did not. Those who did held a certain cachet within the Corps, but neither Holcomb nor Vandegrift let this unduly influence their personnel decisions. Besides, it would have been hypocrit-ical of Vandegrift to disqualify officers from leading divisions and corps because they lacked prewar combat leadership experience when he himself spent World War I in Haiti. The reality was that by World War II almost every long-serving Marine officer had come under fire at some point in his career—if not in France in World War I, then probably in Cuba, Nicaragua, Haiti, or the Dominican Republic.

During the Pacific War, sixteen officers ran the Corps' six divisions and two corps overseas for a significant amount of time, but only five of them—Cates, del Valle, Erskine, Rockey, and Shepherd—were still leading their outfits when the conflict ended. In short, eleven officers lost their com-mands for one reason or another. Moreover, most of them did not see much action at the head of their units. Barrett, Marston, and Vogel never got the opportunity to command in battle. Cates, del Valle, Erskine, Rockey, Shepherd, and Julian Smith participated in only one operation apiece. Of the remaining officers, four—Rupertus, Turnage, Vandegrift, and Watson—each took part in two engagements. Holland Smith oversaw, but did not command, in three battles, and Geiger and Schmidt partook in four apiece.

The high turnover rate might suggest that the commandants did a poor job of selecting top-level combat commanders, but a closer look provides some qualification. Of the eleven officers removed from their posts, three—Vandegrift, Holland Smith, and Geiger—were elevated to more prestigious and responsible positions as rewards for their performances on the battlefield. The Corps' small high-level officer corps, the episodic nature of the conflict, and the commandants' desire to rest their division and corps commanders meant that many officers were rotated home to assume important stateside positions. There they could relay their hard-won knowledge to others, relax with their families, and give eager colleagues their chance to lead big units in action. There was, in short, nothing dishonorable about it. Two of the remaining nine officers—del Valle and Watson—undoubtedly fit into this category. Rupertus and Turnage's cases were less clear. Although Rupertus certainly had trouble on Peleliu, Vandegrift did not know the full extent of those problems when he ordered him to run the Marine Corps Schools. As for Turnage, Vandegrift had doubts about him from the time he took over the 3rd Marine Division, but there is no evidence that these concerns motivated his decision to remove Turnage from his division.

Bringing officers back home for reassignment also provided a face-saving way of removing those from division and corps command who did not live up to expectations. Some of these men failed not on the battlefield, but beforehand, in planning, training, and coordinating their expeditions. These included Marston and Vogel. Holland Smith did a fine job organizing amphibious operations, but his inability to get along with others as time went on undermined his effectiveness and contributed to Vandegrift's decision to kick him upstairs to a stateside assignment. Vandegrift did not exactly sabotage Julian Smith's career, but instead appointed him to jobs further and further removed from combat leadership positions until Smith found himself serving stateside. Holcomb would no doubt have ordered Barrett home upon learning of Halsey's discontent with him, but Barrett's death precluded it.

MAKING THE GRADE

Evaluating the Marine Corps' division and corps commanders in the Pacific War is a thorny and subjective undertaking. Although the Marine Corps gained considerable renown in the conflict, its combat generals remain

✗ YOU SAID IT   SOME OF THIS BOOK IS
VERY GOOD — SOME NOT SO MUCH!

virtually unknown. Most World War II buffs remain far more familiar with Iwo Jima than with Schmidt's actions there. These Marines are not nearly as famous as Army generals—among them Dwight Eisenhower, Omar Bradley, George Patton, and Douglas MacArthur—or even naval leaders, such as Nimitz and Halsey. Several reasons account for their historical anonymity.

For one thing, the nature of the American counteroffensive across the Pacific made it difficult for Marine generals to distinguish themselves. In every Marine operation save Guadalcanal, the Navy first secured control of the seas around and skies above the targeted island before the leathernecks landed. From that point on, the isolated Japanese garrison could only decline in strength, being denied reinforcement or support. On the other hand, the assailing Marines benefited from overwhelming firepower, numbers, and materiel. For the Americans, absent a fit of astounding incompetence, success was all but guaranteed once the Marines came ashore. The only unanswered questions were how long it would take for the Marines to achieve their objective and how many casualties they would sustain in the process. This did not mean that victory came easily, but rather could largely be predicted. By this measurement, all the Marine Corps' division and corps leaders had to do was perform competently, a low bar not conducive to demonstrations of genius.

Military operations are extraordinarily complicated undertakings. This was particularly true in the Pacific War because assailing Japanese-held islands usually required intricate coordination among Army, Navy, and Marine officers. Getting the military pieces assembled properly, however, almost always guaranteed victory for the Americans because of their materiel and numerical superiority. The Marine Corps' contribution stood as merely one component in an enormous interservice military machine. The key was in the preparation. It required considerable skill for Marine generals to organize, equip, train, and plan the Corps' part of these operations. Such unglamorous, albeit vital, work, however, has not attracted attention or garnered glory. History, after all, remembers those who make their marks on the battlefield, not in the conferences beforehand. Holland Smith, for example, did a fine job preparing for the Gilbert, Marshall, and Mariana operations, but overcoming the bureaucratic and logistical obstacles he faced in the office is not as impressive as outmaneuvering the enemy in the field.

Marine division and corps commanders had few opportunities to demonstrate the kind of tactical proficiency that characterizes great combat generals. Most Marine battles occurred on islands whose small size and difficult terrain made it almost impossible to engage in the kind of grand maneuvers that brought fame to some of their Army counterparts in North Africa and Europe. There was, for example, no tactical finesse to the Marine victory at Tarawa. Instead, Marine generals usually had to rely on frontal assaults to achieve their objectives. To be sure, doing so required talent and determination. Marine generals trained and encouraged their leathernecks to overcome Japanese positions with tank-infantry cooperation, flamethrowers, demolitions, small units, and air and artillery support. These hard-won, nitty-gritty skills rarely brought Marine generals much acclaim, then or later. The devil may have been in the details, but fame and glory were not to be found.

In evaluating Marine Corps division and corps commanders, one must keep in mind that the playing field for them was by no means level or fair. Generals operated in environments and under conditions in which they often had little control, making it difficult to objectively assess their abilities. Bad geography, hydrography, and terrain sometimes hobbled able generals. Tarawa's horrific tides, for example, tarnished Julian Smith's record. On the other hand, Schmidt's, Watson's, and Cates' reputations benefited from fighting on Tinian's flat and open terrain. Marine generals were also dependent on the Navy, and later the Army, for their success or failure. Marine generals did not determine Pacific War strategy, so they often had little say about the targets that the Joint Chiefs of Staff and Navy selected. If the objective was weakly defended and the Navy or Army or both provided plenty of support, a Marine general could still do well. Geiger, for instance, profited from extensive naval support in seizing Guam. Conversely, the Navy's refusal to provide a sufficiently sustained preliminary bombardment at Iwo Jima might have made Schmidt's, Erskine's, Cates', and Rockey's tasks more difficult.

Marine generals could also do little about the quality of the opposition. Ineffective Japanese opposition on Roi-Namur made Schmidt look good, but ferocious Japanese resistance at Peleliu undermined Rupertus' reputation. Leadership mattered as well. A poor corps commander could interfere with a division chief's efforts to do his job, whereas good leadership at the corps level made running a division easier. Certainly Geiger's actions at Okinawa

contributed to the good work del Valle and Shepherd did there. These limitations do not excuse a general's poor performance—after all, good generalship means overcoming difficulties—but rather help explain them.

Six Marine generals led corps overseas in World War II: Barrett, Geiger,
Schmidt, Holland Smith, Vandegrift, and Vogel. Of these men, Geiger was
probably the most capable. He participated in more successful operations—
Bougainville, Guam, Peleliu, and Okinawa—at that level than any other corps
commander in the Marines. Superiors, staffers, subordinates, and Army and
Navy officers all praised his leadership abilities. Of course, he was not perfect. On Peleliu, for instance, he failed to oversee Rupertus effectively, thus
prolonging that miserable battle. Even so, he repeatedly demonstrated a thorough knowledge of logistics, combined arms, organization, and planning.
He got along well with almost everyone, despite his distant and somewhat
forbidding personality. He was personally courageous even by Marine standards. Although the usual geographic constrictions limited his opportunities
to display much tactical prowess, he consistently fought aggressively, unre-
mittingly, and intelligently. Geiger's performance on Guam highlighted all
his best qualities, which were largely responsible for the Americans' victory
there. It is ironic that the most proficient and successful high-level Marine
corps commander was not an infantryman or artilleryman, but an airman.

Holland Smith was a fine general up to the point that his humanity got
the better of him. His expressive and sensitive nature constituted both a
strength and weakness. On the one hand, his grasp of logistics, organization,
training, and planning easily equaled Geiger's. His intelligence, explosive
temperament, self-confidence, and outspokenness enabled him to stand up
to Kelly Turner, protect Marine prerogatives, cut through red tape, and get
to the heart of matters. These qualities played no small role in U.S. victory
in the Gilberts, Marshalls, and Marianas. On the other hand, his emotion-
alism and tactlessness eventually metastasized into a self-pity, alienation, and
paranoia that ruined his career.

Saipan had been Smith's first opportunity to lead the V Amphibious
Corps in action. There, his inexperience and prejudice contributed to his
misunderstanding and mishandling the Army's 27th Division. Although
Smith's decision to relieve the 27th Division commander, Ralph Smith,
probably had little impact on the battle's outcome, it poisoned Army-Marine

relations and hurt Smith's standing in the Pacific Ocean Area. When Army and Navy leaders showed more interest in putting the ensuing controversy behind them instead of assessing blame, Smith concluded that the higher-ups were persecuting him. His growing mistrust of Nimitz and others led Vandegrift to question his fitness for his job. Vandegrift eventually kicked Smith upstairs to Fleet Marine Force commander and later transferred him out of the Pacific.

Schmidt succeeded Holland Smith as V Amphibious Corps commander. His record, while not as distinguished as Smith's or Geiger's, was an honorable one that befitted his competent, conventional, and staid personality. He benefited enormously from inheriting the well-oiled amphibious machine that Smith had built, leading the corps through Tinian and Iwo Jima. Schmidt recognized the advantages of landing on Tinian's poorly defended northwestern coast, a move that proved to be the key to the Marines' quick and comparatively inexpensive victory there. He also deserved praise for organizing and planning the ground portion of the Iwo Jima operation. Iwo Jima turned out to be the Marine Corps' costliest Pacific War battle, but Schmidt had little say in some of the decisions that contributed to the bloodletting, such as the Navy's truncated preliminary bombardment, Holland Smith's refusal to commit the 3rd Marine Division's last regiment, and the decision to assail such a well-defended island in the first place. There was nothing brilliant about Schmidt's performance on Iwo Jima, but his steady hand helped the leathernecks overcome the determined Japanese opposition.

Vandegrift served two short stints as head of the I Amphibious Corps in between his more celebrated roles as 1st Marine Division commander and commandant. He replaced Vogel from July to September 1943 and a couple of weeks later, returned for a month after Barrett's death. Neither tenure included the kind of heavy combat Geiger, Holland Smith, and Schmidt saw while leading their corps, but Vandegrift nonetheless did a fine job. During his first assignment running the corps, he cleaned up much of the administrative and organizational mess that Vogel had left behind. In doing so, he restored the Navy's confidence in the Marine Corps' ability to wage war in the South Pacific. If it had not been for Vandegrift's efforts, the Army and Navy might have relegated the Marine Corps to the sideline of the Pacific War. During Vandegrift's second round at corps command, he got the Bougainville operation back on track and then led the amphibious assault on the island. Although he left the beachhead after only a day, his quiet competence did much to make the operation run as smoothly as it did. His actions at the head of the I Amphibious Corps were unglamorous and pedestrian, but still confirmed Holcomb's wisdom in selecting Vandegrift to succeed him as commandant.

Geiger, Schmidt, Holland Smith, and Vandegrift were on the whole successful corps commanders. The same cannot be said of Barrett and Vogel. They did not fail on the battlefield, but instead proved themselves unable to master the mundane yet vitally difficult tasks of organization, management, and planning. For Vogel the consensus was that Holcomb had given him a job beyond his limited intellectual abilities. Running the I Amphibious Corps was simply too much for him. Barrett was a more impressive man, but the awesome responsibility of leading troops into a battle that would undoubtedly see some of them killed unnerved and paralyzed him. In the

Not true

end, Halsey manufactured the relief of both officers before they could cause more damage in the field.

Twelve officers led Marine Corps divisions overseas for prolonged periods during the conflict: Cates, del Valle, Erskine, Marston, Rockey, Rupertus, Schmidt, Shepherd, Julian Smith, Turnage, Vandegrift, and Watson. Because of the geographic and topographical limitations under which the Marines labored, few of them had much opportunity to distinguish themselves on the battlefield, so it is difficult to draw fine distinctions among them all. That said, most of them—Cates, del Valle, Erskine, Rockey, Schmidt, Shepherd, Turnage, and Watson—proved to be fine and capable division commanders. None of these eight officers made mistakes serious enough to jeopardize victory in the operations in which they participated at the head of their divisions. Instead, they all fought professionally, tenaciously, and aggressively. Although some in the Marines attempted to rate them, such assessments tended to be too subjective to be of much value. For example, Vandegrift and Holland Smith's high opinion of Erskine's abilities was based at least in part on their personal fondness for the man. The fact is that two-thirds of the Marine Corps' division leaders demonstrated sufficient skill to win their engagements in a timely manner.

The records of three of the four remaining division commanders—Marston, Rupertus, and Julian Smith—are problematic. Like Barrett and Vogel at the corps level, Marston was relieved before he got the opportunity to lead his outfit in combat. Marston's inability to successfully manage the 2nd Marine Division was probably exacerbated by his struggle with malaria. Whatever the source of Marston's ineffectiveness, Holcomb opted to bring him home. Rupertus performed satisfactorily at the head of the 1st Marine Division at Cape Gloucester, but at Peleliu his inadequate generalship undoubtedly prolonged that wretched battle. On Peleliu Rupertus' mercurial personality, hatred of the Army, inability to get around and see his *NOT* leathernecks, and use of unimaginative tactics did little to serve the Ameri- *TRUE* cans' cause. Julian Smith did as well as could be expected in organizing and planning the 2nd Marine Division's assault on Tarawa. Once the fighting began, however, poor communications prevented him from exerting much authority over his men. It is not uncommon for generals to lose control of most elements of an engagement after the first shots are fired, but this truism was particularly striking in Smith's case. Smith would in all likelihood have been a satisfactory combat general, but he never had the chance to prove himself because Vandegrift transferred him to an administrative post.

Vandegrift's case was unique among the Corps' World War II division commanders because he led the 1st Marine Division on Guadalcanal, a campaign much different from the eleven other major Marine Corps operations in the Pacific War. On Guadalcanal the Americans were untested in amphibious assaults, initially had inadequate resources, failed to quickly secure air and naval supremacy, faced significant logistical difficulties, fought mostly on the defensive, and confronted a formidable foe who still possessed operational mobility. There was, in short, nothing certain or inevitable about the outcome. Although Vandegrift did not see the campaign through to the end, he was still key to the U.S. victory. He organized and planned the invasion despite a short timetable, limited supplies, and insufficient intelligence. Once ashore, he recognized that Guadalcanal's airfield was more important than occupying the rest of the island and deployed his leathernecks accordingly. Remaining on the defensive enabled him to repel several piecemeal and poorly coordinated Japanese counterattacks. Vandegrift's serenity and quiet competence under the desperate circumstances on the island were to his credit, but he still made mistakes. His efforts to assume the offensive proved to be only marginally successful, demonstrating that assailing the Japanese required more skill than fighting them from behind prepared positions. It also took him longer than it should have to purge his division of underachieving high-ranking officers. Even so, his performance on Guadalcanal justified Holcomb's confidence in him and paved the way for his ascension to commandant.

Nope! .

THE UPSHOT

The Marine Corps played a major part in the Pacific War against Japan. Marines fought in the South Pacific, spearheaded the Navy's Central Pacific offensive, and helped seize the islands necessary for the final assault on Japan. In the process, the Corps proved itself by winning the significant battles for Guadalcanal, Tarawa, and especially Iwo Jima. Unfortunately, the Army and Navy's strategic acumen did not always match Marine valor. Of the Marine Corps' twelve major amphibious assaults, a third of them—Tarawa, Cape Gloucester, Peleliu, and Iwo Jima—were of questionable strategic value and not worth the high price the Marines paid for them. Even so, most Marine generals accepted their sometimes-dubious assignments with little complaint, often with good reasons driving their stoicism.

For one thing, the Marines had limited representation on the councils that determined Pacific War strategy, so by the time Marine generals saw their objectives, it was often too late to change them. Besides, Marines were accustomed to obeying orders, not questioning them. This can-do attitude extended to the very top of the Corps' hierarchy. Vandegrift, for instance, deeply regretted Marine casualties at Tarawa and elsewhere, but saw them as the price to be paid in a total war, not as evidence of the Navy's strategic mismanagement. Marine generals, sensitive to charges of institutional superfluousness, were eager to demonstrate their usefulness to the rest of the military establishment, Congress, and the public. Balking at their missions might cast doubt on the need for a Marine Corps. When Vogel questioned the New Georgia operation, for example, a disgusted Halsey turned to the Army and left the Corps on the sideline until Vandegrift restored Navy confidence in the Corps. As a result of these concerns, thousands of

Marines were killed and wounded not only to further the war effort, but also to demonstrate the Corps' relevance.

There was nothing preordained about the war's outcome and the Marine Corps' role in it. At the conflict's start, the Corps possessed an untested amphibious doctrine, an uncertain relationship with the Army, and limited resources. To demonstrate its relevance to national security, the Marines had to prove their outfit capable of conducting the amphibious operations that provided its raison d'être. Its commandants also had to identify high-level commanders to run the large combat units deployed overseas. If the initial amphibious assaults had failed, the Joint Chiefs of Staff might well have sidelined the Corps and given the Army the task of leading the offensive through the Southwest Pacific to Japan. The Marines could have ended up spending the conflict as a tiny organization providing shipboard security, guarding Navy bases, and undertaking reconnaissance missions. Fortunately for the Marines, their equipment, doctrine, tactics, and especially commanders proved the Corps' ability to successfully storm hostile beaches. Holcomb and Vandegrift deserve credit for finding enough good combat commanders among their limited pool of high-ranking officers to lead their divisions and corps to victory. In doing so, these generals not only helped to win the Pacific War, but also secured for the Marine Corps a prominent postwar role in the U.S. military.

ONE OF THE MAJOR PROBLEMS WITH THIS BOOK IS CHErrY PICKING — LOOK AT THE Bibliography/NOTES

Notes

INTRODUCTION

1. Stephen R. Taaffe, *Marshall and His Generals: U.S. Army Commanders in World War II* (Lawrence: University Press of Kansas, 2011), 11.

CHAPTER ONE. SEMPER FI

1. Earl Ellis, "Advanced Base Force Operations in Micronesia," https://www.ibiblio.org/hyperwar/USMC/ref/AdvBaseOps/Advanced-2.html, 41.
2. Quoted in Jeter A. Isely and Philip A. Crowl, *The U.S. Marines and Amphibious War: Its Theory, and Its Practice in the Pacific* (Princeton, New Jersey: Princeton University Press, 1951), 19–20.
3. Archibald Vandegrift, as told to Robert B. Asprey, *Once a Marine: The Memoirs of General A. A. Vandegrift* (New York: W. W. Norton & Company, 1964), 93.
4. See John L'Estrange, in Henry Berry, *Semper Fi, Mac: Living Memories of the U.S. Marines in World War II* (New York: Quill, 1982), 166.
5. William Hawkins, in Berry, *Semper Fi*, 39–40.
6. Vandegrift, *Once a Marine*, 93. See also Gerald Thomas, interview by Benis Frank, 1966, Marine Corps Historical Division, Marine Corps University, 49; Julian Smith, interview by Benis Frank, 1973, Marine Corps Historical Division, Marine Corps University, 166.
7. Thomas, interview, 49; Frederick Henderson, interview by Benis Frank, 1976, Marine Corps Historical Division, Marine Corps University, 16–17, 25, 181; Dewitt Peck, interview by Benis Frank, 1967, Marine Corps Historical Division, Marine Corps University, 55; Francis Mulcahy, interview by Benis Frank, 1967, Marine Corps Historical Division, Marine Corps University, 82; Henry Buse Jr., interview by Benis Frank, 1986, Marine Corps Historical Division, Marine Corps University, 65; Graves Erskine, interview by Benis Frank, 1975, Marine Corps Historical Division, Marine Corps University, 115; Pedro del Valle, *Semper Fidelis: An Autobiography* (Hawthorne, California: Christian Book Club of America, 1976), 110; Robert Hugh Williams, *The Old Corps: A Portrait of the U.S. Marines between the Wars* (Annapolis, Maryland: Naval Institute Press, 1982), 115.
8. Henderson, interview, 29.

9. Victor Krulak, interview by Benis Frank, 1973, Marine Corps Historical Division, Marine Corps University, 48; Thomas, interview, 44, 94; Henderson, interview, 181; Buse, interview, 18, 24; Erskine, interview, 116–17, 120–21; Robert Luckey, interview by Benis Frank, 1973, Marine Corps Historical Division, Marine Corps University, 13; Edwin Pollock, interview by Thomas Donnelly, 1977, Marine Corps Historical Division, Marine Corps University, 100; Roy Robinson, interview by Benis Frank, 1973, Marine Corps Historical Division, Marine Corps University, 57.

10. Erskine, interview, 121.

11. Thomas, interview, 94; Henderson, interview, 16–17, 25, 181; Mulcahy, interview, 82; Norman V. Cooper, *A Fighting General: The Biography of Gen Holland M. "Howlin' Mad" Smith* (Quantico, Virginia: Marine Corps Association, 1987), 88; Erskine, interview, 119.

12. Erskine, interview, 18.

13. Keller Rockey to Jeter Isely, 17 March 1950, Harry Schmidt Papers, Hoover Institution Archives, box 1, folder 3. See also Vandegrift, *Once a Marine*, 87–91; Oliver Smith, interview by Benis Frank, 1973, Marine Corps Historical Division, Marine Corps University, 79–80; Thomas, interview, 160; Vernon Megee, interview by Benis Frank, 1973, Marine Corps Historical Division, Marine Corps University, session 3, 234; Julian Smith, interview, 178, 180; Louis Jones, interview by Thomas Donnelly, 1973, Marine Corps Historical Division, Marine Corps University, 9; Erskine, interview, 128; Robert Williams, interview by Benis Frank, 1983, Marine Corps Historical Division, Marine Corps University, 65–66; William Worton, interview by Benis Frank, 1973, Marine Corps Historical Division, Marine Corps University, 57, 67; Williams, *Old Corps*, 114.

14. Thomas, interview, 201, 204; Merrill Twining, interview by Benis Frank, 1967, Marine Corps Historical Division, Marine Corps University, 85–87, 203; Frederick Roy, interview by Benis Frank, 1976, Marine Corps Historical Division, Marine Corps University, 30–31; Omar Pfeiffer, interview by L. E. Tatem, 1974, Marine Corps Historical Division, Marine Corps University, 193–94, 241–43; Austin Brunelli, interview by Norman Anderson, 1984, Marine Corps Historical Division, Marine Corps University, 37; Harold Deakin, interview by Benis Frank, 1988, Marine Corps Historical Division, Marine Corps University, 34.

15. Vandegrift, *Once a Marine*, 87–91; Thomas, interview, 192–93; Thomas Holcomb to Archibald Vandegrift, 15 December 1942 and 18 August 1943, Archibald Vandegrift Papers, Marine Corps Historical Division, Marine Corps University, box 2; Holcomb to George Marshall, 7 August 1942, Thomas Holcomb Papers, box 5; Gerald Thomas, unpublished memoirs (chap. 2), Gerald Thomas Papers, Marine Corps Historical Division, Marine Corps University, box 2, 12–13.

16. Holcomb to Holland Smith, 22 October 1943, Holcomb Papers, box 2.

CHAPTER TWO. WAGING WAR IN THE MOST REMOTE PLACE ON EARTH

1. Alfred Noble, interview by L. E. Tatem, 1968, Marine Corps Historical Division, Marine Corps University, 76; Peck, interview, 42–43; Richmond Kelly Turner to Schmidt, 29 March 1949, Schmidt Papers, box 1, folder 3.

2. Vandegrift, *Once a Marine*, 119; Twining, interview, 178–79, 180–81, 184, 190, 219–20; Julian Smith, interview, 170; Robert Blake, interview by Benis Frank, 1968, Marine Corps Historical Division, Marine Corps University, 84; Buse, interview, 48; Lewis Fields, interview by Thomas Donnelly, 1976, Marine Corps Historical Division, Marine Corps University, 147; Joseph Burger, interview by Benis Frank, 1969, Marine Corps Historical Division, Marine Corps University, 158–59; John Masters, interview by Thomas Donnelly, 1977, Marine Corps Historical Division, Marine Corps University, 65–68; Merrill Twining, *No Bended Knee: The Battle of Guadalcanal*, ed. Neil G. Carey (New York: Ballantine Books, 1996), 53, 146.

3. Twining, interview, 190; Erskine, interview, 216; Holcomb to Vandegrift, 21 August 1940, Holcomb Papers, box 1; Holcomb to Vandegrift, 14 August 1942, Holcomb Papers, box 2; Holcomb to Philip Torrey, 4 October 1941, Holcomb Papers, box 1; Holcomb to John Marston, 22 November 1941, Holcomb Papers, box 4; Holcomb memo, n.d., Holcomb Papers, box 6.

4. Vandegrift, *Once a Marine*, 18–19, 104–5, 110; Thomas, interview, 98; Twining, interview, 131–32, 176–77, 209; Robert Kilmartin, interview by Benis Frank, 1979, Marine Corps Historical Division, Marine Corps University, 273; Fletcher Pratt, *The Marines' War: An Account of the Struggle for the Pacific from Both American and Japanese Sources* (New York: William Sloane Associates, 1948), 8–9; Thomas, unpublished memoirs (chap. 1), Thomas Papers, box 2, 7–8.

5. Vandegrift, *Once a Marine*, 153.

6. Vandegrift, 119, 153; Pfeiffer, interview, 163–64; Twining, interview, 165, 178–79, 204; Erskine, interview, 183; Robert Sherrod, *On to Westward: War in the Central Pacific* (New York: Duell, Sloan and Pearce, 1945), 247–50, 255; George Carroll Dyer, *The Amphibians Came to Conquer: The Story of Admiral Richmond Kelly Turner*, vol. 1 (Washington, D.C.: Department of the Navy, 1972), 410, 453–54, 592–94; Dyer, *The Amphibians Came to Conquer*, vol. 2, 853–54, 1160–61; George van Deurs, *The Reminiscences of Rear Admiral George van Deurs* (Annapolis, Maryland: U.S. Naval Institute Press, 1974), 509–11; Robert Hogaboom, interview, Holcomb Papers, box 23, 181–82.

7. Vandegrift, *Once a Marine*, 120; Thomas, interview, 103; Twining, interview, 180–81, 184–85; Dyer, *The Amphibians Came to Conquer*, vol. 1, 299–302.

8. Vandegrift, *Once a Marine*, 18–19. See also Thomas, unpublished memoirs (chap. 1), Thomas Papers, box 2, 15.

9. Thomas, interview, 109; Twining, interview, 206; Robert Tregaskis, *Guadalcanal Diary* (Open Road Media, 2016), 78–80.

10. Vandegrift, *Once a Marine*, 125, 131; Thomas, interview, 110, 116; Twining, interview, 217; Twining, *No Bended Knee*, 70; Dyer, *The Amphibians Came to Conquer*, vol. 1, 337.

11. Vandegrift, *Once a Marine*, 231; Thomas, unpublished memoirs (chap. 1), Thomas Papers, box 2, 23.

12. Vandegrift, *Once a Marine*, 130, 132, 135, 139; Clifton Cates, interview by Benis Frank, 1973, Marine Corps Historical Division, Marine Corps University, 141; Twining, *No Bended Knee*, 198.

13. Vandegrift, *Once a Marine*, 182–83; Pfeiffer, interview, 203–4; Twining, interview, 205–6; Twining, *No Bended Knee*, 142; Dyer, *The Amphibians Came to Conquer*, vol. 1, 455–56; Thomas, unpublished memoirs (chap. 1), Thomas Papers, box 2, 44, 46, 55, 66.

14. Vandegrift, *Once a Marine*, 149.

15. James B. Wellons, "General Roy S. Geiger, USMC: Marine Aviator, Joint Force Commander" (master's thesis, School of Advanced Air and Space Studies, Maxwell Air Force Base, 2007), 13.

16. Roger Willock, *Unaccustomed to Fear: A Biography of the Late General Roy S. Geiger, U.S.M.C.* (Princeton, New Jersey: Roger Willock, 1968), xxiv.

17. Simon Buckner, 13 March 1945, Nicholas E. Sarantakes, ed., *Seven Stars: The Okinawa Battle Diaries of Simon Bolivar Buckner, Jr., and Joseph Stilwell* (College Station: Texas A&M Press, 2004), 21.

18. Wellons, "General Roy S. Geiger," 151. For information on Geiger, see Vandegrift, *Once a Marine*, 149; Willock, *Unaccustomed to Fear*, xiii–xiv, xvii–xx, 242–43, 257–58; Holland M. Smith and Percy Finch, *Coral and Brass* (New York: Charles Scribner's Sons, 1948), 155; Thomas, interview, 136; Merwin Silverthorn, interview by Benis Frank, 1973, Marine Corps Historical Division, Marine Corps University, 302–3, 327; Henderson, interview, 87, 111–12, 113–14; Pfeiffer, interview, 245, 265; Edward Snedeker, interview by L. E. Tatem, 1973, Marine Corps Historical Division, Marine Corps University, 65; Fields, interview, 126; Charles Hayes, interview by Benis Frank, 1970, Marine Corps Historical Division, Marine Corps University, 36–37; Russell Jordahl, interview by Benis Frank, 1970, Marine Corps Historical Division, Marine Corps University, 109–10, 123; Kilmartin, interview, 347–49, 350–51; John McQueen, interview by Benis Frank, 1973, Marine Corps Historical Division, Marine Corps University, 97; Buckner, 13 March 1945, Sarantakes, *Seven Stars*, 21; Henry A. Shaw, Jr., Bernard C. Nalty, and Edwin T. Tumbladh, *Central Pacific Drive: History of U.S. Marine Corps Operations in World War II*, vol. 3 (Washington, D.C.: Government Printing Office, 1966), 433n.

19. Vandegrift, *Once a Marine*, 163; Willock, *Unaccustomed to Fear*, 215–16; Wellons, "General Roy S. Geiger," 92; William F. Halsey and J. Bryan III, *Admiral Halsey's Story* (New York: McGraw-Hill Books, Company, 1947), 174–75; Thomas, interview, 132, 168; Twining, *No Bended Knee*, 129, 153; Vandegrift to Roy Geiger, 14 August 1945, Roy Geiger Papers, Marine Corps Historical Division, Marine Corps University, box 7; Thomas, unpublished memoirs (chap. 1), Thomas Papers, box 2, 71.

20. Kilmartin, interview, 241–43, 300; Thomas, interview, 109, 128, 141; Twining, interview, 131–32, 206, 211–12, 222; Blake, interview, 84; Pollock, interview, 150.

21. Vandegrift, *Once a Marine*, 161–62; Thomas, interview, 141; Twining, interview, 219–20; Buse, interview, 47–48; Vandegrift to W. G. Hawthorne, 19 September 1942, Vandegrift Papers, box 2; Vandegrift to Turner, 24 September 1942, Vandegrift Papers, box 2; Thomas, unpublished memoirs (chap. 1), Thomas Papers, box 2, 48–49.

22. Vandegrift, *Once a Marine*, 161–62; Thomas, interview, 103, 160; Megee, interview, 121; Twining, *No Bended Knee*, 154; Buse, interview, 83; Fields, interview, 73, 145;

Kilmartin, interview, 243–44; Joseph Crousen and Francis McGrath in Berry, *Semper Fi*, 27; Tregaskis, *Guadalcanal Diary*, 129; Vandegrift to Hawthorne, 19 September 1942, Vandegrift Papers, box 2; Holcomb to Vandegrift, 29 September 1942, Vandegrift Papers, box 2; Vandegrift letter, 13 August 1942, Vandegrift Papers, box 2, 14.

23. Halsey and Bryan, *Halsey's Story*, 117.

24. Halsey and Bryan, 117; Vandegrift, *Once a Marine*, 182–85; Thomas, interview, 159–60; Brunelli, interview, 27–28.

25. Thomas, interview, 160.

26. Thomas, unpublished memoirs (chap. 1), Thomas Papers, box 2, 63.

27. Megee, interview, 122; Thomas, unpublished memoirs (chap. 2), Thomas Papers, box 2, 4.

28. Vandegrift, *Once a Marine*, 183; Thomas, interview, 176; Jordahl, interview, 110; Holcomb to John Lejeune, 11 November 1942, Holcomb Papers, box 1; Holcomb to Vandegrift, 13 and 15 December 1942, Holcomb Papers, box 2; Holcomb to Holland Smith, 2 February 1943, Holcomb Papers, box 13.

29. Henderson, interview, 304–12; Frank O. Hough, Verle E. Ludwig, and Henry I. Shaw, Jr., *Pearl Harbor to Guadalcanal: History of U.S. Marine Corps Operations in World War Two*, vol. 1 (Washington, D.C.: Government Printing Office, 1958), 360n; Marston to Clyde Metcalf, 18 September 1943, Julian Smith Papers, Marine Corps Historical Division, Marine Corps University, box 16.

30. The quote is from Henderson, interview, 318. See also Holcomb to Vandegrift, 29 September 1942, Vandegrift Papers, box 2.

31. Lemuel Shepherd, interview by Benis Frank and Robert Heinl Jr., 1967, Marine Corps Historical Division, Marine Corps University, 39.

32. Twining, interview, 251. See also Thomas, interview, 94; Silverthorn, interview, 292; Noble, interview, 49; Shepherd, interview, 7, 10; Peck, interview, 8–9; Kilmartin, interview, 11; del Valle, *Semper Fidelis*, 15; John Seymour Letcher, *One Marine's Story* (Verona, Virginia: McClure Press, 1970), 218–19; Holcomb to Marston, 22 November 1941, Holcomb Papers, box 1, folder 58; Tom FitzPatrick, *A Character That Inspired: Major General Charles D. Barrett, USMC, Amphibious Warfare Pioneer* (Fairfax, Virginia: Tom FitzPatrick, 2003), 292, 293, 376.

33. FitzPatrick, *A Character That Inspired*, 374–75.

34. FitzPatrick, 376, 453; Holcomb to Vandegrift, 14 August 1942, Vandegrift Papers, box 2; Holcomb to Marston, 30 January 1942, Holcomb Papers, box 4; Holcomb to Harold Stark, 24 November 1940, Holcomb Papers, box 13.

35. Thomas, interview, 173; Henderson, interview, 336; Peck, interview, 14–15; Alan Shapley, interview by Thomas Donnelly, 1976, Marine Corps Historical Division, Marine Corps University, 72–73; Julian Smith, interview, 166; Holcomb to Clayton Vogel, 28 January and 13 April 1941, Holcomb Papers, box 1; Marston to Holcomb, 24 March 1942, Holcomb Papers, box 1; Holcomb to Vandegrift, 29 September 1942, Vandegrift Papers, box 2; Holcomb to Vandegrift, 13 December 1942, Vandegrift Papers, box 2.

36. Pfeiffer, interview, 226–28; Twining, interview, 248–49; Julian Smith, interview, 265, 272–73; Burger, interview, 129; Vandegrift to Holcomb, 16 July 1943, Vandegrift

Papers, box 2; Charles Price to Vandegrift, 27 April 1944, Vandegrift Papers, box 2; Dewitt Peck to Holcomb, 26 April 1943, Holcomb Papers, box 6; Holland Smith to Holcomb, 22 June 1943, Holcomb Papers, box 13.

37. Pfeiffer, interview, 226–28; Twining, interview, 248–49; Thomas, unpublished memoirs (chap. 2), Thomas Papers, box 2, 7.

38. Peck to Holcomb, 26 April 1943, Holcomb Papers, box 6. See also Twining, interview, 248–49; Holcomb to Vandegrift, 29 June 1943, Vandegrift Papers, box 2; Thomas, unpublished memoirs (chap. 2), Thomas Papers, box 2, 7.

39. Holcomb to William Halsey, 12 March 1943, Holcomb Papers, box 6.

40. Pfeiffer, interview, 232–33; Vandegrift to Holland Smith, 27 March 1944, Holland Smith Papers, Auburn University Libraries; Holcomb to Vandegrift, mid-April and 29 June 1943, Vandegrift Papers, box 2; Vandegrift to Holcomb, 1 April and 16 July 1943, Vandegrift Papers, box 2; Holcomb to Halsey, 12 March 1943, Holcomb Papers, box 6; Peck to Holcomb, 26 April 1943, Holcomb Papers, box 6; Holland Smith to Holcomb, 22 June 1943, Holcomb Papers, box 13.

41. Holcomb to Vandegrift, early April and 11, 13, 18, and 27 August 1943, Vandegrift Papers, box 2; Vandegrift to Holcomb, 16 July and 16 October 1943, Vandegrift Papers, box 2; Vandegrift to Julian Smith, 17 July 1943, Vandegrift Papers, box 2; Holcomb to Ernest King, 12 August 1943, Vandegrift Papers, box 6.

42. Vandegrift to Holcomb, 10 July 1943, Vandegrift Papers, box 2.

43. Henderson, interview, 337; Twining, *No Bended Knee*, 229; Holcomb to Vandegrift, 15 July 1943, Holcomb Papers, box 1; Peck to Holcomb, 26 April 1943, Holcomb Papers, box 6; Holcomb to Vandegrift, 17 and 29 July 1943, Vandegrift Papers, box 2; Vandegrift to Holcomb, 23 August 1943, Vandegrift Papers, box 2; Thomas, unpublished memoirs (chap. 2), Thomas Papers, box 2, 7, 9.

44. FitzPatrick, *A Character That Inspired*, 453.

45. FitzPatrick, 463; Vandegrift to William Rupertus, 26 July 1943, Vandegrift Papers, box 2; Holcomb to Vandegrift, 6 and 27 August 1943, Vandegrift Papers, box 2; Vandegrift to Holcomb, 18 August 1943, Vandegrift Papers, box 2; Peck to Holcomb, 26 April 1943, Holcomb Papers, box 6; Holcomb to Charles Barrett, 28 July 1943, Holcomb Papers, box 6; Holland Smith to Holcomb, 22 June 1943, Holcomb Papers, box 13.

46. Vandegrift to Holcomb, 16, 22, and 26 July 1943, Vandegrift Papers, box 2; Holcomb to Vandegrift, 29 July and 6 August 1943, Vandegrift Papers, box 2.

47. Vandegrift, *Once a Marine*, 220, 229; Raymond Murray, interview by Benis Frank, 1988, Marine Corps History Division, Marine Corps University, 97; Robert Cushman, interview by Benis Frank, 1984, Marine Corps Historical Division, Marine Corps University, 167; Buse, interview, 74; Jordahl, interview, 123; Kilmartin, interview, 135; Letcher, *One Marine's Story*, 294.

48. Henderson, interview, 337–40; Vandegrift to Holcomb, 26 July and 26 August 1943, Vandegrift Papers, box 2; Vandegrift to Rupertus, 26 July 1943, Vandegrift Papers, box 2; Twining, *No Bended Knee*, 234–36; FitzPatrick, *A Character That Inspired*, 515, 516–17.

49. Twining, *No Bended Knee*, 239.

50. Vandegrift, *Once a Marine*, 222; Noble, interview, 85; Twining, *No Bended Knee*, 234–36; Vandegrift to Holcomb, 14 October 1943, Vandegrift Papers, box 2.

51. Henderson, interview, 340; Twining, *No Bended Knee*, 234–36, 239; Vandegrift to Holcomb, 14 October 1943, Vandegrift Papers, box 2; Holcomb to Vandegrift, 22 October 1943, Vandegrift Papers, box 2.

52. Peck, interview, 9; FitzPatrick, *A Character That Inspired*, 503–5, 516–17, 523–24; D. L. Brewster to Holcomb, 10 October 1943, Holcomb Papers, box 6.

53. Holcomb to Harry Schmidt, 18 October 1943, Holcomb Papers, box 6.

54. Pfeiffer, interview, 244–45; Burger, interview, 137–38; Robinson, interview, 87; Fitz-Patrick, *A Character That Inspired*, 542; Vandegrift to Holcomb, 14 October 1943, Vandegrift Papers, box 2; Brewster to Holcomb, 10 October 1943, Holcomb Papers, box 6.

55. Vandegrift, *Once a Marine*, 227; Halsey and Bryan, *Halsey's Story*, 174–75; Thomas, interview, 183; Henderson, interview, 341; Noble, interview, 86; Vandegrift to Holcomb, 14 October 1943, Vandegrift Papers, box 2; Thomas unpublished memoirs (chap. 2), Thomas Papers, box 2, 12.

56. Holcomb to Schmidt, 18 October 1943, Holcomb Papers, box 6.

57. Vandegrift, *Once a Marine*, 227; Halsey and Bryan, *Halsey's Story*, 174–75; Thomas, interview, 187; Pfeiffer, interview, 244–45; Snedeker, interview, 66; Vandegrift to Geiger, 6 April 1943, Vandegrift Papers, box 2; Vandegrift to Holcomb, 22 July 1943, Vandegrift Papers, box 2; Holcomb to Vandegrift, 19 October 1943, Vandegrift Papers, box 2; Holcomb to Albert Fisher, 19 November 1943, Holcomb Papers, box 7; Holland Smith to Holcomb, 13 and 20 October 1943, Holcomb Papers, box 13.

58. George C. McMillan et al., *Uncommon Valor: Marine Divisions in Action* (Washington, D.C.: Infantry Journal Press, 1946), 89.

59. Vandegrift, *Once a Marine*, 229–30; Noble, interview, 86; Letcher, *One Marine's Story*, 253.

60. Snedeker, interview, 66.

61. Henry I. Shaw, Jr. and Douglas T. Kane, *Isolation of Rabaul: History of U.S. Marine Corps Operations in World War II*, vol. 2 (Washington, D.C.: Government Printing Office, 1963), 294.

62. Henderson, interview, 367.

63. Wellons, "General Roy S. Geiger," 113n; Oliver Smith, interview, 120; Henderson, interview, 367, 368; Buse, interview, 48, 60–62; Deakin, interview, 44–45, 47; Fields, interview, 128–29; James H. Hallas, *The Devil's Anvil: The Assault on Peleliu* (Westport, Connecticut: Praeger, 1994), 14.

64. Vandegrift, *Once a Marine*, 224; Holland Smith to Vandegrift, 19 December 1940, Vandegrift Papers, box 1; Vandegrift to W. L. Calhoun, 17 July 1943, Vandegrift Papers, box 2; Vandegrift to Rupertus, 17 July 1943, Vandegrift Papers, box 2; Vandegrift to Holcomb, 9 May and 18 August 1943, Vandegrift Papers, box 2; Vandegrift to Roy Hunt, 30 June 1943, Vandegrift Papers, box 2; Holcomb to Vandegrift, 22 October 1943, Vandegrift Papers, box 2.

65. Shepherd, interview, 164–65; Shaw and Kane, *Isolation of Rabaul*, 305; Vandegrift to Holcomb, 6 October 1943, Vandegrift Papers, box 2; Holcomb to Schmidt, 10 September 1943, Holcomb Papers, box 6.

66.   Quoted in Shaw and Kane, *Isolation of Rabaul*, 375.
67.   Fields, interview, 111–12.
68.   Shaw and Kane, *Isolation of Rabaul*, 370.
69.   The quote is from Buse, interview, 62. See also Oliver Smith, interview, 111–13; Deakin, interview, 42, 44–45; Geiger to Vandegrift, 25 March 1944, Vandegrift Papers, box 2.
70.   Shepherd, interview, 164–65.
71.   Fields, interview, 112. See also Vandegrift to Rupertus, 7 January 1944, William Rupertus Papers, Marine Corps Historical Division, Marine Corps University, box 1; Vandegrift to Holland Smith, 15 March 1944, Holland Smith Papers.

CHAPTER THREE. CENTRAL PACIFIC OFFENSIVE

1.   Smith and Finch, *Coral and Brass*, 17.
2.   Krulak foreword to Cooper, *Fighting General*.
3.   Krulak, interview, 44–46; Silverthorn, interview, 395; Shepherd, interview, 107; del Valle, *Semper Fidelis*, 113–14; Megee, interview, 32; Jordahl, interview, 123; Erskine, interview, 181–83, 375; Sherrod, *On to Westward*, 256–57; Williams, *Old Corps*, 117; Letcher, *One Marine's Story*, 361; Holcomb to Douglas McDougal, 30 January 1941, Holcomb Papers, box 1, folder 48.
4.   Quoted in Dyer, *The Amphibians Came to Conquer*, vol. 2, 600.
5.   Erskine, interview, 181–83.
6.   The quote is from Robinson, interview, 82. See also Thomas, interview, 191; Pfeiffer, interview, 230–31; Cooper, *Fighting General*, 102; Holcomb to Vandegrift, 18 August 1943, Vandegrift Papers, box 2; Holcomb to George Dyer, 5 March 1961, Holcomb Papers, box 13; Holland Smith to Holcomb, 22 June 1943, Holcomb Papers, box 13.
7.   The quote is from Holland Smith to Holcomb, 6 September 1943, Holcomb Papers, box 13. See also Smith and Finch, *Coral and Brass*, 136–38; Pfeiffer, interview, 230–31; Cooper, *Fighting General*, 92–94, 105; Holcomb to Vandegrift, 31 August 1943, Vandegrift Papers, box 2.
8.   Quoted in Cooper, *Fighting General*, 105.
9.   Cooper, 105, 115; Smith and Finch, *Coral and Brass*, 109–10; Dyer, *The Amphibians Came to Conquer*, vol. 2, 1145; Erskine, interview, 334, 336; Joseph Stewart, interview by Benis Frank, 1973, Marine Corps Historical Division, Marine Corps University, 10; Vandegrift to Holcomb, 9 August 1943, Vandegrift Papers, box 2; Holcomb to Vandegrift, 19 November 1943, Vandegrift Papers, box 2; Holland Smith to Holcomb, 8 November 1943, Holcomb Papers, box 13.
10.   Vandegrift, *Once a Marine*, 243–44; Smith and Finch, *Coral and Brass*, 115–16; Taaffe, *Marshall and His Generals*, 148–51.
11.   Vandegrift, *Once a Marine*, 80; Smith and Finch, *Coral and Brass*, 184; Cooper, *Fighting General*, 150; Charles Banks, interview by Benis Frank, 1974, Marine Corps Historical Division, Marine Corps University, 27; Erskine, interview, 115, 119, 203–4, 375; Turner to Schmidt, 29 March 1949, Schmidt Papers, box 1, folder 3.

12. Shaw, Nalty, and Tumbladh, *Central Pacific Drive*, 27–28; Dyer, *The Amphibians Came to Conquer*, vol. 2, 618–19; Smith and Finch, *Coral and Brass*, 114.

13. Henderson, interview, 313; Julian Smith, interview, 263, 266, 343–46; Holcomb to Stanley Hornbeck, 3 August 1937, Holcomb Papers, box 1; Holcomb to Marston, 21 March 1939 and 23 March 1942, Holcomb Papers, box 1; Vandegrift to Holcomb, 1 April 1943, Vandegrift Papers, box 2; Holland Smith to Holcomb, 22 June 1943, Holcomb Papers, box 13.

14. Marston to Vogel, 2 April 1943, Holcomb Papers, box 6.

15. Vandegrift to Holcomb, 1 April 1943, Vandegrift Papers, box 2; Marston to Julian Smith, 18 September 1943, Julian Smith Papers, box 16; Marston to Metcalf, 18 September 1943, Julian Smith Papers, box 16; Marston to Holcomb, 2 April 1943, Holcomb Papers, box 6; Holcomb to Vogel, 26 April 1943, Holcomb Papers, box 6; Holcomb to Marston's wife, 5 April 1943, Holcomb Papers, box 6.

16. Murray, interview, 147.

17. Harriotte "Happy" Bird Smith, *But, That's Another Story* (New York: Vantage Press, 1992), 231–34.

18. Krulak, interview, 8; Henderson, interview, 182; Julian Smith, interview, 168–70, 185, 212; Buse, interview, 8–9; Smith, *But, That's Another Story*, 137, 219–21; Robert Sherrod, *Tarawa: The Story of a Battle* (Fredericksburg, Texas: Admiral Nimitz Foundation, 1973), 24.

19. Julian Smith to Little, 11 August 1942, Julian Smith Papers, box 15.

20. Julian Smith, interview, 260, 262; Twining, *No Bended Knee*, 229; Smith, *But, That's Another Story*, 235–36; Holcomb to Vandegrift, 22 October 1943, Vandegrift Papers, box 2; Julian Smith to Ann Ashurst, 1 September 1943, Julian Smith Papers, box 15; Holcomb to Vogel, 26 April 1943, Holcomb Papers, box 6; Vogel to Holcomb, 20 May 1943, Holcomb Papers, box 6; Holcomb to Holland Smith, 2 February 1943, Holcomb Papers, box 13.

21. Julian Smith, interview, 344.

22. Julian Smith, interview, 265–67, 275–76, 346–48, 349–50; Vandegrift to Holcomb, 10 and 16 July 1943, Vandegrift Papers, box 2; Julian Smith to Vandegrift, 22 July and 16 August 1943, Vandegrift Papers, box 2; Vandegrift to Julian Smith, 17 July and 1 September 1943, Julian Smith Papers, box 16; Vogel to Holcomb, 20 May 1943, Holcomb Papers, box 6; Julian Smith to Holcomb, 22 July 1943, Holcomb Papers, box 6.

23. Quoted in Cooper, *Fighting General*, 105. See also Holland Smith to Holcomb, 20 and 28 October 1943, Holcomb Papers, box 13.

24. Holcomb to Holland Smith, 22 October 1943, Vandegrift Papers, box 2.

25. The quote is from Smith, *But, That's Another Story*, 245. See also Clayton Barrow, "The Stick Wavers," *Naval History* 4, no. 1 (1980): 31; Julian Smith, "Tarawa," U.S. Naval Institute *Proceedings* 79, no. 11 (November 1953): 1167–68, 1171.

26. Smith and Finch, *Coral and Brass*, 119–21, 123–24; Julian Smith, interview, 297; Cooper, *Fighting General*, 115.

27. Smith and Finch, *Coral and Brass*, 129.

28. Smith and Finch, 130; Smith, *But, That's Another Story*, 245; Julian Smith to Vandegrift, 10 December 1943, Vandegrift Papers, box 2.

29. Vandegrift, *Once a Marine*, 235.
30. Smith and Finch, *Coral and Brass*, 112.
31. Sherrod, *Tarawa*, 196.
32. Smith and Finch, *Coral and Brass*, 125–26, 133; Cooper, *Fighting General*, 124; Holland Smith to Vandegrift, 7 December 1943, Holland Smith Papers; Vandegrift to Holland Smith, 14 December 1943, Holland Smith Papers; Holcomb to Julian Smith, 25 November 1943, Holcomb Papers, box 1; Julian Smith to Vandegrift, 13 December 1943, Vandegrift Papers, box 2; Holland Smith to Holcomb, 29 November 1943, Holcomb Papers, box 13; Holcomb to Holland Smith, 25 November 1943, Holcomb Papers, box 13.
33. The quote is from Holcomb to James Forrestal, 28 June 1943, Holcomb Papers, box 6. See also John Russell to Holcomb, 18 July 1943, Holcomb Papers, box 1; Holcomb to Vandegrift, 13 December 1942, Vandegrift Papers, box 2; Barrett to Holcomb, 13 July 1943, Holcomb Papers, box 6.
34. Actually, in November 1940 Holcomb told Admiral Harold Stark that if Roosevelt did not want to appoint him to a second term as commandant, he recommended Holland Smith for the job, with Philip Torrey, Vandegrift, and Barrett as alternatives. He gave priority to Smith because he was the most senior. Perhaps he figured that Vandegrift would not be ready for the post until after Smith was commandant. See Holcomb to Stark, 24 November 1940, Holcomb Papers, box 13. See also Holcomb memo, n.d., Holcomb Papers, box 6.
35. Vandegrift, *Once a Marine*, 182–83; Holcomb to Vandegrift, 13 December 1942, Vandegrift Papers, box 2; Thomas, unpublished memoirs (chap. 1), Thomas Papers, box 2, 66; Holcomb to Forrestal, 28 June 1943, Holcomb Papers, box 6.
36. Vandegrift, *Once a Marine*, 224; Frank Knox to Holcomb, 1 December 1943, Holcomb Papers, box 7; Holcomb to Vandegrift, 14 July, 11, 13, and 18 August 1943, Vandegrift Papers, box 2; Holcomb to Barrett, 28 July 1943, Holcomb Papers, box 6.
37. Vandegrift to Holcomb, 16 July 1943, Vandegrift Papers, box 2.
38. Thomas, interview, 221–22.
39. See, for instance, Julian Smith, interview, 209–10, 211.
40. The quote and story are from Vandegrift, *Once a Marine*, 236–37.
41. Vandegrift to Geiger, 3 December 1943, Geiger Papers, box 5.
42. Vandegrift, *Once a Marine*, 248–49.
43. Vandegrift, 239; Oliver Smith, interview, 109; Fields, interview, 145; Burger, interview, 149; Vandegrift to Holland Smith, 5 January 1944, Holland Smith Papers; Masters, interview, 71–72; Thomas, unpublished memoirs (chap. 2), Thomas Papers, box 2, 12–13.
44. The quote is from Benis M. Frank and Harry I. Shaw, Jr., *Victory and Occupation: History of U.S. Marine Corps Operations in World War II*, vol. 5 (Washington, D.C.: Government Printing Office, 1968), 414n. See also Vandegrift, *Once a Marine*, 238–39; Thomas, interview, 208–9, 224; Masters, interview, 71–72; Thomas, unpublished memoirs (chap. 2), Thomas Papers, 20–21; Vandegrift to Holcomb, 6 June 1944, Vandegrift Papers, box 2.
45. Holland Smith to Vandegrift, 9 January 1944, Holland Smith Papers.

46. Vandegrift to Holland Smith, 6 October 1944, Holland Smith Papers.

47. Vandegrift, *Once a Marine*, 241, 270–71, 279; Thomas, interview, 222; Silverthorn, interview, 397; Jordahl, interview, 82–83; Kilmartin, interview, 307–8; Pollock, interview, 188; Holland Smith to Vandegrift, 17 December 1943, 9 January and 2 November 1944, Holland Smith Papers; Vandegrift to Holland Smith, 5 and 15 January, and 24 March 1944, Holland Smith Papers; Vandegrift to Harry Pickett, 19 January 1944, Vandegrift Papers, box 2; Vandegrift to Holland Smith, 28 February 1944, Vandegrift Papers, box 2; Vandegrift to Lemuel Shepherd, 21 September 1944, Vandegrift Papers, box 3.

48. Cooper, *Fighting General*, 88.

49. Vandegrift, *Once a Marine*, 241–42, 246; Thomas, interview, 203; Burger, interview, 141–42, 146; Thomas to Graves Erskine, 5 January 1944, Erskine Papers, Marine Corps Historical Division, Marine Corps University, box 4; Thomas, unpublished memoirs (chap. 2), Thomas Papers, box 2, 12–13, 28.

50. Dyer, *The Amphibians Came to Conquer*, vol. 2, 741.

51. Cooper, *Fighting General*, 132–33; Holland Smith to Vandegrift, 17 December 1943, Holland Smith Papers.

52. Holland Smith to Vandegrift, 9 January 1944, Holland Smith Papers.

53. Thomas, interview, 191, 221; Peck, interview, 137; Worton, interview, 68–69; Cooper, *Fighting General*, 146; Holland Smith to Vandegrift, 7 and 17 December 1943, Holland Smith Papers.

54. S. L. A Marshall, *Bringing Up the Rear: A Memoir*, ed. Cate Marshall (San Rafael, California: Presidio Press, 1979), 77–78.

55. Cooper, *Fighting General*, 134–35; Deakin, interview, 23; Holland Smith to Vandegrift, 9 January 1944, Holland Smith Papers; Vandegrift to Holland Smith, 5 and 15 January 1944, Holland Smith Papers.

56. Smith and Finch, *Coral and Brass*, 167; Cooper, *Fighting General*, 163–64, 227; Melvin Krulewitch, interview by Benis Frank, 1970, Marine Corps Historical Division, Marine Corps University, 87, 91–92; Melvin L. Krulewitch, *Now That You Mention It* (New York: Quadrangle, 1973), 97–98; Buckner, 13 March 1945, Sarantakes, *Seven Stars*, 21; Holcomb to Henry Larsen, 2 August 1943, Holcomb Papers, box 1, folder 79.

57. Smith and Finch, *Coral and Brass*, 167; Holcomb to Henry Larsen, 2 August 1943, Holcomb Papers, box 1; Holcomb to Schmidt, 18 October 1943, Holcomb Papers, box 6; Holcomb to Holland Smith, 28 July 1943, Holcomb Papers, box 13; Holcomb to Vandegrift, 6 August and 22 October 1943, Vandegrift Papers, box 2; Vandegrift to Holcomb, 22 July 1943, Vandegrift Papers, box 2.

58. Quoted in Shaw, Nalty, and Tumbladh, *Central Pacific Drive*, 170–71.

59. Pratt, *Marines' War*, 177–78.

60. Smith and Finch, *Coral and Brass*, 147; Holland Smith to Vandegrift, 4 February 1944, Holland Smith Papers.

61. Smith and Finch, *Coral and Brass*, 146.

62. Holland Smith to Vandegrift, 4 February 1944, Holland Smith Papers; Marshall, *Bringing Up the Rear*, 77–78.

63. Smith and Finch, *Coral and Brass*, 148–49; Dyer, *The Amphibians Came to Conquer*, vol. 2, 827, 829; Shaw, Nalty, and Tumbladh, *Central Pacific Drive*, 182.

64.   Harry Hill to Vandegrift, 12 March 1944, Vandegrift Papers, box 2.

65.   Vandegrift, *Once a Marine*, 245; Holland Smith to Vandegrift, 22 February 1944, Holland Smith Papers; Vandegrift to Holland Smith, 27 March 1944, Holland Smith Papers; Hill to Vandegrift, 12 March 1944, Vandegrift Papers, box 2.

66.   Carl W. Proehl, ed., *The Fourth Marine Division in World War II* (Washington, D.C.: Infantry Journal Press, 1946), 58–59.

67.   Smith and Finch, *Coral and Brass*, 153.

68.   Smith and Finch, 156; Holland Smith to Vandegrift, 11 February and 8 March 1944, Holland Smith Papers.

69.   Smith and Finch, *Coral and Brass*, 168–71; Cooper, *Fighting General*, 149; Holland Smith to Vandegrift, 11 February, 18 March, and 2 and 25 May 1944, Holland Smith Papers; Vandegrift to Holland Smith, 5 January 1944, Holland Smith Papers; Sherrod, *On to Westward*, 37–38; Dyer, *The Amphibians Came to Conquer*, vol. 2, 928.

70.   Smith, *But, That's Another Story*, 262–64.

71.   Smith, 260–64; Julian Smith, interview, 314–15, 316–21; Vandegrift to Holcomb, 6 June 1944, Vandegrift Papers, box 2; Holland Smith to Vandegrift, 7 June 1944, Vandegrift Papers, box 2; Vandegrift to Julian Smith, 14 June 1944, Vandegrift Papers, box 2; Holland Smith to Vandegrift, 2 May 1944, Holland Smith Papers.

72.   Vandegrift to Holland Smith, 16 February 1944, Holland Smith Papers.

73.   Holland Smith to Vandegrift, 8 March and 25 May 1944, Holland Smith Papers; Vandegrift to Holland Smith, 5 January 1944, Holland Smith Papers.

74.   John C. Chapin, *Breaching the Marianas: The Battle for Saipan* (Washington, D.C.: United States Marine Corps, 1994), 9.

75.   Cooper, *Fighting General*, 164.

76.   Vandegrift, *Once a Marine*, 287–89; Smith and Finch, *Coral and Brass*, 167; Thomas, interview, 224; Silverthorn, interview, 419; Holland Smith to Vandegrift, 9 January 1944, Holland Smith Papers; Vandegrift to Holland Smith, 16 February 1944, Holland Smith Papers.

77.   Chapin, *Breaching the Marianas*, 2.

78.   Krulewitch, interview, 96; Shaw, Nalty, and Tumbladh, *Central Pacific Drive*, 277.

79.   Holland Smith to Vandegrift, 22 June 1944, Vandegrift Papers, box 2.

80.   The quote is from Sherrod, *On to Westward*, 89. See also Smith and Finch, *Coral and Brass*, 168–75; Erskine, interview, 322–23; Shaw, Nalty, and Tumbladh, *Central Pacific Drive*, 313; Cooper, *Fighting General*, 180.

81.   Shaw, Nalty, and Tumbladh, *Central Pacific Drive*, 330.

82.   Shaw, Nalty, and Tumbladh, 348.

83.   Vandegrift, *Once a Marine*, 268–69; Smith and Finch, *Coral and Brass*, 181; Holland Smith to Vandegrift, 18 July 1944, Holland Smith Papers; Vandegrift to Holcomb, 13 July 1944, Vandegrift Papers, box 2; Vandegrift to Schmidt, 24 July 1944, Vandegrift Papers, box 2.

84.   Taaffe, *Marshall and His Generals*, 150.

85.   Smith and Finch, *Coral and Brass*, 176–79; Holland Smith to Vandegrift, 15 and 18 July 1944, Holland Smith Papers; Holland Smith to Commander, Joint Expeditionary Force, 18 July 1944, Holland Smith Papers, box 1, Marine Corps History Division.

86.   The quote is from Vandegrift to Holland Smith, 22 July 1944, Holland Smith Papers. See also Vandegrift, *Once a Marine*, 260–64; Smith and Finch, *Coral and Brass*, 173–75; Oliver Smith, interview, 150; Cooper, *Fighting General*, 209; Vandegrift to Holland Smith, 10 July 1944, Holland Smith Papers; Graham Barden to Julian Smith, 15 September 1944, Julian Smith Papers, box 17; Vandegrift to Holcomb, 13 July 1944, Vandegrift Papers, box 2; Vandegrift to Holcomb, 5 September 1944, Vandegrift Papers, box 3.

87.   Holland Smith to Vandegrift, 11 October and 2 November 1944, Holland Smith Papers; Buckner, 13 September 1944, Sarantakes, *Seven Stars*, 17; Julian Smith to Thomas, 8 July 1944, Julian Smith Papers, box 17; Vandegrift to Holcomb, 24 November 1944, Vandegrift Papers, box 3; Taaffe, *Marshall and His Generals*, 156–57.

88.   For a ringing defense of the 27th Division, see Harry A. Gailey, *Howlin' Mad vs. the Army: Conflict in Command, Saipan 1944* (Navato, California: Presidio Press, 1966).

89.   See Shaw, Nalty, and Tumbladh, *Central Pacific Drive*, 348.

90.   Smith and Finch, *Coral and Brass*, 202.

91.   Smith and Finch, 202; Holland Smith to Vandegrift, 25 September 1944, Holland Smith Papers; Vandegrift to Holland Smith, 27 March 1944, Holland Smith Papers; Vandegrift to Holcomb, 6 June 1944, Vandegrift Papers, box 2; Vandegrift to Price, 18 September 1944, Vandegrift Papers, box 3; Erskine to Clifton Cates, 26 September 1944, Erskine Papers, box 4.

92.   Holland Smith to Vandegrift, 7 June 1944, Vandegrift Papers, box 2.

93.   Holland Smith to Vandegrift, 4 February and 18 July 1944, Holland Smith Papers; Vandegrift to Holland Smith, 3 December 1943, Holland Smith Papers; Vandegrift to Holcomb, 13 July and 6 October 1943, Vandegrift Papers, box 2; Holland Smith to Vandegrift, 7 June 1944, Vandegrift Papers, box 2; Vandegrift to Schmidt, 24 July 1944, Vandegrift Papers, box 2; Vandegrift to Holland Smith, 27 June 1944, Vandegrift Papers, box 3.

94.   Smith and Finch, *Coral and Brass*, 205–6; Cooper, *Fighting General*, 194–96; Dyer, *The Amphibians Came to Conquer*, vol. 2, 956–57; Harry Hill, "A Perfect Assault," in *The Pacific War Remembered: An Oral History Collection*, ed. John T. Mason (Annapolis, Maryland: Naval Institute Press, 1986), 247–53; Turner to Schmidt, 29 March 1949, Schmidt Papers, box 1, folder 3.

95.   The quote is from Masters, interview, 105. See also Krulak, interview, 48; Thomas, interview, 103; Shepherd, interview, 190; Cates, interview, 205; Megee, interview, 235; Buse, interview, 46–47; Luckey, interview, 204; David Nimmer, interview by Thomas Donnelly, 1970, Marine Corps Historical Division, Marine Corps University, 122; Pollock, interview, 105–6, 108, 109, 164; Robinson, interview, 33; Thomas Barry, in Berry, *Semper Fi*, 94; Tregaskis, *Guadalcanal Diary*, 130.

96.   Cates, interview, 163–64; Holcomb to Vandegrift, 29 September 1942, Vandegrift Papers, box 2; Vandegrift to Holcomb, 6 June 1944, Vandegrift Papers, box 2; Holland Smith to Vandegrift, 7 June 1944, Vandegrift Papers, box 2.

97.   Cates to Vandegrift, 25 August 1944, Vandegrift Papers, box 3; Cates, interview, 180.

98.   Cates to Vandegrift, 25 August 1944, Vandegrift Papers, box 3.

99.   Willock, *Unaccustomed to Fear*, 261–62; Shepherd, interview, 71; Geiger to Vandegrift, 25 March 1944, Vandegrift Papers, box 2; Geiger to Louis Woods, 20

December 1943, Geiger Papers, box 5; Geiger to David Click, 20 August 1944, Geiger Papers, box 5.

100. Erskine to Holland Smith, 25 October 1944, Erskine Papers, box 4; Thomas, interview, 203.

101. Shepherd, interview, 38, 155, 158, 161.

102. Sherrod, *On to Westward*, 272.

103. Krulak, interview, 91–92, 130; Cushman, interview, 149–50; Mulcahy, interview, 87; Justice Chambers, interview by Paul Chambers, 1988, Marine Corps Historical Division, Marine Corps University, 705; McQueen, interview, 95.

104. Vandegrift, *Once a Marine*, 292–93; Shepherd, interview, 71–73, 83–84, 165–66; Luckey, interview, 129; August Larson, interview by Thomas Donnelly, 1975, Marine Corps Historical Division, Marine Corps University, 78; McQueen, interview, 147; Holcomb to Shepherd, 10 June 1941, Holcomb Papers, box 1.

105. Del Valle, *Semper Fidelis*, 142; Wellons, "General Roy S. Geiger," 111; Silverthorn, interview, 325–26, 340; Norman, *Fighting General*, 199; Geiger to Richard Conolly, 9 August 1944, Geiger Papers, box 5.

106. Geiger to Conolly, 9 August 1944, Geiger Papers, box 5.

107. The quote is from George W. Garand and Truman R. Strobridge, *Western Pacific Operations: History of U.S. Marine Corps Operations in World War II*, vol. 4 (Washington, D.C.: Historical Division, Headquarters, U.S. Marine Corps, 1971), 280. See also Wellons, "General Roy S. Geiger," 111; Vandegrift to Holcomb, 5 September 1944, Vandegrift Papers, box 3; Vandegrift to Geiger, 15 August 1944, Geiger Papers, box 7.

108. Quoted in Smith, *But, That's Another Story*, 262.

109. Silverthorn, interview, 323; Julian Smith, interview, 321, 325–26; Holland Smith to Vandegrift, 2 May 1944, Holland Smith Papers; Julian Smith to George Lockwood, 19 June 1944, Julian Smith Papers, box 16; Julian Smith to Rupertus, 10 July 1944, Julian Smith Papers, box 17; Julian Smith to Robert Baer, 26 December 1944, Julian Smith Papers, box 17.

110. Rupertus to Vandegrift, 7 September 1944, Vandegrift Papers, box 3.

111. Wellons, "General Roy S. Geiger," 113–14; Oliver Smith, interview, 132–33; Henderson, interview, 367; Shepherd, interview, 165; Vandegrift to Geiger, 16 May 1944, Vandegrift Papers, box 2; Vandegrift to Rupertus, 24 July 1944, Vandegrift Papers, box 2; Rupertus to Vandegrift, 7 September 1944, Vandegrift Papers, box 3.

112. Oliver Smith, interview, 128; Deakin, interview, 48; Hallas, *Devil's Anvil*, 31; Rupertus to Vandegrift, 13 July 1944, Vandegrift Papers, box 2.

113. Wellons, "General Roy S. Geiger," 114; Oliver Smith, interview, 130; Garand and Strobridge, *Western Pacific Operations*, vol. 4, 279.

114. Oliver Smith, interview, 136–37, 139; Henderson, interview, 364; Garand and Strobridge, *Western Pacific Operations*, vol. 4, 131.

115. Silverthorn, interview, 319.

116. The quotes are from Deakin, interview, 54 and Hallas, *Devil's Anvil*, 233. See also Oliver Smith, interview, 140; Vandegrift to Rupertus, 18 September 1944, Vandegrift Papers, box 3.

117.   Silverthorn, interview, 325–26; Deakin, interview, 53; Craig M. Cameron, *American Samurai: Myth, Imagination, and the Conduct of Battle in the First Marine Division, 1941–1951* (Cambridge: Cambridge University Press, 1994), 148–49; Garand and Strobridge, *Western Pacific Operations*, vol. 4, 165, 185–86, 187–89.
118.   Sherrod, *On to Westward*, 11.
119.   The quote is from Vandegrift to Holland Smith, 26 March 1945, Holland Smith Papers. See also Vandegrift, *Once a Marine*, 278, 285–86; Rupertus to Vandegrift, 7 September 1944, Vandegrift Papers, box 3; Vandegrift to Rupertus, 18 September 1944, Vandegrift Papers, box 3; Vandegrift to Holcomb, 24 November 1944, Vandegrift Papers, box 3; Rupertus to Vandegrift, 25 March 1945, Rupertus Papers, box 1.
120.   Smith, *But, That's Another Story*, 289.
121.   Julian Smith, interview, 336–37; Vandegrift to Holland Smith, 18 October 1944, Holland Smith Papers; Julian Smith to Chester Nimitz, 9 December 1944, Julian Smith Papers, box 17; Julian Smith to Hans and Mellie L'Orange, 12 December 1944, Julian Smith Papers, box 17; Julian Smith to Holland Smith, 12 December 1944, Julian Smith Papers, box 17; Julian Smith to Edgar Bain, 13 December 1944, Julian Smith Papers, box 17; Julian Smith to Dudley Brown, 22 December 1944, Julian Smith Papers, box 17; Vandegrift to Holcomb, 24 November 1944, Vandegrift Papers, box 3; Julian Smith to Vandegrift, 17 February 1945, Vandegrift Papers, box 3; Vandegrift to Julian Smith, 25 March 1945, Vandegrift Papers, box 3.

CHAPTER FOUR. CLOSING IN ON JAPAN

1.   Garand and Strobridge, *Western Pacific Operations*, vol. 4, 448.
2.   Turner to Schmidt, 29 March 1949, Schmidt Papers, box 1, folder 3.
3.   Vandegrift, *Once a Marine*, 280; Holland Smith to Vandegrift, 11 October and 2 November 1944, Holland Smith Papers; Vandegrift to Holland Smith, 18 October 1944, Holland Smith Papers; Buckner, 13 March 1945, Sarantakes, *Seven Stars*, 21; Vandegrift to Schmidt, 19 October 1944, Vandegrift Papers, box 3.
4.   Cooper, *Fighting General*, 221; Vandegrift to Holland Smith, 15 March 1944, Holland Smith Papers; Erskine, interview, 353; Holland Smith to Vandegrift, 7 June 1944, Vandegrift Papers, box 2.
5.   Donn Robertson, interview by Benis Frank, 1976, Marine Corps Historical Division, Marine Corps University, 104.
6.   Vandegrift, *Once a Marine*, 80, 84; Smith and Finch, *Coral and Brass*, 184; Murray, interview, 173; Krulak, interview, 61; Henderson, interview, 193–94, 476; Cushman, interview, 168; Buse, interview, 93; Kilmartin, interview, 9, 10, 194, 201–2, 235; Sherrod, *On to Westward*, 204; Buckner, 13 March 1945, Sarantakes, *Seven Stars*, 21; Walter Rogers to Schmidt, 19 December 1949, Schmidt Papers, box 1, folder 3.
7.   Erskine to Thomas Yancey, 26 October 1944, Erskine Papers, box 4.
8.   The quote is Erskine to Shepherd, 26 October 1944, Erskine Papers, box 4. See also Erskine to Vandegrift, 31 October 1944, Vandegrift Papers, box 3; Erskine to Holland

Smith, 25 October 1944, Erskine Papers, box 4; Hogaboom, interview, Holcomb Papers, box 23, 223–24.

9. Cates to his family, 27 January 1945, Cates Papers, Marine Corps Historical Division, Marine Corps University, box 3.

10. Holland Smith to Vandegrift, 11 October 1944, Holland Smith Papers; Schmidt to Vandegrift, 26 October 1944, Vandegrift Papers, box 3; Cates to his wife and family, 30 September 1944 and 27 January 1945, Cates Papers, box 3.

11. Vandegrift, *Once a Marine*, 241–42.

12. Holcomb to Vandegrift, 27 August 1943, Vandegrift Papers, box 2; Thomas, interview, 203–4; Pfeiffer, interview, 241–43.

13. Thomas Wornham, interview by Benis Frank, 1967–68, Marine Corps Historical Division, Marine Corps University, 64; Robertson, interview, 61, 67; Buckner, 13 March 1945, Sarantakes, *Seven Stars*, 21; *New York Times*, 9 June 1970, 41; Holcomb to Rockey, 2 November 1938, Holcomb Papers, box 1, folder 22; Vandegrift to Holland Smith, 6 October 1944, Holland Smith Papers; Garand and Strobridge, *Western Pacific Operations*, vol. 4, 468; Rogers to Schmidt, 30 March (year unknown), Schmidt Papers, box 1, folder 3.

14. *New York Times*, 9 June 1970, 41; Garand and Strobridge, *Western Pacific Operations*, vol. 4, 468; Holcomb to Vandegrift, 29 September 1942, 6 April and 18 August 1943, Vandegrift Papers, box 2; Vandegrift to Holcomb, 26 August 1943, Vandegrift Papers, box 2; Price to Vandegrift, 27 April 1944, Vandegrift Papers, box 2; Schmidt to Vandegrift, 26 October 1944, Vandegrift Papers, box 3; Holcomb to Schmidt, 10 September 1943, Holcomb Papers, box 6.

15. Holland Smith to Vandegrift, 12 January 1945, Holland Smith Papers.

16. Vandegrift, *Once a Marine*, 280–82; Smith and Finch, *Coral and Brass*, 253–54; Cates, interview, 187; Cooper, *Fighting General*, 227; Holland Smith to Vandegrift, 27 March 1945, Holland Smith Papers; Sherrod, *On to Westward*, 153–54, 158–59; Cates to his wife, 18 February 1945, Cates Papers, box 3.

17. Vandegrift to Schmidt, 19 October 1944, Vandegrift Papers, box 3.

18. Vandegrift to Holland Smith, 22 July and 16 October 1944, Holland Smith Papers; Frank and Shaw, *Victory and Occupation*, vol. 5, 23.

19. Quoted in Garand and Strobridge, *Western Pacific Operations*, vol. 4, 527.

20. Wornham, interview, 82.

21. Schmidt, "Uncommon Valor a Common Virtue," Schmidt Papers, box 1, folder 2.

22. Holland Smith to Vandegrift, 27 February 1945, Holland Smith Papers. See also Schmidt, "Uncommon Valor a Common Virtue," Schmidt Papers, box 1, folder 2; Cates to his wife, 1 March 1945, Cates Papers, box 3.

23. The quote is from Sherrod, *On to Westward*, 213. See also Cushman, interview, 172; Sherrod, *On to Westward*, 212; Letcher, *One Marine's Story*, 362–63; Joseph Alexander, "Combat Leadership at Iwo Jima," *Marine Corps Gazette* 79, no. 2 (February 1995): 69–70; Garand and Strobridge, *Western Pacific Operations*, vol. 4, 586, 592, 633, 643, 669, 688.

24. Wornham, interview, 81; Cooper, *Fighting General*, 234–35, Holland Smith to Vandegrift, 27 February 1945, Holland Smith Papers; Holland Smith to Vandegrift, 21 March 1945, Vandegrift Papers, box 3.

25. Megee, interview, 42–43; Schmidt, "Uncommon Valor a Common Virtue," 2–3; Schmidt to Isely, 11 December 1949, Schmidt Papers, box 1, folder 3.

26. Megee, interview, 43–44; Wornham, interview, 78; Sherrod, *On to Westward*, 204, 207–8; Erskine, interview, 357–59; Alexander, "Combat Leadership at Iwo Jima," 70; Alan Rems, "Letters to Iwo Jima," *Naval History Magazine* 23, no. 1 (2009); Garand and Strobridge, *Western Pacific Operations*, vol. 4, 592; Schmidt to Isely, 11 December 1949, Schmidt Papers, box 1, folder 3; Vandegrift to Holland Smith, 6 March 1945, Vandegrift Papers, box 3; Erskine to Vandegrift, 21 March 1945, Vandegrift Papers, box 3.

27. Sherrod, *On to Westward*, 196.

28. Sherrod, 195–96; Cates, interview, 191; Megee, interview, 43–44; Garand and Strobridge, *Western Pacific Operations*, vol. 4, 669; Cates to Vandegrift, 11 March 1945, Vandegrift Papers, box 3; Cates to his wife, 18 February, 1 and 16–17 March 1945, Cates Papers, box 3.

29. Wornham, interview, 64, 81; Robertson, interview, 61, 67; Rockey to Isely, 17 February 1950, Schmidt Papers, box 1, folder 3.

30. Quoted in Cooper, *Fighting General*, 232.

31. Wornham, interview, 78–79; Erskine, interview, 357; Rems, "Letters to Iwo Jima"; Garand and Strobridge, *Western Pacific Operations*, vol. 4, 608, 608n; Schmidt to Isely, 11 December 1949, Schmidt Papers, box 1, folder 3; Robert Heinl to Schmidt, 16 September 1960, Schmidt Papers, box 1, folder 4.

32. Cates to his family, 16–17 March 1945, Cates Papers, box 3.

33. Vandegrift to Holland Smith, 17 March 1945, Holland Smith Papers.

34. Vandegrift, *Once a Marine*, 280–83; Vandegrift to Holland Smith, 10 and 26 March 1945, Holland Smith Papers; Vandegrift to Holland Smith, 6 March 1945, Vandegrift Papers, box 3; Holland Smith to Vandegrift, 21 March 1945, Vandegrift Papers, box 3; Vandegrift to Rose Rowell, 3 April 1945, Vandegrift Papers, box 3; Vandegrift to Holcomb, 7 April 1945, Vandegrift Papers, box 3; Vandegrift to Schmidt, 14 August 1945, Vandegrift Papers, box 3.

35. Quoted in Cooper, *Fighting General*, 234.

36. Holland Smith to Vandegrift, 11 October and 2 November 1944, 12 January and 27 March 1945, Holland Smith Papers; Vandegrift to Holland Smith, 18 October 1944, Holland Smith Papers; Holland Smith to Vandegrift, 21 March 1945, Vandegrift Papers, box 3; Taaffe, *Marshall and His Generals*, 298–99.

37. The quote is from Van Deurs, *Reminiscences*, 503. See also Oliver Smith, interview, 152, 155–56, 162–63; Silverthorn, interview, 339; Shepherd, interview, 71; Vandegrift to Holland Smith, 26 March 1945, Holland Smith Papers; Buckner, 7 February 1945, Sarantakes, *Seven Stars*, 19; Vandegrift to Holcomb, 24 November 1944, Vandegrift Papers, box 3.

38. Henderson, interview, 346.

39. Twining, interview, 128.

40. Twining, interview, 127–28; Vandegrift, *Once a Marine*, 161–62; Henderson, interview, 182; Shapley, interview, 100; Julian Smith, interview, 41; Chambers, interview, 247; Kilmartin, interview, 290–92.

41.   Deakin, interview, 57–58.

42.   Deakin, interview, 61, 64–65; Krulak, interview, 91–92; Del Valle, *Semper Fidelis*, 139; Frank and Shaw, *Victory and Occupation*, vol. 5, 87; Vandegrift to del Valle, 24 August 1943, Vandegrift Papers, box 2.

43.   Vandegrift, *Once a Marine*, 270; Thomas, interview, 203–4; Shepherd, interview, 167; Holcomb to Vandegrift, 4 November 1943, Vandegrift Papers, box 2; Vandegrift to Holcomb, 13 July 1944, Vandegrift Papers, box 2; Vandegrift to Holcomb, 5 September 1944, Vandegrift Papers, box 3; Thomas, unpublished memoirs (chapter 2), Thomas Papers, box 2, 22–23.

44.   Quoted in Laura Homan Lacey, ed., *Stay Off the Skyline: The Sixth Marine Division on Okinawa—An Oral History* (Washington, D.C.: Potomac Books, 2005), 83.

45.   Oliver Smith, interview, 158; Krulak, interview, 91–92; Holland Smith to Vandegrift, 25 February 1945, Holland Smith Papers; Vandegrift to Holland Smith, 18 October 1944, Holland Smith Papers; Luckey, interview, 160; James H. Hallas, *Killing Ground on Okinawa: The Battle for Sugar Loaf Hill* (Westport, Connecticut: Praeger, 1996), 16; Holcomb to Vandegrift, 22 October 1943, Vandegrift Papers, box 2; Shepherd to Vandegrift, 4 September 1944 and 12 March 1945, Vandegrift Papers, box 3; Geiger to Vandegrift, 2 February 1945, Geiger Papers, box 6.

46.   Holland Smith to Vandegrift, 27 March 1945, Holland Smith Papers; Frank and Shaw, *Victory and Occupation*, vol. 5, 66–67.

47.   Sherrod, *On to Westward*, 280.

48.   George McMillan, *The Old Breed: A History of the First Marine Division in World War II* (Nashville, Tennessee: Battery Press, 2001), 362; McMillan et al., *Uncommon Valor*, 52; James Belote and William Belote, *Typhoon of Steel: The Battle for Okinawa* (New York: Harper and Row, 1970), 73–74; Vandegrift to Rowell, 3 April 1945, Vandegrift Papers, box 3; Vandegrift to Holcomb, 7 April 1945, Vandegrift Papers, box 3.

49.   Vandegrift, *Once a Marine*, 287–89; Oliver Smith, interview, 169–70; Krulak, interview, 95; Thomas, interview, 227; Silverthorn, interview, 153–54; Shepherd, interview, 29.

50.   Oliver Smith, interview, 165–67; Krulak, interview, 91–92; Shepherd, interview, 83–84; Victor Bleasdale, interview by Benis Frank, 1984, Marine Corps Historical Division, Marine Corps University, 280–84; Deakin, interview, 62; Larson, interview, 91, 103; McQueen, interview, 111; Buckner, 15 April 1945, Sarantakes, *Seven Stars*, 40; Hallas, *Killing Ground*, 161, 180.

51.   Oliver Smith, interview, 165–66; Krulak, interview, 91–92; del Valle, *Semper Fidelis*, 157; Buckner, 3 May and 3 June 1945, Sarantakes, *Seven Stars*, 50, 71.

52.   Wellons, "General Roy S. Geiger," 129–30; Oliver Smith, interview, 175–76; Silverthorn, interview, 325–26, 339, 346; Snedeker, interview, 81–82; Geiger to Vandegrift, 26 June 1945, Geiger Papers, box 6.

53.   Oliver Smith, interview, 156; Silverthorn, interview, 375–76; Geiger to Peck, 10 July 1945, Geiger Papers, box 6.

54.   Vandegrift, *Once a Marine*, 292–93; Frank and Shaw, *Victory and Occupation*, vol. 5, 125; Vandegrift to Shepherd, 11 June 1945, Vandegrift Papers, box 3; Vandegrift to Geiger, 6 July 1945, Vandegrift Papers, box 3; Vandegrift to Geiger, 15 August 1945, Geiger Papers, box 7.

55. Jordahl, interview, 127–28; Frank and Shaw, *Victory and Occupation*, vol. 5, 398.

56. Vandegrift, *Once a Marine*, 292–93; Thomas, interview, 228–29; Silverthorn, interview, 394–95; Cooper, *Fighting General*, 242; Vandegrift to Nimitz, 7 May 1945, Vandegrift Papers, box 3.

57. Smith and Finch, *Coral and Brass*, 1–2; Holland Smith to Vandegrift, 19 June 1945, Vandegrift Papers, box 3.

58. Silverthorn, interview, 327, 395; Vandegrift to Nimitz, 7 May 1945, Vandegrift Papers, box 3; Vandegrift to Geiger, 6 July 1945, Vandegrift Papers, box 3; Geiger to Vandegrift, 26 June 1945, Geiger Papers, box 6; Roy Owsley to Elmer Salzman, 22 July 1945, Geiger Papers, box 7; Vandegrift to Geiger, 15 August 1945, Geiger Papers, box 7.

59. Holcomb to Vandegrift, 9 July 1945, Vandegrift Papers, box 3.

60. Vandegrift to Holland Smith, 10 July 1944, Holland Smith Papers; Vandegrift, *Once a Marine*, 287–89.

61. Vandegrift, *Once a Marine*, 292–93; Del Valle, *Semper Fidelis*, 161; Vandegrift to Geiger, 6 July 1945, Vandegrift Papers, box 3; Holcomb to Vandegrift, 9 July 1945, Vandegrift Papers, box 3; Geiger to Vandegrift, 18 July 1945, Geiger Papers, box 7; Geiger to del Valle, 28 July 1945, Geiger Papers, box 7; Del Valle to Geiger, 20 July 1945, Geiger Papers, box 7.

62. Vandegrift, *Once a Marine*, 292–93; Vandegrift to Geiger, 6 July 1945, Vandegrift Papers, box 3; Shepherd to Vandegrift, 8 July and 14 August 1945, Vandegrift Papers, box 3; Geiger to Vandegrift 18 July 1945, Geiger Papers, box 7.

Bibliography

PRIMARY SOURCES

Berry, Henry. *Semper Fi, Mac: Living Memories of the U.S. Marines in World War II*. New York: Quill, 1982.

Del Valle, Pedro. *Semper Fidelis: An Autobiography*. Hawthorne, California: Christian Book Club of America, 1976.

Halsey, William F., and J. Bryan III. *Admiral Halsey's Story*. New York: McGraw-Hill Book Company, 1947.

Hunt, George P. *Coral Comes High*. New York: Harper and Brothers, 1946.

King, Ernest J., and Walter Muir Whitehill. *Fleet Admiral King: A Naval Record*. New York: Da Capo Press, 1976.

Krulak, Victor H. *First to Fight: An Inside View of the U.S. Marine Corps*. New York: Naval Institute Press, 2013. eBook Collection, EBSCOhost.

Krulewitch, Melvin L. *Now That You Mention It*. New York: Quadrangle, 1973.

Lacey, Laura Homan, ed. *Stay Off the Skyline: The Sixth Marine Division on Okinawa—An Oral History*. Washington, D.C.: Potomac Books, 2005.

Letcher, John Seymour. *One Marine's Story*. Verona, Virginia: McClure Press, 1970.

Marshall, S. L. A. *Bringing Up the Rear: A Memoir*. Edited by Cate Marshall. San Rafael, California: Presidio Press, 1979.

Sarantakes, Nicholas E., ed. *Seven Stars: The Okinawa Battle Diaries of Simon Bolivar Buckner, Jr., and Joseph Stilwell*. College Station: Texas A&M Press, 2004.

Sherrod, Robert. *On to Westward: War in the Central Pacific*. New York: Duell, Sloan and Pearce, 1945.

———. *Tarawa: The Story of a Battle*. Fredericksburg, Texas: Admiral Nimitz Foundation, 1973.

Sledge, E. B. *With the Old Breed at Peleliu and Okinawa*. Novato, California: Presidio Press, 1981.

Smith, Harriotte "Happy" Byrd. *But, That's Another Story*. New York: Vantage Press, 1992.

Smith, Holland M., and Percy Finch. *Coral and Brass*. New York: Charles Scribner's Sons, 1948.

Smith, Larry, ed. *Iwo Jima: World War II Veterans Remember the Greatest Battle of the Pacific*. New York: W. W. Norton & Company, 2008.

Tregaskis, Richard. *Guadalcanal Diary*. Open Road Media, 2016.

Twining, Merrill B. *No Bended Knee: The Battle of Guadalcanal*. Edited by Neil G. Carey. New York: Ballantine Books, 1996.

Van Deurs, George. *The Reminiscences of Rear Admiral George van Deurs.* Annapolis, Maryland: U.S. Naval Institute Press, 1974.

Vandegrift, Archibald, as told to Robert B. Asprey. *Once a Marine: The Memoirs of General A. A. Vandegrift.* New York: W. W. Norton & Company, 1964.

Williams, Robert Hugh. *The Old Corps: A Portrait of the U.S. Marine Corps between the Wars.* Annapolis, Maryland: Naval Institute Press, 1982.

SECONDARY SOURCES

Alexander, Joseph H. "Combat Leadership at Iwo Jima." *Marine Corps Gazette* 79, no. 2 (February 1995): 69–70.

———. *Utmost Savagery: The Three Days at Tarawa.* Annapolis, Maryland: Naval Institute Press, 1995.

Arthur, Robert A., and Kenneth Cohlmia. *The Third Marine Division.* Nashville, Tennessee: Battery Press, 1988.

Barrow, Clayton. "The Stick Wavers." *Naval History* 4, no. 1 (1980): 28–32.

Belote, James, and William Belote. *Typhoon of Steel: The Battle for Okinawa.* New York: Harper and Row, 1970.

Bergerud, Eric. *Touched with Fire: The Land War in the South Pacific.* New York: Viking, 1996.

Cameron, Craig M. *American Samurai: Myth, Imagination, and the Conduct of Battle in the First Marine Division, 1941–1951.* Cambridge: Cambridge University Press, 1994.

Cass, Bevan G., ed. *History of the Sixth Marine Division.* Nashville, Tennessee: Battery Press, 1987.

Chapin, John C. *Breaching the Marianas: The Battle for Saipan.* Washington, D.C.: U.S. Marine Corps, 1994.

Clark, George B. *United States Marine Corps Generals in World War II: A Biographical Dictionary.* Jefferson, North Carolina: McFarland & Co., 2008.

Condit, Kenneth W., John H. Johnstone, and Ella W. Nargele. *A Brief History of Headquarters Marine Corps Staff Organization.* Washington, D.C.: Historical Division, U.S. Marine Corps, 1971.

Cooper, Norman V. *A Fighting General: The Biography of Gen Holland M. "Howlin' Mad" Smith.* Quantico, Virginia: Marine Corps Association, 1987.

Coram, Robert. *Brute: The Life of Victor Krulak, U.S. Marine.* New York: Little, Brown and Company, 2010.

Daugherty, Leo J., III. *Pioneers of Amphibious Warfare, 1898–1945: Profiles of Fourteen American Military Strategists.* London: McFarand and Co., 2009.

Dyer, George Carroll. *The Amphibians Came to Conquer: The Story of Admiral Richmond Kelly Turner.* 2 vols. Washington, D.C.: Department of the Navy, 1972.

FitzPatrick, Tom. *A Character That Inspired: Major General Charles D. Barrett, USMC, Amphibious Warfare Pioneer.* Fairfax, Virginia: Tom FitzPatrick, 2003.

Ford, Douglas. "Brute Force or Combat Finesse? The Evolving Role of Firepower in US Amphibious Operations against the Imperial Japanese Forces, 1941–1945." *War in History* 23 (2016): 341–61.

Frank, Benis M. *Okinawa: The Great Island Battle.* New York: Elsevier-Dutton, 1978.

Frank, Benis M., and Henry I. Shaw, Jr. *Victory and Occupation: History of U.S. Marine Corps Operations in World War II*, vol. 5. Washington, D.C.: Government Printing Office, 1968.

Frank, Richard B. *Guadalcanal*. New York: Random House, 1990.

Gailey, Harry A. *Howlin' Mad vs. the Army: Conflict in Command, Saipan 1944*. Navato, California: Presidio Press, 1986.

———. *The Liberation of Guam, 21 July–10 August 1944*. Navato, California: Presidio Press, 1988.

Garand, George W., and Truman R. Strobridge. *Western Pacific Operations: History of U.S. Marine Corps Operations in World War II*, vol. 4. Washington, D.C.: Historical Division, Headquarters, U.S. Marine Corps, 1971.

Gregg, Charles T. *Tarawa*. New York: Stein and Day, 1984.

Hallas, James H. *The Devil's Anvil: The Assault on Peleliu*. Westport, Connecticut: Praeger, 1994.

———. *Killing Ground on Okinawa: The Battle for Sugar Loaf Hill*. Westport, Connecticut: Praeger, 1996.

Hammel, Eric. *Guadalcanal: Starvation Island*. New York: Crown Publishers, Inc., 1987.

Haskew, Michael E. *The Marines in World War II*. New York: St. Martin's Press, 2016.

Hill, Harry. "A Perfect Assault." In *The Pacific War Remembered: An Oral History Collection*, edited by John T. Mason, 247–53. Annapolis, Maryland: Naval Institute Press, 1986.

Hoffman, Jon T. *Chesty: The Story of Lieutenant General Lewis B. Puller, USMC*. New York: Random House, 2001.

Hough, Frank O., Verle E. Ludwig, and Henry I. Shaw, Jr. *Pearl Harbor to Guadalcanal: History of U.S. Marine Corps Operations in World War II*, vol. 1. Washington, D.C.: Government Printing Office, 1958.

Isely, Jeter A., and Philip A. Crowl. *The U.S. Marines and Amphibious War: Its Theory, and Its Practice in the Pacific*. Princeton, New Jersey: Princeton University Press, 1951.

Johnston, Richard W. *Follow Me! The Story of the Second Marine Division in World War II*. Nashville, Tennessee: Battery Press, 1987.

La Bree, Clifton. *The Gentle Warrior: General Oliver Prince Smith, USMC*. Kent, Ohio: Kent State University Press, 2001.

Lacey, Sharon Tosi. *Pacific Blitzkrieg: World War II in the Central Pacific*. Denton: University of North Texas Press, 2013.

Lorelli, John A. *To Foreign Shores: U.S. Amphibious Operations in World War II*. Annapolis, Maryland: Naval Institute Press, 1995.

Marling, Karal Ann, and John Wetenhall. *Iwo Jima: Monuments, Memories, and the American Hero*. Cambridge, Massachusetts: Harvard University Press, 1991.

Mason, John T., ed. *The Pacific War Remembered: An Oral History Collection*. Annapolis, Maryland: Naval Institute Press, 1986.

McMillan, George. *The Old Breed: A History of the First Marine Division in World War II*. Nashville, Tennessee: Battery Press, 2001.

McMillan, George, et al. *Uncommon Valor: Marine Divisions in Action*. Washington, D.C.: Infantry Journal Press, 1946.

Millett, Allan R. *In Many a Strife: General Gerald C. Thomas and the U.S. Marine Corps, 1917–1956*. Annapolis, Maryland: Naval Institute Press, 1993.

Millett, Allan R., and Jack Shulimson, eds. *Commandants of the Marine Corps.* Annapolis, Maryland: Naval Institute Press, 2004.

———. *Semper Fidelis: The History of the United States Marine Corps.* New York: Free Press, 1991.

Moskin, J. Robert. *The U.S. Marine Corps Story.* New York: McGraw-Hill Book Company, 1987.

Pratt, Fletcher. *The Marines' War: An Account of the Struggle for the Pacific from Both American and Japanese Sources.* New York: William Sloane Associates, 1948.

Proehl, Carl W., ed. *The Fourth Marine Division in World War II.* Washington, D.C.: Infantry Journal Press, 1946.

Rems, Alan. "Letters to Iwo Jima." *Naval History Magazine* 23, no. 1 (2009).

Russ, Martin. *Line of Departure: Tarawa.* Garden City, New York: Doubleday and Company, 1975.

Shaw, Henry I., Jr., and Douglas T. Kane. *Isolation of Rabaul: History of U.S. Marine Corps Operations in World War II*, vol. 2. Washington, D.C.: Government Printing Office, 1963.

Shaw, Henry I., Jr., Bernard C. Nalty, and Edwin T. Tumbladh. *Central Pacific Drive: History of U.S. Marine Corps Operations in World War II*, vol. 3. Washington, D.C.: Government Printing Office, 1966.

Smith, Julian. "Tarawa." U.S. Naval Institute *Proceedings* 79, no. 11 (November 1953): 1167–71.

Taaffe, Stephen R. *Marshall and His Generals: U.S. Army Commanders in World War II.* Lawrence: University Press of Kansas, 2011.

Ulbrich, David J. *Preparing for Victory: Thomas Holcomb and the Making of the Modern Marine Corps, 1936–1943.* Annapolis, Maryland: Naval Institute Press, 2011.

———. "The U.S. Marine Corps, Amphibious Capabilities, and Preparations for War with Japan." *Marine Corps University Journal* 6, no. 1 (2015): 71–105.

Wellons, James B. "General Roy S. Geiger, USMC: Marine Aviator, Joint Force Commander." Master's thesis, School of Advanced Air and Space Studies, Maxwell Air Force Base, 2007.

Wheeler, Richard. *Iwo.* New York: Lippincott & Crowell, 1980.

———. *A Special Valor: The U.S. Marines and the Pacific War.* New York: Harper and Row, 1983.

Willock, Roger. *Unaccustomed to Fear: A Biography of the Late General Roy S. Geiger, U.S.M.C.* Princeton, New Jersey: Roger Willock, 1968.

ARCHIVAL SOURCES

Auburn University Libraries
Holland Smith Papers

Hoover Institution Archives
Harry Schmidt Papers

Marine Corps History Division, Marine Corps University
Oral Histories
Chester Allen, Charles Banks, Robert Blake, Victor Bleasdale, Thomas Bourke, Alpha Bowser, Wilburt Brown, Austin Brunelli, Joseph Burger, Henry Buse Jr., Clifton Cates,

Justice Chambers, Robert Cushman, Raymond Davis, Harold Deakin, Graves Erskine, Lewis Fields, George Good, Jr., Charles Hayes, Frederick Henderson, Leo Hermle, Louis Jones, Russell Jordahl, Robert Kilmartin, Victor Krulak, Melvin Krulewitch, August Larson, Robert Luckey, John Masters, John McQueen, Vernon Megee, Francis Mulcahy, Raymond Murray, David Nimmer, Alfred Noble, Dewitt Peck, Omar Pfeiffer, Edwin Pollock, Lewis Puller, Donn Robertson, Roy Robinson, Frederick Roy, Lawson Sanderson, Adolph Schwenk, Alan Shapley, Lemuel Shepherd, Merwin Silverthorn, Julian Smith, Oliver Smith, Edward Snedeker, Joseph Stewart, Gerald Thomas, Merrill Twining, Robert Williams, Ralph Wismer, Thomas Wornham, and William Worton

Papers
Clifton Cates, Pedro del Valle, Graves Erskine, Roy Geiger, Thomas Holcomb, William Rupertus, Lemuel Shepherd, Holland Smith, Julian Smith, Gerald Thomas, Archibald Vandegrift, Clayton Vogel, and Thomas Watson

United States Army Heritage and Education Center
Senior Officer Oral History Program
J. Lawton Collins

Index

Advanced Base Force Operations in Micronesia, 9

Agana, Guam, 128, 129

Agat, Guam, 128

amphibious warfare: difficulties of, 3–4, 9–10; Marine Corps commitment to, 8, 9, 10, 13, 180, 181, 193

Angaur, Palau Islands, 131, 133, 137

Aola Bay, Guadalcanal, 33

Army, Tenth, 160, 163, 167, 168, 170, 172, 173

Army, United States: in Bougainville operation, 60; in Cape Gloucester operation, 64; Central Pacific offensive role, 75, 109; compared to Marine Corps, 5, 8, 14, 187; and Dual Drive Offensive, 69–70; in Gilbert Islands campaign, 76, 78, 81, 82, 84, 87; in Guadalcanal campaign, 40–43; in Iwo Jima operation, 159; in Mariana Island campaign, 108, 112, 113, 114, 126, 129; in Marshall Islands campaign, 95, 97, 98, 100, 101, 103, 104; in New Georgia operation, 49; in Okinawa campaign, 160–61, 167, Pacific War command structure, 20–21; in Peleliu operation, 133, 137–38, 140; relationship with Marine Corps, 6, 16, 22, 51, 64, 75, 93, 97–98, 101–2, 103, 108–9, 115–18, 129, 141, 150–51, 172, 188–89, 193; size of, 3

Army Air Forces, 45, 69, 106, 141, 159, 160, 174

Asan, Guam, 128, 129

Aslito Airfield, Saipan, 112

atolls, 76

atomic bomb, 144, 178

Attu, Aleutian Islands, 73

Auckland, New Zealand, 27

Australia, 20, 23, 41, 44, 69, 70, 144

Ayers, Russell, 104

B-29 Superfortress Bomber, 69, 120, 145, 159, 178

Barnett, George, 14, 122

Barrett, Charles: appointed I Amphibious Corps commander, 52; appointed 3rd Marine Division commander, 47; background and character, 46–47; commands brigade in Samoa, 47; death of, 57; evaluation of, 46, 47, 68, 181, 183, 184, 185, 188, 189, 190, 191; opinion of Rockey, 52; opinion of Turnage, 52–53; problems as I Amphibious Corps commander, 54–56; relieved as I Amphibious Corps commander, 56

Bataan, Philippines, 22–23, 32

Batchelder, Merton, 123

Belleau Wood, Battle of, 8

Betio, Tarawa: geography, 20; Marine assault on, 83–85; terrain, 76

Bleasdale, Victor, 167, 171

Bonin Islands, 145

Bougainville, Solomon Islands: aftermath and consequences, 61; command structure for, 54; fighting on, 59–60; geography, 54; Japanese strength on, 54; Marine landing on, 59–60; and navy role, 56, 60; planning and preparations for, 54–56, 58; role in Guadalcanal campaign, 34; terrain, 54

INDEX

About the Author

Stephen R. Taaffe is a professor of history at Stephen F. Austin State University in Nacogdoches, Texas, where he specializes in U.S. military history. He received his bachelor's degree from Grove City College in Grove City, Pennsylvania, and his graduate degrees from Ohio University in Athens, Ohio.

The Naval Institute Press is the book-publishing arm of the U.S. Naval Institute, a private, nonprofit, membership society for sea service professionals and others who share an interest in naval and maritime affairs. Established in 1873 at the U.S. Naval Academy in Annapolis, Maryland, where its offices remain today, the Naval Institute has members worldwide.

Members of the Naval Institute support the education programs of the society and receive the influential monthly magazine *Proceedings* or the colorful bimonthly magazine *Naval History* and discounts on fine nautical prints and on ship and aircraft photos. They also have access to the transcripts of the Institute's Oral History Program and get discounted admission to any of the Institute-sponsored seminars offered around the country.

The Naval Institute's book-publishing program, begun in 1898 with basic guides to naval practices, has broadened its scope to include books of more general interest. Now the Naval Institute Press publishes about seventy titles each year, ranging from how-to books on boating and navigation to battle histories, biographies, ship and aircraft guides, and novels. Institute members receive significant discounts on the Press' more than eight hundred books in print.

Full-time students are eligible for special half-price membership rates. Life memberships are also available.

For a free catalog describing Naval Institute Press books currently available, and for further information about joining the U.S. Naval Institute, please write to:

Member Services
U.S. Naval Institute
291 Wood Road
Annapolis, MD 21402-5034
Telephone: (800) 233-8764
Fax: (410) 571-1703
Web address: www.usni.org